The Project Management Scorecard

**IMPROVING
HUMAN
PERFORMANCE
SERIES**

The Project Management Scorecard

Measuring the Success of Project Management Solutions

Jack J. Phillips, Ph.D.
Timothy W. Bothell, Ph.D.
G. Lynne Snead

An Imprint of Elsevier Science

Amsterdam   Boston   London   New York   Oxford   Paris
San Diego   San Francisco   Singapore   Sydney   Tokyo

Library of Congress Cataloging-in-Publication Data

Phillips, Jack J., 1945–
  The project management scorecard : measuring the success of project management solutions / Jack J. Phillips, Timothy W. Bothell, G. Lynne Snead.
    p. cm.—(Improving human performance series)
  Includes bibliographical references and index.
  ISBN 0-7506-7449-0 (alk. paper)
  1. Project management. 2. Project management—Evaluation. I. Bothell, Timothy W. II. Snead, G. Lynne. III. Title. IV. Series.

HD69.P75 P49 2001
658.4'04—dc21

                                                                2001052837

British Library Cataloguing-in-Publication Data
A catalogue record for this book is available from the British Library.

The publisher offers special discounts on bulk orders of this book.
For information, please contact:
Manager of Special Sales
Elsevier Science
225 Wildwood Avenue
Woburn, MA 01801–2041
Tel: 781-904-2500
Fax: 781-904-2620

For information on all Butterworth–Heinemann publications available, contact our World Wide Web home page at: http://www.bh.com

10 9 8 7 6 5 4 3 2 1

Printed in the United States of America

Contents

PART III

Key Issues with the Measures

PART IV

Challenges

Preface

As the practice of scorecard measurement becomes more the norm than the exception, human performance practitioners and professionals of many disciplines need examples of scorecards for specific disciplines and activities. One process generating an urgent need for scorecard application is the field of project management.

Within almost every industry, employees in many different jobs are required to manage a project or multiple projects. Today, few employees find their workplace free from competing priorities, critical deadlines, excessive workloads, and unexpected interruptions. The meaning of the word "project" today is broad. In fact, most employees can be thought of as project managers because they simultaneously juggle many priorities on the job. This is why many organizations spend a great deal of time and money working to improve the management of projects. This is also the reason many organizations want to justify the efforts and resources for improving project management using a balanced set of measures that considers the effectiveness of projects from all angles. As a result, organizations need a "Project Management Scorecard."

Project management is an ideal process to evaluate and measure. The reasons for this are:

- ☐ Projects focus on objectives and outcomes.
- ☐ Projects contain processes (most of which are measurable).

☐   For many projects, the end in mind is directly related to the sales, production, or overall profitability of organizations.

☐   The individual tasks of projects are typically specific, measurable, and time-dimensioned.

☐   Most projects contain a budget for which project managers of this modern age are increasingly accountable.

To effectively manage and measure projects, managers rely on effective processes, techniques, and approaches to guide them in their work. This book will provide readers with a step-by-step approach for measuring project success and for setting up a project management scorecard. Busy professionals without the time to become experts in measurement will quickly find tools to manage and measure projects within their fast-paced, cost-conscious organizations.

INTEREST IN SCORECARD MEASURES

Scorecards are categories of key measures that evaluate the effectiveness of organizations, divisions within organizations, programs, projects, and sometimes multiple projects. Scorecard measures have become one of the most challenging and intriguing issues facing the performance improvement field. The interest in key measures during the 1990s was phenomenal in part due to one key measure called *return on investment (ROI)*. The topic appeared on almost every conference and convention agenda. Articles on ROI appear regularly in practitioner and research journals. Several books have been developed on the topic, and consulting firms have sprung up almost overnight to tackle this critical and important issue. However, ROI is only one of many key measures important to scorecards. Scorecards often include customer satisfaction measures, operational efficiency measures, revenue measures, employee satisfaction measures, and milestone measures for goals that build on the accomplishment of other goals. All of these measures are typical in many scorecards and all are growing in strategic importance in most organizations.

Several issues are driving the increased interest in, and application of, the scorecard process. Pressure from clients and senior managers to show the return on their training investment is an influential driver. Competitive economic pressures are causing intense scrutiny of all expenditures, including all project costs. Total quality management, re-engineering, and continuous process improvement have created a renewed interest in measurement and evaluation, including measuring the effectiveness of project management. The general trend toward accountability with all staff support groups is causing some managers to measure their own contribution to the organization's bottom line. These and other factors have created an unprecedented wave of applications of a comprehensive ROI scorecard process.

NEEDED: AN EFFECTIVE PROJECT MANAGEMENT SCORECARD

The challenging aspect of a project management scorecard is the nature and accuracy of its development. The process often seems very confusing because it is surrounded by models, formulas, and statistics that often frighten even the most capable practitioners. Coupled with this concern are misunderstandings about scorecards—the process and the gross misuse of measurement techniques in some organizations. These issues sometimes leave practitioners with a distaste for evaluation and measurement.

Unfortunately, for project managers today, accountability scorecards cannot be ignored. To admit to clients and senior managers that the impact of managing projects well cannot be measured is to admit that learning does not add value, or that project management should not be subjected to accountability processes, or that all projects are equally managed, leading to similar results. In practice, the project management scorecard is the perfect tool to improve the outcomes of projects. The scorecard must be explored, considered, and ultimately implemented in most organizations.

What is needed is a rational, logical approach that can be simplified and implemented within the current budget constraints and resources of the organization. This book presents a proven scorecard process, based on almost twenty years of development and refinement. It is a process that is rich in tradition and modified to meet the demands facing most project managers.

The project management scorecard described in this book meets the requirements of three very important groups. First, the project managers who have used evaluation models and implemented ROI or scorecard processes in their organizations continue to report their satisfaction with the process and the success that it has achieved. The scorecard process presented here is user-friendly, easy to understand, and has been proven to pay for itself time and time again. A second important group, the clients and senior managers who must approve project budgets, want measurable results, preferably expressed as a return on investment. The ROI process within the scorecard has fared well with these groups. Senior managers view the process as credible, logical, practical, and easy to understand from their perspective. More importantly, they buy into the process, which is critical for their future support. The third important group is the evaluation researchers who develop, explore, and analyze new processes and techniques. When exposed to this scorecard in a two-day or one-week workshop, the researchers, without exception, give this process very high marks. They often applaud the strategies for isolating the effects of quality project management and the strategies for converting data to monetary values. Unanimously, they characterize the project management scorecard process as an important contribution to the field.

WHY THIS BOOK AT THIS TIME?

Currently, there is no book that offers a comprehensive, practical presentation on a project management scorecard, using a process that meets the demands of the three groups previously described. Most models and representations of the scorecard process ignore, or provide very little insight into, the two key elements essential to developing the scorecard: isolating the effects of project management solutions and converting data to monetary values. Recognizing that there are many other factors that will have an influence on output results, this book provides various strategies to isolate the effects of project management solutions, far more than any other presentation on the topic. Not enough attention has been provided to the issue of assigning monetary values to the benefits derived from quality project management. This book presents various strategies for converting data to monetary values.

TARGET AUDIENCE

This book should be of interest to anyone involved in project management solutions, measurement and evaluation, and performance improvement, and anyone managing a project or multiple projects. The primary audience is project managers or project management trainers. This book should also be of interest to evaluators looking for specific application examples of the ROI process to project management. In addition, employees of most any industry will find valuable insights into project management from this book.

STRUCTURE OF THIS BOOK

This book is written to provide the reader with a brief introduction to the project management process and an overview of the entire process needed to develop the project management scorecard. Chapters in the book will explain the methodology required for each step in the project management scorecard. The book provides a description of how each step in the process is applied to evaluating project management, and also provides tools that readers can use to begin their project management evaluation efforts.

CHAPTER DESCRIPTIONS

Chapter 1: Project Management Issues and Challenges

This chapter will review current issues and challenges that organizations today experience because of poor project management skills. Real-life examples that detail the costs of failed projects will be included in this chapter.

Chapter 2: The Project Management Process

This chapter will introduce the reader to effective project management processes. It reviews proven methods for handling multiple priorities and for organizing projects from beginning to completion. The chapter will be organized according to the four-step project management process. Content in this chapter will include:

- [ ] Identifying expectations (Step 1—Visualize)
- [ ] Clarifying a project's vision (Step 1—Visualize)
- [ ] Creating a plan (Step 2—Plan)
- [ ] Implementing the plan (Step 3—Implement)
- [ ] Monitoring a project's progress (Step 3—Implement)
- [ ] Evaluating a project's success (Step 4—Close)

Also, the planning of measurement practices that can be used with each step in the project management process will be briefly described.

Chapter 3: Project Management Solutions

This chapter reviews possible solutions for project management improvement. Across many well-managed projects, there are common success factors. Quality projects include a uniform process, an effective tool set, proper training, clear roles and responsibilities, and other factors. This chapter reviews these important factors.

Chapter 4: The Project Management Scorecard

Chapter 4 describes the project management scorecard and how organizations are tackling this important issue. Best practices, which form the basis for the book, are briefly described. Various return on investment criteria and requirements are presented to build a foundation for the remainder of the book. This chapter presents a brief summary of the model for those who are being introduced to the process for the first time.

Chapters 5 Through 10: How to Measure . . .

Chapters 5 through 10 outline how to measure each component of a project management scorecard. Methodologies are outlined and tools are illustrated, giving the reader a step-by-step process for using the scorecard.

Chapter 11: Monitoring the True Costs of the Project Solution

Chapter 11 details specifically what types of costs should be included in the project cost formula. Different categories and classifications of costs are explored in this chapter, with the goal of developing a fully loaded cost profile for each project scorecard.

Chapter 12: How to Isolate the Effects of Project Management Solutions

This chapter presents what is perhaps the most important aspect of the scorecard process. Ranging from the use of a control group arrangement to obtaining estimates directly from participants, various strategies are presented that can determine the amount of improvement that is directly linked to the project management. The premise of this chapter is that there are many influences on business performance measures, with project management being only one of them. Methods best suited for isolating the effects of project management will be discussed in greater detail.

Chapter 13: How to Convert Business Measures to Monetary Values

Chapter 13 presents an essential step for developing an economic benefit from project management. Ranging from determining the profit contribution of an increased output to using expert opinion to assign a value to data, various strategies to convert both hard and soft data to monetary values are presented along with project management examples.

Chapter 14: Forecasting ROI: How to Build a Business Case for the Project Management Solution

Many projects don't go further than the planning stage, for appropriate reasons. However, some projects never leave the idea stage, due to poor business relevance. All projects can be subjected to a simple forecasting process to determine if they should move from ideas to plans to action. This chapter will provide the reader with a methodology to determine if ideas should become projects.

Chapter 15: How to Provide Feedback and Communicate Results to the Client

Chapter 15 addresses a variety of reporting issues. To implement the project management scorecard effectively requires a plan for how the data will be used. This chapter identifies the important issues that must be tackled for the scorecard process to become a productive, useful, and long-lasting process that will drive continuous improvement.

Chapter 16: Overcoming Resistance and Barriers to the Project Management Solution

Chapter 16 addresses a variety of implementation issues. To implement the scorecard process effectively requires following logical steps and overcoming several hurdles. This chapter reviews implementation issues.

Acknowledgments

From Jack Phillips

No book is the sole work of the authors, but rather a collaboration of the many people who have helped along the way. Several groups have contributed to the completion of this book and deserve recognition. Our valuable clients provided us the opportunity to apply these processes. Many have given us tremendous latitude to work on projects within their organization; we have learned from each and every assignment.

The individuals who helped develop this manuscript deserve special recognition. I appreciate the efforts of my co-authors, Lynne Snead and Tim Bothell, in making this book a reality. Tim was very diligent in taking rough material and converting it into useable manuscript. Lynne shared her expertise in project management and found time to make a significant contribution, particularly with the material in the front section of the book. Joyce Alff, our internal editor, did a superb job of making the initial draft more readable and understandable. Finally, several people helped type the manuscript, including my assistant, Francine Hawkins, who kept us on schedule in spite of our efforts.

We appreciate the efforts of the editorial staff at Butterworth-Heinemann to add this book to our Improving Human Performance series. Jennifer Pursley has been very conscientious in making sure that this publication is available to the right audience. Thanks, Jennifer.

Finally, my appreciation goes to my spouse and partner, Patti. This book would not be possible without her support. Her assistance was invaluable in developing some of the materials, structuring the book, and helping with some of the initial writing and editing. My thanks go to Patti for her enduring efforts to make our publications much better. Go, girl!

From Tim Bothell

What I know about project management, evaluation, and ROI, I learned from obtaining advanced degrees, from Lynne Snead, from Brent Peterson, from Richard Sudweeks, from Adrian Van Monfrans, and from Jack J. Phillips. Most of what I have learned about both project management and measuring the return on investment of project management, I have learned from serving many clients and from managing my own evaluation projects. I am grateful for these people and for that experience.

In addition to the aforementioned people, I would especially like to thank my wife Sheri for her constant support and understanding of my work.

I thank my family for their toleration of multiple projects. I thank my co-authors, Jack Phillips and Lynne Snead, for this exciting opportunity, and all the staff at Franklin Covey who have helped me learn and grow.

From Lynne Snead

Everything I know about project management I learned from someone or somewhere. In my eleven years as a project management trainer and consultant, most of what I have learned has come from my clients and classroom participants. It would be impossible for me to acknowledge them all, but I appreciate the tremendous depth they have added to my learning and knowledge.

Behind the scenes support often means the difference between a successfully completed project and one that never gets off the drawing board. There are many who, in some way, made this possible for me. I thank my co-authors, Jack Phillips and Tim Bothell, for this exciting opportunity, Stephen M.R. Covey and Vandy Evans for their encouragement and support, Judy Ball for editing help and knowing how to make a project fun, Carol Dombrowski for her excellent illustration work, and the staff at Franklin Covey, who have helped me learn and grow in this wonderful business.

To my incredible family, I give thanks for not only tolerating the long hours of my work, but also for being the best cheerleaders and supporters I could ever hope for. You are the wind beneath my wings.

Note: Limited portions of this book were taken from three other books that discuss this process. These sources are:

Phillips, Jack J., Ron D. Stone, and Patricia Pulliam Phillips. *The Human Resources Scorecard*. Boston: Butterworth-Heinemann, 2001.

Phillips, Jack J. *The Consultant's Scorecard*. New York: McGraw-Hill, 2000.

Phillips, Jack J. *Return on Investment in Training and Performance Improvement Programs*. Boston: Butterworth-Heinemann, previously published by Gulf Publishing Co., 1997.

PART I

Setting the Stage

CHAPTER 1

Project Management Issues and Challenges

Together, failed and poorly managed projects cost U.S. companies and government agencies an estimated $145 billion per year (Field, 1997). The estimated costs for failed projects in the United States is more than twice that of the estimated amount of money spent on all training and performance improvement efforts combined in the United States in 1999, which was $62.5 billion (*Training Magazine*, 1999). Of the estimated $62.5 billion spent on training and performance improvement efforts, about 17 percent was spent on project management training (*Training & Development Magazine*, Jan. 2000). Thus, on average in the United States, organizations spend approximately $10 billion to fix a $145 billion per year problem. How can a problem so large receive such little attention?

Some employees feel that they are not project managers or that project management failures are not a problem within their fields or disciplines. However, all employees are project managers, and some to a greater extent than others.

There are numerous examples of failed projects. Some disciplines suffer from more failures than other disciplines. For instance, within the information technology field, an estimated 40 percent of IT application development projects are cancelled before completion (Field, 1997).

Today, competition and a global marketplace have created a demand for better, faster, and more cost-effective projects. Yet in many organizations, there are no formal processes or methodologies for the effective selection and management of projects. In the past, project management was about "figuring it out as we go," or about relying on just a few within the organization who were inherently good at managing projects. Today, this is not acceptable. With the high cost of project failure, it is not smart business to let individuals and teams "figure it out as they go," with the hope that they will be good at it.

There are many drivers behind the need for improved project management. Robert Happy, founder and president of the Project Consulting Group of Novato, California, described some of these drivers when he said:

> As the world economy progresses and globalization becomes a way of life for all of us, there is extraordinary pressure for organizations to be more proactive and to respond more quickly than ever before to market and customer needs. While the demand for customized solutions increases daily, time to market and shorter product development life cycles are the key to obtaining and maintaining market share. Add to this the requirement by management to do more with less and it becomes clear why Project Management is growing fast.

The demand to do more with less places pressure on a wide variety of individuals to be part owners in managing projects. A project is defined as "a complex series of non-routine tasks directed to meet a specific goal" (Franklin Covey, 1999).

While an employee's job title may not be that of project manager, each individual in an organization is, in essence, a project manager, even if what that person is managing is simply a piece of a larger project. More employees than ever before need better project management skills. Tom Peters, in *Reinventing Work: The Project 50*, points out that projects are a significant part of what makes up most employees' jobs and that these employees should be creating what he calls "WOW projects"—projects that matter and in which participants are passionate about the outcome (Peters, 1999).

Twenty years ago, it was common to have a job where the responsibilities from one day to the next were often routine and predictable. Now, every day can be unique. A greater percentage of an employee's daily responsibilities is made up of a unique series of non-routine tasks called "projects." Because of these trends, every organization should be contemplating questions like those in Figure 1-1.

Project Management Needs Assessment

Please circle the letter that best represents your response.

	A	B	C	D	E
• What percentage of the organization's projects are a means to strategic initiatives?	A 1–20%	B 21–40%	C 41–60%	D 61–80%	E 81–100%
• Does the organization use resources wisely?	A Never	B Seldom	C Sometimes	D Often	E Always
• Does the organization understand and manage workload capabilities effectively?	A Never	B Seldom	C Sometimes	D Often	E Always
• Does the organization always clearly understand customers' needs and expectations (internal and/or external)?	A Never	B Seldom	C Sometimes	D Often	E Always
• Does your organization have an effective project management process that is used consistently?	A Never	B Seldom	C Sometimes	D Often	E Always
• Do you personally have effective project management tools that you use consistently?	A Never	B Seldom	C Sometimes	D Often	E Always
• Do you personally manage daily workload (multiple priorities) effectively?	A Never	B Seldom	C Sometimes	D Often	E Always
• What percentage of projects you work on will be cancelled or changed before you finish them?	A 1–20%	B 21–40%	C 41–60%	D 61–80%	E 81–100%
• Do you always clearly meet customers' needs and expectations (internal and/or external)?	A Never	B Seldom	C Sometimes	D Often	E Always
• Do you manage projects effectively?	A Never	B Seldom	C Sometimes	D Often	E Always
• What percentage of your projects fail?	A 1–20%	B 21–40%	C 41–60%	D 61–80%	E 81–100%
• Do you know what the cost of those failed projects are?	A Never	B Seldom	C Sometimes	D Often	E Always
• Do you know on an annual basis, how much is wasted on poorly managed or failed projects?	A Never	B Seldom	C Sometimes	D Often	E Always
• Do you feel clear about your role and responsibilities within your organization?	A Never	B Seldom	C Sometimes	D Often	E Always
• Do you understand what decisions you are responsible for?	A Never	B Seldom	C Sometimes	D Often	E Always

← Project Management Need for Improvement Continuum →

Lots of Improvement Needed 17–35	Some Improvement Needed 36–65	Little Improvement Needed 66–85

Figure 1-1. Project management needs assessment.

Scoring for Figure 1-1: Give yourself 1 point for each "A" you marked, 2 points for each "B" you marked, 3 points for each "C" you marked, 4 points for each "D" you marked, and 5 points for each "E." Then, total your scores. Use your total score to see where on the need for improvement continuum you fall.

REASONS FOR FAILED OR POORLY MANAGED PROJECTS

Why do projects fail in an organization? Here are the top reasons most people give—regardless of the type of business environment they come from:

- ☐ Lack of a clear or common vision or goal
- ☐ Changing direction mid-project
- ☐ Conflicting priorities
- ☐ Unrealistic expectations
- ☐ Not enough resources (time, money, equipment, knowledge, or expertise)
- ☐ Poor communication
- ☐ Unmet customer expectations
- ☐ Poor planning or no planning
- ☐ No clear methodology
- ☐ No clear understanding of what needs to be done (who is going to do it, by when, and at what price)
- ☐ Scope change
- ☐ No buy-in and support from key stakeholders
- ☐ Poor leadership

Projects do not fail because technically oriented project management procedures did not work. Almost never do workers say, "We failed because we didn't do our PERT diagram correctly." Projects fail because of what some call "soft" issues; however, there is nothing "soft" about the cost of failed projects.

WHAT IS THE COST OF A FAILED OR POORLY MANAGED PROJECT?

This is an important question that rarely gets a clear answer. Yet, the answer to this question can be costly. The following cites some examples:

☐ A major restaurant chain manages a routine project to revise its menu in hundreds of restaurants around the United States. Because of poor project definition up front, lack of a clear work breakdown, missed deadlines, and not understanding the impact of last-minute changes, a project that should have cost $500,000 costs over $2 million. (Client preferred not to be identified.)

☐ A component manufacturer bids a project at $150,000 that ended up costing $450,000 to complete. Because no change documentation existed, the manufacturer was responsible for the price difference. The client told them that if they had clearly understood at the beginning of the project what the actual cost would be, they would have been willing to pay that cost. (Client preferred not to be identified.)

☐ A joint undertaking between Marriott Corp., Hilton Hotels Corp., Budget Rent a Car, and AMR Information Services (AMRIS) was begun to create a computer system called Confirm. Four years later, after complaints around the product definition, missed deadlines, overwhelming numbers of changes, poor project management skills and poor communication practices, AMRIS wrote off $213 million in expenses related to the project and then litigation began. AMRIS sued Marriott, Hilton and Budget for $70 million, Hilton counter-sued for $175 million, Marriott for $65 million, and Budget for over $500 million. The participants settled the differences out of court (Flowers, 1996).

The cost of failed or poorly managed projects in an organization may or may not be of this magnitude, but the relative effects remain the same.

In addition to the direct costs of a failed project, there are possible hidden costs or lost opportunity costs of project failures, and associated consequences of simply not doing a project well. These can include:

☐ Excessive use of resources
☐ Unmet client needs
☐ Low employee morale
☐ High employee turnover
☐ Longer time to market
☐ Less successful projects in a year than should be possible

Often these hidden costs or lost opportunity costs may be difficult to pinpoint, but the costs are there, directly or indirectly. Projects fail because of poor project management practices such as:

- ☐ Poor creativity and visioning skills
- ☐ Poor communication skills
- ☐ Poor interview skills
- ☐ Poor planning skills
- ☐ Over-allocating resources
- ☐ No clear work breakdown
- ☐ Ineffective workload management skills
- ☐ Poor delegation and follow-through practices
- ☐ Poor tracking, monitoring, and managing skills
- ☐ No common process or methodology

SUCCESS FACTORS

Although managing projects may appear to be a "soft skill," these so-called "soft" skills, when ineffectively practiced, can consistently result in poor or failed projects. In fact, the failure to use effective project management skills can double, or even triple, the costs of a project. Thus, what is the savings for managing a project well? The savings could be tremendous.

Determining whether an organization is working on the right projects at the right time is a key success factor. The following questions may help determine whether it is the right project at the right time:

- ☐ Are resources being wasted in the organization by work being done on low-priority projects?
- ☐ Are ideas that are not clearly defined, being prematurely tossed over the wall as assignments to an already busy staff?
- ☐ Are projects being implemented that are not in support of the organization's mission, vision, values, and strategic initiatives?
- ☐ Does the organization practice the prioritization technique known as "last one over the wall is the highest priority"?
- ☐ Can the organization afford to cancel projects in the implementation stage that never should have been started in the first place?

Wasted resources, undefined ideas, projects unaligned strategically, and misunderstood priorities can choke the resource capabilities within many organizations and contribute to high stress, low morale, and poor project performance.

STRATEGIC PLANNING PYRAMID

What is missing in most organizations is an understanding of the organization's highest priorities. Operating practices that ensure that decisions and activities focus on those priorities are essential to successful projects. A model, called the Strategic Planning Pyramid™, can be used by any organization to clarify and communicate priorities, aid in decision-making, and focus activities on priorities (Franklin Covey, 1999).

As Figure 1-2 shows, the Strategic Planning Pyramid™ starts with a clear understanding of an organization's mission, vision, and values (what is most important to the organization). It then clarifies long-range goals and/or strategic initiatives, specifies projects required to accomplish those goals and initiatives, and focuses activities to complete the resulting projects.

The foundation of the model is based upon clarifying statements in terms of what is most important to the organization. While the language can vary from one organization to the next, typical terms for these statements are:

☐ Mission: A statement of who or what the organization is—its purpose
☐ Vision: A statement of what the organization wants to be in its future
☐ Values: Principles and qualities that guide the organization's decisions, behaviors, and operations

Figure 1-2. The strategic planning pyramid™.

The next level in the model clarifies long-range goals to help in the realization of the mission, vision, and values. Some organizations call these *strategic initiatives*. For the purpose of this book, *long-range goals* and *strategic initiatives* are used interchangeably. The important thing to realize about goals and initiatives at this level is that they are often large, long-range, and "big-picture" oriented. For work at this level to be accomplished, it often needs to be clarified into smaller, more specific, manageable, intermediate goals.

Intermediate goals are the next level in the model. These are specific projects. Projects are a complex series of non-routine tasks directed to meet a specific goal. It may take several projects to successfully complete a long-range goal or strategic initiative.

The top of the model describes the process whereby activities from the projects need to result in daily activities performed by employees of the organization. The project is clarified in terms of what needs to be done, by whom, and by when. Keep in mind that it is often not the management of a particular project that causes a challenge; it is dealing with multiple projects. Every individual within an organization needs to be able to answer two key questions on a regular basis: "How does what I do fit with what matters most to this organization?" and "What do I need to do today?" This is workload management and is at the top of the pyramid.

The Strategic Planning Pyramid™ becomes a model of vision, communication, planning, and decision-making throughout an organization. Any proposed project is checked back to the model to ensure it supports the organization's mission, vision, values, goals, and strategies. Any project that does not fit the model is a candidate for a clear "No."

Another model, covered in the next chapter, will discuss a project management process to use with the Strategic Planning Pyramid™. The Four-Step Project Management Process™ aids project success by providing a consistent step-by-step methodology (Franklin Covey, 1999). This process will provide a common language that can be used throughout the organization, as well as some key go/no-go decision points to ensure an organization is working on the right projects at the right time.

FINAL THOUGHTS

Failed and poorly managed projects cost companies and government agencies billions of dollars every year, yet, in many organizations, there are no formal processes for the effective selection and management of projects. To overcome the failures of poorly managed projects and the consequences in lost profitability, misuse of resources, unmet client needs, and low employee morale, organizations must look at the reasons projects are not successful. They must also recognize that every individual in the organization is, to some degree, a project manager. Understanding the organization's priorities and putting in place operating practices to ensure that decisions and activities focus on those priorities is essential to successful projects. The Strategic Planning Pyramid™ can help any organization in this process.

REFERENCES

Field, Tom. "When Bad Things Happen to Good Projects." *CIO Magazine*, October 15, 1997, as reported by the Standish Group International Inc.

Flowers, Stephen. *Software Failure: Management Failure*. University of Brighton, UK. John Wiley & Sons, 1996, 31–41.

Franklin Covey Project Management – An In Depth Approach. 1999. A two-day seminar. Salt Lake City: Copyright Franklin Covey Co., 1999.

"Industry Report 1999," *Training Magazine*, October 1999, p. 40.

Peters Tom. *Reinventing Work. The Project 50: Fifty Ways to Transform Every Task into a Project that Matters*. New York, NY: Alfred A. Knopf, Inc., 1999, 3–20.

"1999 State of the Industry Report," *Training & Development Magazine*, Supplement, January 2000, p. 10. Adapted from Figure 5: "Course Type as Percentage of Training Expenditures."

CHAPTER 2

The Project Management Process

The Four-Step Project Management Process™ provides a methodology that can be used throughout any organization, regardless of the type of project that is being managed. The benefit of the process is that it is a constant that anyone in the organization can learn, share, and repeat. It is easier to become a process expert than a project expert because, by definition, projects are goal driven, unique, and temporary, meaning there is no such thing as "Last time we did this. . . ." When adhered to, another benefit of the process mentality rather than the project mentality is that the step-by-step process builds solutions that avoid the most common reasons for project failure.

While the project management process remains a repeatable formula, the same is not true of the tools used to help manage projects. These vary tremendously and can be customized according to availability, needs, styles, and preferences. Project management tools, however, are dependent upon the process used to manage the project. This chapter will not attempt to focus on the wide variety of tools available, but rather, the focus will be on a process that will guide the project toward a successful completion, a process that can be used with any choice of tools. The presentation of specific methods is beyond the scope of this book and is contained in other works.

PROCESS OVERVIEW

There are four steps to the project management process: Visualize, Plan, Implement, and Close (see Figure 2-1). The primary principle in the Visualize stage is to begin with the end in mind. This stage focuses on the creation of a shared vision statement, which is created with input from the project key stakeholders. (While this sounds like an obvious place to start, keep in mind that most projects start in the Implement stage.)

The Plan stage equates to the "how to" stage of the process. How will the project be accomplished? This stage looks at project constraints, potential hot spots, and a clear work breakdown defining what needs to be done, by whom, by when, and at what cost.

The third stage, Implement, puts the plan into effect. This stage involves management of the workload, communication issues, delegation and follow-through skills, monitoring and controlling the project, and making changes and adjustments.

The final stage in the process, Close, looks at bringing a project through to successful completion, finalizing project documentation, and evaluating the return on investment of the project.

Within the process, there are two checkpoints to ensure that the project is headed in the right direction (according to the organization's mission, vision, values, goals, strategies, and available resources). A conscious decision about whether to continue with or stop the project is made at each of the two checkpoints. Figure 2-2 shows these checkpoints.

Upon completion of the Visualize stage, much has been learned about the project. This is the first opportunity to decide if the project should continue (discussed in a later section). This first go/no-go decision point is simply a preliminary decision. A "no" at this point indicates the project is not the right project at the right time and indicates either a definite "no" or perhaps a "no, not now." In the latter case, the project may be revisited at another time. A "yes" simply indicates that key criteria have been met and it is worthwhile to continue to the Plan stage.

The Plan stage is the opportunity to clarify the rest of the vital information needed to make a final go/no-go decision on the project. Here, the detailed project plan will specify what work needs to be done, what resources are needed to do it, and what the time requirement is for the project. This is the level of detail necessary for the final decision to continue to the Implement stage.

Figure 2-1. Project management process.

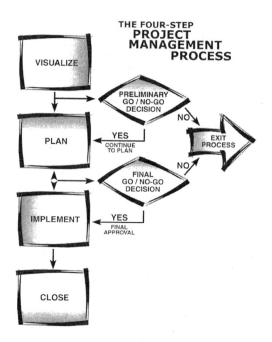

Figure 2-2. Checkpoints within the project management process.

The purpose of the decision checkpoints is to ensure that a project idea:

☐ has a fair opportunity to be creatively explored and clarified *before* it is implemented, and

☐ that should not be continued is halted, sooner rather than later, thereby avoiding the high cost (and common practice) of aborting projects in the Implement stage.

Performing the two-decision checkpoints effectively will increase the return on investment (ROI) of any project. Increased understanding of what a project looks like will lead to a better-managed project, which generally leads to a better ROI. Likewise, a project that was halted early rather than later in the project management process will always save organizations time, money, and resources, which will improve the ROI of the organizations' project management processes.

FOLLOWING THE PROCESS

Visualize

The Project Management Institute's *Guide to the Project Management Body of Knowledge* refers to project management as "the application of knowledge, skills, tools, and techniques to project activities in order to meet or exceed stakeholder needs and expectations from a project . . . [and] invariably involves balancing competing demands among scope, time, cost, and quality and stakeholders with differing needs and expectations . . ." (Project Management Institute, 1996).

Many of the challenges faced while managing projects are captured in the above quote. We have all heard the statement from a customer or boss: "That is not what I wanted." One key reason for project failure is different visions of the desired end result. Blame is often the by-product. We wonder, "Why didn't they tell me that?" This is, however, a reactive view of the problem.

There is a cartoon that shows programmers working at their computers and the team leader speaking to them as he turns to leave the room. The caption reads, "You all start coding. I'll go ask the customer what they want." Our environment has often become more technology-driven than passionately customer-driven. If we understand the nature of such issues, we are able to shift to a proactive approach that will circumvent these issues in the future. However, visualizing the end result of a project requires much more than just understanding what needs and expectations need to be met—and much more than balancing priorities between time, cost, scope, and quality.

Visualizing the end result of a project requires a detailed understanding of what key business or organizational results will be improved by both the outcomes of the project and effectively managing the project. Understanding the organizational results impacted by the project helps project managers visualize the evaluation that should be implemented throughout the project.

The Good News

As Mahan Khalsa says in his book, *Let's Get Real or Let's Not Play: The Demise of Dysfunctional Selling and the Advent of Helping Clients Succeed*, the good news is, when it comes right down to it, "We both want the same thing. We both want a solution that truly meets the client's needs." We need to learn how to mutually explore with the client the shared outcome of that solution (Khalsa, 1999). Khalsa's book is devoted to learning how to help clients succeed and knowing how to ask the right questions. As project managers, if we understand that key stakeholders are our clients, and that helping clients succeed is our mission, our paradigm shifts to help us understand that we are partners in that process. With that paradigm we can work with our clients (project owners, sponsors, yes, even our boss is our client) to create the win-win situation that comes from a solution that truly meets their needs.

If key stakeholders do not provide clear information up front about what the end results of the project should be, it will most likely be for one or more of the following reasons:

- ☐ They don't know.
- ☐ They don't receive the right questions.
- ☐ They are afraid they will not be listened to.
- ☐ They don't understand the end results in terms of organization-wide, bottom-line results and project outcomes.

A vital skill for project managers is to be expert interviewers. They need to know how to ask the right questions. The questions need to be so good, in fact, that they will enable us to elicit information the key stakeholder hadn't even thought of yet. The following practice will provide a proactive approach to clarifying the needed information. When practiced diligently, this will preclude ever hearing the statement, "That's not what I wanted." Vision statements describing the end result of the project are co-created with key stakeholders.

The first step in the Visualize process is to identify the project's key stakeholders. While stakeholders are those affected by a project, *key* stakeholders are those who have the ability to ultimately determine if the project is a success or a failure. These often include the customer, boss, project sponsor or owner, as well as the project manager and key members of the project team. If the members of this group (our clients) have different visions of the end result, the project is doomed to fail before it ever begins.

Ensuring that this group has the same vision of the end result requires an up-front investment in the creation of a vision statement that the key stakeholders share and support. Many project managers are reluctant to invest this time up front in the project, and prefer to jump right into the work. Results are predictable, however, if this investment is skipped. Expert project managers are those who are willing to invest the time and effort needed in this process. In fact, if this one stage of the process is done well, the next three don't need to be done perfectly, and the project can still succeed. If this stage is not done well, however, it doesn't matter how well the next three are done—the project will fail.

Once the key stakeholders have been identified, it is time to find out what they have in mind about the project. Asking vague questions like "What do you want here?" or "What should this look like?" most often leads to vague answers about whose job it is to figure that out. Instead, approach key stakeholders with questions they *can* and *want* to answer. You are treating each key stakeholder as though he or she is your client and you are conducting a client interview.

Key Stakeholder/Client Interview

There are five interview questions to ask of key stakeholders (clients); however, there are two keys to a successful interview experience:

☐ There must be a clear understanding of the underlying principle in operation. It's difficult to meet a need you don't understand.
☐ The questions must be smooth and comfortable and you can't use what you don't remember. Write it down and practice, practice, practice.

The five questions are:

1. As you think about success on this project (client name), tell me, what kinds of things are important to you?
2. Anything else?
3. What are your priorities for these things?
4. If all the success factors you have described are achieved, which bottom-line organizational results (e.g., reduced turnover, increased production, increased sales, reduced operating costs) will be most improved by completing the project?
5. What costs will be avoided by successfully managing the project well?

The first question works because it is open to what the client *does* know about the project. With the first question, it is important to ask for further clarification on any points where the terminology may be vague. For example, "The term 'data management system' means different things to different people. Tell me more about what you mean when you use that term," or, "Tell me more about what this data management system would accomplish."

The second question is a real key to success during the interview. This prompts the stakeholders to go deeper. You are helping your client think it through. This may be (and probably is) the first time your client has given it this much thought. Don't ask this question once or twice and then bail out. It is often the last item that you gently pushed for that may bring up a critical success factor. Keep asking until he or she says, "No, there is nothing else."

The third question helps to recap all of the things that have been discussed and then places a priority on the list. This is a critical part of understanding the client's needs. You are working to co-create a clear vision and understanding of what the project is to accomplish.

The fourth question gives stakeholders the opportunity to think about what the return on investment will be if the project is completed successfully. This information can be extremely important when it comes to the checkpoints or go/no-go decisions. Return on investment is a comparison of the financial benefits of a successfully completed project to the costs of the project. If the successfully completed project will increase sales by 10 percent and that 10 percent increase will account for more money than the costs of the project, the predicted ROI is positive. Stakeholders may not be used to thinking in these terms and they may need some instruction in order to predict the ROI of the project outcome.

The fifth question allows the stakeholders to respond to how the return on investment will be greater if the project is managed well. Every missed deadline costs more money in salary and time put toward the project.

Most likely, there are multiple key stakeholders and a number of interviews will have been conducted. Information will be obtained from each of them, which can be used to compile a vision statement. A vision statement can then be written into a document that clarifies the project in terms of a short, but clear, description of the project and a prioritized list of the desired results. It should meet the SMART criteria: Specific, Measurable, Achievable, Relevant, and Time-Dimensioned. *Anything beyond this list of desired results in this document is beyond the scope of the project.*

A good vision statement document includes the following items:

☐ Project title
☐ Starting date
☐ Due date
☐ Project manager
☐ Project description: (what, where, and by when)
☐ Prioritized list of desired results (deliverables, outcomes, and accomplishments of the project)
☐ A statement detailing how the project meets the organization's strategic initiatives and outlining which organizational results will be most improved by the outcomes of the project.
☐ List of the key stakeholders

If there is a conflict between any of the key stakeholders, this is the best place in the process to discover and resolve that conflict, rather than during the later stages of the project. The vision statement document requires an approval from each of the key stakeholders in order to proceed to the next stage of the process. That approval is the first of two go/no-go decision points.

There are some challenges during the Visualize stage. Taking the time to find out the information up front is a challenge. Staying out of the task level of details—the work that needs to be done and who is going to do it—is also a challenge. This stage is not about identifying the work that needs to be done. That is accomplished in the Plan stage. The Visualize stage is simply about beginning with the end in mind. When it is done, what does it look like, what does it accomplish, and how will we know success when we see it; how will the organization's bottom line be better?

Go/No-Go Checkpoint Number One

At the end of the Visualize stage of the process, the project is evaluated with the following criteria in mind:

☐ Will the project deliver the stakeholders' desired results?
☐ Does the project vision statement meet the SMART (Specific, Measurable, Achievable, Relevant, Time-Dimensioned) criteria?
☐ Does the project support organizational and personal mission, vision, and values?

□ Will the project improve key organizational results?
□ Is the predicted ROI of the project positive?

This is a preliminary checkpoint. A "yes" here indicates that the project, in general, is worth pursuing. However, the rest of the needed information required for a final decision will be the result of the Plan stage.

Plan

The Plan stage is the "how to" stage of the project. It involves seven steps. The advantage of a planning process is that it provides a common methodology that can be learned, shared, and repeated.

Steps one through four need to be done in sequential order. Steps five through seven can be done in any sequence, depending on the tools that are used. For example, you may choose paper Gantt-style charts, spread sheets, or project software.

Step One: Discuss and Prioritize the Triple Constraint with Key Stakeholders

There are three different kinds of performance specifications that affect every project.

1. Quality/scope
2. Time
3. Costs (to be compared with predicted financial benefits)

The triple constraint can be a confusing concept, but it is an important one to understand and manage early in the planning process. How we plan and manage the project depends upon an understanding of the constraints, which can be prioritized differently on any given project.

Quality and scope are inextricably linked. Quality refers to the level of excellence devoted to the project, whereas scope designates the size of the project and its features. The time constraint clarifies how long the project will take. The cost constraint clarifies the resources needed by the project and how much it will cost. To understand if there is flexibility around the costs, the costs can be compared to what the return on the costs will be.

There is a relationship of trade-offs between these three constraints, meaning that as one performance factor becomes a priority, it may require a sacrifice from another. Typically, a project will have one or two fixed constraints, requiring the remaining constraint(s) to be flexible. If the first constraint is fixed, the second and third constraints need to remain flexible in order to accomplish the highest-priority constraint. If the first two constraints are both fixed, then the third constraint must remain flexible to accomplish the first two. For example, a project that needs to be done fast, and with high quality/scope consideration, will typically have a higher cost. A project that has a tight budget, yet for which the quality/scope is also important, will require more time to complete. A project with tight time and budget constraints will require a trade-off from the features (scope) or the performance specifications (quality) of the project.

Ultimately, the best combination is a balance of the three project constraints. In addition, if we continuously improve our projects from past experience, the paradigm for future projects can be: "better, faster, and cheaper than ever before."

Step Two: Explore and Manage Possible Hot Spots

In order for a project to succeed, it is necessary to involve team members in the process of brainstorming to identify potential hot spots on a project. *Hot spots* are factors that could cause difficulty or cause the project to fail. Involving the team in this activity takes advantage of the expertise and knowledge provided by team members. No single person can provide the knowledge and insight provided by the entire team. This collective knowledge provides insights into the Plan stage that can help avoid and/or manage these potential hot spots.

When potential hot spots are identified by the team, rank them in terms of the level of risk. A simple five-point scale can help in the process, as follows:

1. Causes minor adjustments
2. Sacrifices the lowest-priority performance factor
3. Sacrifices the medium-priority performance factor
4. Sacrifices the highest-priority performance factor
5. Causes total failure

For hot spots that are ranked a 3, 4, or 5, brainstorm with the team to find ways to avoid the potential hot spot and ways to manage it if it does occur. Detailed action plans can be produced where needed on the potential hot spots with the highest risk. The risk scale provides additional insights into the next go/no-go decision stage. A high-risk project may be a candidate for a "no" at the next decision point.

Step Three: Break the Project Work Down into Manageable Pieces (Work Breakdown Structure)

Why is this important? Many projects are begun at task level without a clear understanding of the work that is required. This leads to a "what's next" practice of figuring it out as it goes. The result is longer project life cycles, resource conflicts, and poor communication and accountability practices. Doing the work breakdown structure successfully means there is clear understanding up front about what needs to be done, by when, by whom, and what resources will be required in order to do it.

The work breakdown organizes work according to categories. The largest work categories are called *major pieces. Phase* is also a popular term. Sub-categories are called *minor pieces,* which are optional, and are used only if a major category is large and needs to be broken down further for clearer categorization. The major or minor pieces can then be broken down into *task detail.* Tasks are the action steps that need to be done, and should be expressed as verbs. Project detail should be broken down as far as necessary for clear accountability.

For example, a project meant to develop a new training program would begin with a skeleton of the major pieces:

- ☐ Needs assessment
- ☐ Defining vision, scope, and major objectives
- ☐ Curriculum development
- ☐ Materials development
- ☐ Testing/revisions
- ☐ Presenter training
- ☐ Program release (kick-off)
- ☐ Budget/resources

The major piece of curriculum development might be broken down into three minor pieces (sub-categories).

1. Content
2. Exercises
3. Pre- and post-assessment

Each of the minor pieces can then be developed into a task list of the action steps needed to accomplish the work.

Project Team Assignments

Project Title:				Project Manager:							
Start Date:				Target Finish:					Actual Finish:		

Team Member →											
Pieces/Tasks Description	Due Date	Hours	✓	Due Date	Hours	✓	Due Date	Hours	✓	Due Date	Hours	✓
			☐			☐			☐			☐
			☐			☐			☐			☐
			☐			☐			☐			☐
			☐			☐			☐			☐
			☐			☐			☐			☐
			☐			☐			☐			☐
			☐			☐			☐			☐
			☐			☐			☐			☐
			☐			☐			☐			☐
			☐			☐			☐			☐
			☐			☐			☐			☐
			☐			☐			☐			☐
			☐			☐			☐			☐
			☐			☐			☐			☐
			☐			☐			☐			☐
			☐			☐			☐			☐
			☐			☐			☐			☐
			☐			☐			☐			☐
			☐			☐			☐			☐
			☐			☐			☐			☐
			☐			☐			☐			☐
			☐			☐			☐			☐

Figure 2-3. Work breakdown. © 1999 Franklin Covey Co. Used with permission.

A project to remodel a home could start with the following major pieces:

- ☐ Contractor
- ☐ Design
- ☐ Materials
- ☐ Construction
- ☐ Budget/resources

The step to select the contractor is broken down into minor pieces:

- ☐ Recommendations
- ☐ Interview
- ☐ References/inspections
- ☐ Final selection

All tasks on the project should be a subset of a major or minor piece of the project. A minor piece is completed as a result of the tasks beneath that minor piece being completed. A major piece is completed as a result of all of the minor pieces beneath it being completed.

Planning, Scheduling, Tracking, and Communication Tools

At this point, a tool is needed that can aid in the remainder of the planning of the project. Gantt-style charts (sequential and chronological lists) are helpful because, when done properly, they provide vital data about the project in a visual format. This kind of data display is key to both planning and communication on the project. With projects consisting of more than a hundred tasks, project software is very helpful. With projects of a few hundred or thousands of tasks, it is essential.

While software can be complex and difficult to use, there are several keys to success:

- ☐ Having and using a clear process to help define the data prior to the data entry stage
- ☐ Organizing the data effectively at the beginning of the data entry
- ☐ Working the tool one column at a time as opposed to entering data from left to right a row at a time
- ☐ Clarifying task duration and task relationships and letting the software calculate the dates accordingly rather than entering data

into the start- and end-date columns (unless it is a set date). This allows the software to make the necessary adjustments as things change.

Step Four: Organize and Enter the Pieces and Tasks into the Chosen Project Management Scheduling Tool (Paper Schedule or Project Software)

Sequencing the pieces and tasks prior to any data entry into a paper or software scheduling tool is a key to making the most effective use of the tool. Sequencing means listing pieces and tasks in the order they must be done. Sequence the major pieces first. This may be subjective at this level because multiple pieces may be going on simultaneously. However, where the sequencing of pieces is obvious, list them accordingly. Then, within each major piece, sequence the minor pieces. The order of events within a major piece is usually clearer. Within each minor piece, sequence the tasks.

As the pieces and tasks are listed, slightly indent minor pieces under major pieces, and further indent tasks under the minor pieces. Outlining the data makes the flow of the events of the project easier to understand. Now that the pieces and tasks are organized, the next step is to clarify the duration of each task.

Step Five: Determine Task Duration

Working the tool one column at a time allows one to clearly focus on one topic at a time. Go down the list and estimate the time necessary to complete each task. Don't enter data for major and minor pieces at this level. That will eventually be calculated as a sum total of the time frames for each related task.

Step Six: Clarify Task Relationships

This is done in a column entitled "Predecessors" on a paper form, and done as a linking activity in software. There are several kinds of task relationships. Parallel or concurrent tasks can be done at the same time. There are different kinds of dependencies, but for the purpose of this work only finish-to-start relationships are discussed. These dependency tasks require the completion of other tasks before they can be started.

Beside each task in the Predecessors column of the form, simply list the tasks that must be completed first. With project software, follow

Project Timetable

Use project management software such as Microsoft Project or On Target to complete your project schedule. Fill in the following information from your schedule.

Item #	✓	ABC	Project Task	Resource Names	Predecessors	Duration	Start Date	Target Finish	Actual Finish	Planning Notes	Costs Est.	Costs Act.
	☐											
	☐											
	☐											
	☐											
	☐											
	☐											
	☐											
	☐											
	☐											
	☐											
	☐											
	☐											
	☐											
	☐											
	☐											
	☐											
	☐											
	☐											
	☐											
	☐											
	☐											
	☐											

Figure 2-4. Project timetable or Gantt chart.

your software package instructions on linking to the tasks that need to be completed first.

At this point, linking the task relationships is made easier by the fact that the data have already been entered sequentially and organized by major and minor pieces. This creates a logical flow of activities and is easier to work with than a list of tasks that has not been organized in this way. Many who have not organized the data effectively to begin with have experienced disappointing, and sometimes disastrous, results after clicking on the "Sort by Date" button of the software because it destroys the logical flow of organized data.

Step Seven: Determine Resources and Budget

This step can be done within the project software or on a separate spreadsheet. The major advantage of leaving the resource and budget clarification until the last step is that it is based on information clarified in the previous steps. The estimate should be based on how the project is done, in what time frame, and with what resources.

This technique is far more effective than random budget estimates, which are often provided at the time the project assignment is made. Unless these up-front budgets are based on good data from past experience of similar projects, they are often rough-guess estimates based on little or no data.

Go/No-Go Checkpoint Number Two

At this point, the data needed to make the final go/no-go decision should be complete. The project data now include a clear understanding of what the project is and what it will accomplish (from the Visualize stage), as well as a clear understanding of the work breakdown, what needs to be done, who will do it, by when, and at what cost compared to the predicted financial benefits.

Questions for Checkpoint Number Two are:

1. Can the project meet the prioritized performance factors?
2. Is the risk level on hotspots acceptable and manageable?
3. Are the resources available and is the timeline realistic?
4. Are the predicted financial benefits greater than the predicted costs?

These are the questions to consider in the process of deciding whether to continue to the Implement stage or exit the process. Any project proceeding through this checkpoint should have every possible chance of succeeding. The investment in the Visualize and Plan stages can pay huge dividends when undesirable projects are eliminated early in the process. Those that continue to the Implement stage are the high-priority, high return-on-investment projects that now have the highest potential for success.

Celebrate the Early "No's"

It is important in an organizational culture to understand and support the process by celebrating the clear "no's." Success comes from enough clear "no's" to reserve the resources and energy needed for what Tom Peters calls the "WOW" projects—the high-priority, high ROI projects that matter most and are about the business of mission, vision, values, goals, and strategies. Create a corporate culture where clear, fast "no's" are a cause for celebration, as opposed to a sign of failure.

Implement

Implementation is the key to the top of the Strategic Planning Pyramid. The best work breakdowns are of no value if the project does not translate into clear work assignments and daily workload management. A key challenge for most individuals in the workplace today comes from the fact that they must balance project work as well as other daily tasks unrelated to their specific projects. This is the workload management part of the process, where individuals responsible for the work coordinate the tasks, activities, and information into their schedules (Snead, 1997).

Regardless of what type of daily planning system is used, effective management of time, information, and tasks (workload management) is essential in order to manage a project successfully. If the individual's systems and tools do not promote effective workload management, the project work will not be accomplished effectively.

Implementation is made up of two key functions:

1. Doing the work that is in the plan
2. Managing and controlling the project and the communication, including making necessary changes and adjustments needed on the project

Workload Management—Doing the Work

Effective workload management requires a daily planning system that includes three capabilities—the ability to track prioritized daily tasks, schedules, and information.

Differences Between a "To Do" List and a Prioritized Daily Task List

A "To Do" List is a dynamic list of things to do and tasks that cannot be planned and prioritized into specific days. A Prioritized Daily Task List is a dated task list. Each day can be planned and prioritized independently. This is vital to success on a project because of the high number of tasks, the importance of the schedule, and the need to coordinate project tasks with other daily tasks.

Time Activation

Follow the plan and schedule the workload by using a technique called Time Activation. Time Activation answers three questions:

1. What needs to be done?
2. When does it need to occur?
3. Where is the information stored?

How to Do It

Select a specific task for which you are responsible. Working from the project plan, enter a Time Activation reference into your daily planning system on the first date you will begin work on this project. A Time Activation reference includes:

☐ A reference to the project by name
☐ An indication of where the needed information is located (usually a file name)
☐ A reminder to forward the Time Activation reference to the next date work is required on the project, after that day's work is complete (TAF = Time Activate Forward). For example: Client Project (ClientProj.mpp)/TAF. Here, the "mpp" refers to a computer file within the project management software program.

Another example might be: Remodel Project (PT3)/TAF. Here, the "(PT3)" refers to project tab number three in a project notebook. Once the project is entered into the task portion of a day, the next step is to determine how much time will need to be spent on the project that day. Then block time to work on the project in the appointment schedule portion of the planning system. The reason this works is because of the level of detail in the work breakdown structure. When this process is resisted, often the day is spent on non-project tasks and the project spills over into non-working hours.

Communication, Management, and Control of the Project

The best means of communication, management, and control during the project is with regularly scheduled review meetings. Standard practice in many organizations is often to get together only when there is a problem. This is built-in crisis management! Regularly scheduled review meetings are an opportunity to get core members of the team together for progress checks, updates and revisions, and clear communication with the whole team.

This works because:

- [ ] The team has a clear vision.
- [ ] The work breakdown shows details, responsibilities, and time-lines.
- [ ] The review meeting is a reality check. It answers questions such as:

    What has been done?

    What still needs to be done?

    What issues, problems, or changes still exist? These can be spotted on the horizon as opposed to waiting until the crisis arises.

- [ ] In the world of electronic communication, there is no substitute for meeting face to face.

The plan can be revised and the effects of changes communicated to the team on a regular basis. This is the method for continuous management, control, and communication during the project. A colleague told a story recently of a large company who had people working on a project that had already been cancelled. *They had never been notified.* DON'T SELL THIS TECHNIQUE SHORT. This is a powerful method that ensures up-to-date information and excellent communication opportunities.

Managing Changes

Another key control point throughout the Implement stage is an effective change management process. Many organizations experience out-of-control project environments simply because there is no formal change methodology in place. This is only effective when the key stakeholders were involved in the initial Visualize stage to begin with. The Visualize stage serves to dramatically reduce the number of needed changes because changes are often a result of the key stakeholders not thinking the project through from the beginning. This process eliminates that problem, thus requiring fewer changes.

For the few changes that are necessary, the process should require documentation on the reasons for the proposed change, the impact on the quality/scope, time, and cost, as well as the sign-off of key stakeholders. It is amazing how many times the need for a change simply goes away once the impact on the project is clearly understood.

Close and Evaluate

The remainder of this book will outline how to evaluate the success of project management systems including return on investment. This can be accomplished by implementing the Project Management Scorecard, which will be described in the remainder of the book. Yet, a few ideas will be mentioned here.

The key activities in this stage of the project are to complete the project and the documentation, and evaluate and learn for the future. Every project should be a learning experience.

Because of the measurable components in the vision statement, the first part of the evaluation is clear. The basis of the evaluation is simply whether the project successfully accomplished the desired results or not. In addition to that, however, each stage in the process should be considered.

On a 1–5 scale, evaluate how specific practices were performed during each of the stages in the Four-Step Project Management Process—Visualize, Plan, Implement, and Close. Get this input from each key member of the team, not just the project manager. Different insights are important.

Take time with the team to brainstorm ideas for solutions to some of the specific problem areas. This provides valuable documentation that can be filed with the project and utilized in future similar projects.

These data provide measurable tracking and a comparison over time, which is especially valuable in an organization utilizing a project management office (discussed in the next section). One of the advantages of a project management process is that it can be continuously improved.

FINAL THOUGHTS

The four steps in the project management process, Visualize, Plan, Implement, and Close, provide a methodology that can be used by any organization. This process remains a constant, repeatable formula to build solutions that avoid the most common reasons for project failure. Within the process, there are two go/no-go checkpoints that offer an opportunity to decide whether the project should continue. To ensure the success of a project, the project team should compile a shared vision statement with input from key stakeholders. This vision statement provides a detailed understanding of key business or organization results that will be improved by the outcomes of the project.

REFERENCES

Covey, Stephen R. *The Seven Habits of Highly Effective People.* New York: Simon & Schuster, 1989.

A Guide to the Project Management Body of Knowledge. Project Management Institute Standards Committee, The Project Management Institute, 1996, 6.

Khalsa, Mahan. *Let's Get Real or Let's Not Play.* Salt Lake City, Utah: Franklin Covey Co., 1999.

Snead, G. Lynne. *To Do, Doing, Done: A Creative Approach to Managing Projects & Effectively Finishing What Matters Most.* New York: Simon & Schuster, 1997.

FURTHER READING

Buttrick, Robert. *The Interactive Project Workout*, 2nd ed. London: Financial Times Prentice-Hall, 2000.

Cohen, Dennis J. and Robert J. Graham. *The Project Manager's MBA: How to Translate Project Decision into Business Success.* San Francisco: Jossey-Bass, 2001.

Frame, J. Davidson. *Managing Projects in Organizations: How to Make the Best Use of Time, Techniques, and People.* San Francisco: Jossey-Bass, 1987.

Greer, Michael. *The Project Manager's Partner: A Step-by-Step Guide to Project Management.* HRD Press, Inc. and ISPI, 1996.

Russell, Lou. *Project Management for Trainers: Stop "Winging It" and Get Control of Your Training Projects.* Alexandria, VA: American Society for Training and Development, 2000.

CHAPTER 3

Project Management Solutions

The project management scorecard measures the impact of solutions designed to improve the project management process. Regardless of the type of solution, the project management scorecard can isolate the impact of the solution, capture six types of data, and show success. This chapter examines solutions such as specific software, training, or web tools that prove helpful in solving project management challenges. It also explores the issue of creating an effective project management culture within the organization. Solutions should support a sound project management process, based on sound principles, and aid the implementation of the process. When solutions are used in the absence of a sound process, and without skills to use the tools effectively, the project management process typically is not successful.

It is a common occurrence within organizations for solutions to become the focus of the process and the investment. With technology changes today, tools change quickly. Whatever is standard in organizations at this time is likely to be soon outdated. Long-term, effective, project management solutions need to be interdependent of the tools used to implement them, and the solutions need to stand the test of time.

While exploring and designing solutions to solve project management challenges, it is important to understand the types of solutions that are available, and to understand that different project management solutions have an impact at one or more of the Four Levels of Effectiveness™: personal, interpersonal, managerial, and organizational.

(These levels will be explained later in this chapter). Many organizations have been unsuccessful at implementing culture-wide project management solutions because they lack understanding of the different levels of effectiveness and one or more of the levels were neglected.

This chapter will examine what project management solutions are intended to accomplish, the various stages of solving project management challenges, the readiness for these solutions, and the mapping of specific types of solutions for each level of effectiveness.

PROJECT MANAGEMENT SOLUTIONS— PAST AND FUTURE

Most organizations, no matter how large, start from entrepreneurial beginnings, with associates doing little with regard to project management. Each individual and department manages projects differently, and while some are inherently good at it, many are not. Scattered and limited project management efforts are not effective as organizations grow and deal with limited resources and demanding competition. On the other hand, some organizations have implemented project management methodologies that are complicated and understood only by a few professionals with highly specialized training. Often these methodologies are too complex to be used effectively throughout the organization. Regardless of the reasons for project failure, as our economy progressively becomes a world economy and globalization creates extraordinary competition, the need for better project management performance is clear.

Recent statistics indicate that 30 percent of organizational projects end up being canceled before completion, and that over half run as high as 190 percent over budget and many are over the original time estimates for completion (*PM Network Magazine*, January 2001). This type of high project failure rate has simply become unacceptable to many organizations.

Project challenges result in what can be summed up as the "Big Four":

☐ Cost overruns
☐ Time overruns
☐ Customer dissatisfaction
☐ Staff turnover and low morale

Currently, effective project management solutions focus on the following desired results and accomplishments:

- ☐ Increase the effectiveness of organization-wide project management practices
- ☐ Create effective scorecard system and ROI practices
- ☐ Provide a common practice and methodology (language) throughout an organization and key checkpoints within the practice
- ☐ Ensure that projects are tied to organizational strategies and initiatives
- ☐ Create a management culture that's willing and able to make good decisions about what to pursue and what not to pursue, resulting in projects that are strategically relevant
- ☐ Create proficiencies in effective implementation of project and workload management practices
- ☐ Provide tools to reinforce and aid in the application of an effective process
- ☐ Create a management culture that's effective and realistic about what can be done with limited resources

THREE STAGES OF PROJECT MANAGEMENT EFFECTIVENESS IMPLEMENTATION

The high cost of the project management is caused by poor or non-existent project management practices. When project managers understand this issue, they take steps to deal with these problems. Robert Happy, consultant and founder of the Project Consulting Group, of Novato, California, has specialized in helping organizations implement project management solutions for over ten years. Robert's Effective PM™ process focuses on the developmental stages that organizations move through as they try to solve critical issues. This process has three stages, what Robert calls a "crawl, walk, run" approach. This approach acknowledges that lasting project management solutions are not implemented in a single-step project solution. The three stages are:

Stage 1—Recognition

Stage 2—Acceptance

Stage 3—Effectiveness

Stage 1, Recognition, is characterized by a realization that the organization needs to take action. This realization is often implemented by a small group or a single person, and not yet recognized as a key strategic initiative by management. Typical solutions may be a band-aid approach; for example, perhaps a few individuals are sent to software training or new project management software is purchased but installed sporadically. The typical results in this stage are small islands of success but without integration or significant support, and often result in frustration over the complexities of the tools and the lack of consistent use throughout the organization.

Stage 2, Acceptance, reflects a commitment to invest in expanded project management solutions beyond the "hit and run" approach (Stage 1: Recognition). Some efforts are successful and yet major support and funding is usually still lacking. Typical solutions may be to identify internal resources and to dedicate some time to the process and the development of tools. Typically, the results are that some benefit is realized, but that only islands or pockets of success exist. There are still major inconsistencies between departments and resistance to the process exists in various places throughout the organization.

In Stage 3, Effectiveness, as the initiative gains support from senior management, organizations fund the initiative and commit full-time internal resources. Knowledge transfers from external consultants to internal staff, and training begins to take hold and make a significant difference in the behaviors of employees. Typical solutions at this stage are to set up Project Management Offices or Centers for Excellence. Organizational standards and processes and custom tools are implemented. Typically, these centers become the "place to go" for project help, and organization-wide acceptance begins to spread. Muscle memory is created; in other words "...this is just how we manage our projects here" might be a familiar phrase.

CHANGING CORPORATE CULTURES: READINESS FOR PROJECT MANAGEMENT SOLUTIONS

When considering the creation of a project management culture, several key strategic questions are important:

- ☐ Is the need great enough to sustain the commitment to the work?
- ☐ Will the benefits outweigh the costs?
- ☐ Who cares about the cultural change—not just this month, but next year, in three years, in five years?
- ☐ What will the long-term impact be to the organization?
- ☐ If the organization is not ready, what needs to happen to make it ready?

Warning: THIS IS NOT FOR THE WEAK AT HEART!

Early efforts can create success that can have a tremendous and immediate return on investment. Even in an environment seriously challenged with project management problems, success can be realized early on, and the ROI can increase over time with continued dedication and focus on long-term solutions.

The biggest reason for failure in trying to create corporate-wide project management effectiveness stems from simple resistance. The more we are aware of the reasons for resistance, the more we are able to successfully manage the project as an organizational change initiative.

Some resistance comes from fear of change. Many individuals within organizations fear accountability and are not accustomed to processes and structures that may, at first, feel like they limit freedom and creativity. Often individuals are hesitant to support project management efforts because they may fear that this will increase workload or the initiative may not be supported because of limited resources.

Another factor that contributes to failure in creating corporate-wide project management effectiveness is the existence, in most organizations, of the biggest enemy of effective project management practices: the manager who does not know the difference between an idea and a project. He or she may have no filtering system to prioritize relevant ideas over low-priority project ideas, and may make vague assignments to staff without helping to clarify the project vision. Furthermore, the manager may force the project to begin in the implementation stage, with no idea as to what is required to fund the project nor what costs will be incurred in comparison to project benefits. He or she may also have no idea how many projects are currently underway competing for limited resources, and may constantly change ideas and visions about the project during the implementation stage. To make matters worse, he may think hammering harder will drive staff to successfully complete pet projects on time. This type of manager wreaks havoc within an organization and can single-handedly waste millions of dollars of precious resources, and drive valuable talent away from the organization. An environment that condones the activities from this style of manager is not ready for this kind of culture change and will never successfully adopt effective project management practices.

Creating support for proper and effective project management practices is in-and-of itself a project. Begin the process of gaining support for effective project management by asking questions of key stakeholders within the organization to thoroughly understand the project management challenges and key issues they face. Then involve these "clients" in the creation of a vision for a better environment. Where there is participation and involvement, there is buy-in.

Regardless of the solutions that are prescribed, effectiveness translates to the people who are working on those solutions. *People* create success. If people are not helped by the solutions, they will not use them. If the tools are too difficult to understand and to use, the people will not use them. If the solutions are implemented but not supported, people will not use them. If you solve these "hot spot" challenges by forming partnerships with the organization's key stakeholders, success can be achieved.

A good example of this principle of needing key stakeholder support for effective project management effectiveness is as follows: Prior to conducting PM training for a particular organization, an online project management health assessment was given to the participants. Data were captured about the current project management challenges, and these data helped to paint a graphic picture of the current environment within this organization, including the frustrations felt by the participants that made it difficult for them to effectively do their work. Each PM class began with the organization's Executive VP of Strategic Planning, who explained that the increased value to this organization for creating a successful project management environment was estimated to be between 300 and 500 million dollars over the next three to five years. The impact this announcement had upon the participants of each class was remarkable. The interest, commitment, and buy-in far exceeded the norm. The moral: this type of "pep talk" should be repeated in all project management training programs in order for effective PM training to take place.

Successful project managers understand the high cost of poorly managed projects. They fully comprehend that the cost of poorly managed projects is no longer acceptable, and they understand the potential ROI from solving the problems. They understand that an effective project management process is not designed to limit creativity, but rather to limit premature implementation. They are willing to embrace change and will manage change throughout the project, following an effective project management process, and utilizing a "crawl, walk, run" approach that builds buy-in and continuous improvement as the project grows.

THREE TYPES OF SOLUTIONS: PROCESS, TOOLS, AND TRAINING

Organizations that have attempted to implement company-wide project management solutions have often failed due to a narrow focus on one kind of solution. Some have put a process in place without the necessary training and tools to enable employees to effectively use the process. Some have put tools in place, only to assume employees would be motivated to figure out how to use them on their own. Others have provided training, without the necessary organization-wide understanding and support of the material. Creating project management solutions that work involves three different kinds of solutions—process, tools, and training—all vital to accomplish a holistic solution.

Process Solutions

In some organizations, each group, department, or individual managing a project is doing so differently. In others, the process in place is so complicated that only a few professionals can use it effectively. A key to success is to understand that an effective project management *methodology* is critical for an effective solution. An effective project management methodology is a process that is successful regardless of (1) the scope and size of a project, (2) the tools used for the project, and (3) the people working on the project. A consistent process provides a common language and approach that can be developed for repeated use, thus avoiding a common pitfall of treating each new project like something that has never been done before. The methodology provides a clear understanding of the work to be accomplished as well as clear check-off points, such as the process outlined in Chapter 2.

One of the first issues to address with teams who have graduated from project management training is to identify where they are in the process. One of the best ways to stay on track in the process is to have a checklist of the steps and items in the project management process, starting with a vision statement and concluding with the communication of the process results. Such a checklist is provided in later chapters.

Software and Technology Tools

The tools used on a project can vary significantly from paper and pencil to sophisticated and expensive hardware and software. Tools can be flexible, depending on culture and environment, individual working styles and preferences, and cost. The tools should exist to support the implementation of the process. They can be as basic as simple, generic project management templates or as sophisticated as customized templates designed to fit specific business needs.

Software and technology tools can vary from the use of project management software by an individual to the use of industry-wide hardware and software that tracks and manages project timelines and resources over multiple projects, allowing key personnel to check a project's progress at any time and from almost any location throughout the world with Internet access. Software and technology tools:

☐ Improve planning and communication
☐ Increase speed in terms of analysis and reporting
☐ Improve the ability to change and update plans
☐ Provide the opportunity to run what-if scenarios
☐ Compile the data to view and share across the organization

The disadvantages of such tools are:

☐ They can be very expensive.
☐ They require a significant learning curve.
☐ If they are too difficult, no one will use them.
☐ If there is no perceived value to the user, no one will use them.
☐ They may be outdated by noon tomorrow.

The most sophisticated and most expensive technology tools will be ineffective if the information they produce does not turn into real work for employees on a daily basis. Most employees are challenged by multiple projects at one time. Information on these multiple projects needs to be effectively tied to individual planning systems; otherwise, work will never be successfully translated into daily workload for the individuals responsible for the work. In fact, if individuals can't manage their time and information, they can't successfully manage projects.

Training Solutions

Processes and tools, without the training and knowledge about how to *apply* the process and *use* the tools, are useless. Many project managers have learned this the hard way. Just ask the project manager who thought just *having* project management software was the answer to his project management problems. He purchased it and loaded it on everyone's computers, thinking that taking these steps would solve the problem. End of story.

Even with training, most individuals find that they are ill prepared to use software and other tools because the training was focused on the tools themselves and did not cover a sound project management practice or process. The answer to creating skills is in effective training, and effective training is not accomplished as a single event.

The most effective training approach is a threefold approach that encompasses pre-event preparation, training, and then follow-up support. Pre-work helps prepare the student to learn; the training is designed around the needs and learning styles of the audience; and follow-up work helps reinforce the desired behaviors in an on-the-job setting.

Preparation for Training

Participants need to know why the training is relevant? What's in it for them? What's in it for the organization? Remember the client who explained at the beginning of each class that the value difference over three to five years could be 300 to 700 million dollars? This was part of a pre-assessment process and also served to uncover the challenges these participants were going to face. This information enables a trainer to direct the experience appropriately to those challenges. This is often the difference between participants as knowledge seekers—anxious to learn and apply what they have learned—versus prisoners, who are attending training because they have to be there.

Reading supportive material on project management—what it is, how it's done, and what a difference it can make—is helpful as pre-work. This provides hooks for learning and stimulates thoughts about the relevance of the training prior to the actual training experience. Pre-work may also include preparing an individual project assignment for participants to work on throughout the training experience. These activities set the stage for good training.

The Training

The training event needs to be relevant to the audience's current knowledge, work environment, and existing challenges, and should take into consideration all kinds of learning styles through the use of good materials, appropriate examples, and hands-on practice.

Follow-up Support

For training to result in changed behaviors, there must be effective follow-up after training has been completed. *Most training benefit is lost over time without this, and this is where most training initiatives fail.* Employees are used to seeing initiatives come and go. "Will this be another one?" they may ask. Practice and coaching must be provided until the skill and knowledge transfer becomes complete. The objective is for these new skills and tools to become cellular memory over time and for support to permeate throughout the whole organization. In other words: "This is just how we manage projects around here; it is the way it should be done; it is the way we do it."

A clear example of the need for such support is shown by a recent visit with one organization. In the organization, one individual was particularly excited about the skills she had learned during the training program. She spent the next weekend developing a Gantt chart for a project for which her boss was responsible. She presented the chart to him on Monday morning, only to have him briefly glance at it and set it down on the corner of his desk. Not only did he not understand how to read a Gantt chart, but he perceived anything that had task responsibilities clearly spelled out, with individual names and dates attached to them, as a threat. Needless to say, her motivation to continue using the tools she had learned during her training was severely hampered.

Contrast the above story to the company with a "Project Management Innovation Center," where employees can go to trained coaches for help on their projects, either as individuals or as a project team, to get a customized workshop. This particular organization publishes a newsletter detailing specific lessons learned from real project teams, and details millions of dollars of project return on investment. The organization has helped to create a project management culture by learning to crawl, then walk, and is in the process of learning to run!

Some of the critical questions to ask about this ongoing support of PM are the following:

Who's supporting the process?

Where in the organization is good PM becoming part of the overall goals and expectations? Where can an individual trying new skills, tools, and knowledge go for support and coaching?

Is on-site coaching available?

Is telephone coaching available?

Are supervisors acting as mentors and role models?

Have those supervisors had additional training?

Many times, a supervisor who is trying to coach has had the same level of training as the employee. Advanced project management training is needed, and training in coaching skills is also helpful. Other questions include:

Is a Project Management Office, created within the organization, available for help?

Is web support available?

Is just-in-time training now available for the team with a project assignment to help them implement what they have learned—on a *real* project.

Organizations who can answer "yes" to the majority of these questions will be the ones to foster effective project management, which in turn will translate to greater return on investment. The Appendix details a case study where an effective project management culture was implemented at Abbott Laboratories.

MAPPING SOLUTIONS TO FOUR LEVELS OF PROJECT MANAGEMENT EFFECTIVENESS

Another key to success is understanding that project management effectiveness occurs at four levels—personal, interpersonal, managerial, and organizational—as shown in Figure 3-1.

While solutions can address specific issues at any of the four levels, in order to holistically provide lasting solutions throughout an entire culture, solutions must be present at all four levels. If the focus is on organizational change initiatives, it is critical that the other types of change not be ignored. Any level that is neglected tends to be the one that unravels the work accomplished at the other levels.

Remember the manager who didn't understand the Gantt chart and was intimidated by it? This was the result of one of the four levels being neglected.

A SUCCESSFUL APPROACH—INSIDE OUT AND OUTSIDE IN, SIMULTANEOUSLY

Inside-Out Approach

Inside-out training begins at a personal level and works on individual skills development and changing individual behaviors. This training

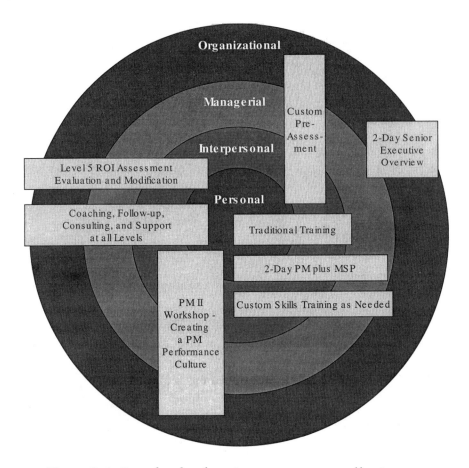

Figure 3-1. Four levels of project management effectiveness.
© *1999 Franklin Covey Co. Used with permission.*

includes learning and utilizing a project management methodology, PM skills, and tools. It may also include other needed skills, such as time management or communication skills.

The next level out is interpersonal skills. This level is influenced as individuals begin to use the skills they have learned while working together. If other individuals in the environment are not trained in the understanding and support of the needed process, skills, and tools, it is difficult to get beyond a personal level of effectiveness. Additional training that may be helpful at this level is communication, team-building, creating trust, or negotiating.

The next level is the managerial level. As individuals have learned the needed skills and have been supported while working together, these same individuals can impact others at a managerial level. It is, however, difficult to set management expectations, coach others, and support the use of new skills, tools, and processes at this level unless additional, advanced training has taken place. This may include more advanced project management, meeting management, and team and leadership skills training. This is where the outside-in approach is vital.

Outside-In Approach

This approach begins at an organizational level. It requires support from senior executives who understand the cost of existing project management challenges and are committed to the creation of an effective organization-wide project management culture. Otherwise, effectiveness tends to build throughout the personal and interpersonal levels, but does not create significant change throughout the management and organizational level.

At an organizational level, it is vital that the organization's mission, vision, and governing values drive the project management process. This ensures that the project management process is in alignment with the organizational strategy, and that the appropriate project management solution is selected. The organizational level is also the place for the creation of organizational systems, structures, and processes—in short, the environmental solutions. A key question to ask here is: Do the systems, structures, and processes within this organization support the desired results of the organization?

From outside-in, support at a managerial level can now begin to create an effective project management environment. With additional, advanced training, managers now have an opportunity to set clear expectations about the processes, have tools and reporting procedures to be used, and can provide coaching and mentoring support. Managers get what they teach, coach, and accept in return. Managers are responsible for the alignment of projects to strategies, and for properly allocating resources to project teams.

PROJECT MANAGEMENT OFFICE

The organizational level can be aided by the creation of a Project Management Office (PMO), which can support the environment through training, coaching, and the careful selection and scheduling of projects and resources. A PMO can help create a learning organization that continuously develops and improves upon its project management culture over time. The existence of a PMO often stands as the difference between organizations that are successful over time in the creation of a project management environment versus those who create only small, sometimes temporary, islands of success.

There are many different types of PMOs, from the one-person office offering a few services to a full-blown PMO that houses all the company's project management services (Block and Frame, 1998). Many function effectively and provide valuable service to an organization. Others function poorly—only as gatekeepers for the organization's projects.

The goal of a PMO should be to support the organization's mission, vision, values, and strategic initiatives through the effective implementation of the "right" projects.

An effective PMO can provide the following services:

- ☐ Oversight of project process and methodology
- ☐ Training
- ☐ Administrative support
- ☐ Project scheduling
- ☐ Resource management
- ☐ A project visibility room
- ☐ Coordination of project review meetings
- ☐ Project documentation
- ☐ Return on investment evaluation assistance

The PMO can also provide:

- ☐ Coaching, mentoring, and training
- ☐ Help with the creation of effective vision statements
- ☐ Encouragement in the pursuit of high ROI projects
- ☐ Assistance with the creation of the project plan
- ☐ Help with coordinating resources for multiple projects
- ☐ Help with scheduling and acquiring resources
- ☐ Some control over project costs

PMO Success Story

At CIGNA HealthCare of Arizona, the Project Management Office (PMO) assists employees in developing their creative ideas into approved projects. The PMO, in the context of project management, assists employees in making "go/no-go" decisions on projects on a regular basis. The PMO is charged with ensuring that projects are aligned with CIGNA's strategic goals: standardizing project management and reporting activities, providing a discipline for managing complexity in projects, and implementing a business case approach for determining and monitoring the net benefit of projects.

This PMO recognized that frequently the best ideas for successful projects come from front-line employees. Front-line employees do not typically have the ear or eyes of senior management to approve projects. Knowledge of this gap influenced the PMO to develop a process to assist employees in getting their project ideas heard and approved. This process includes idea generation, engagement of the PMO to assist with business case development, presentation to middle and senior management for approval, and PMO support throughout the effort.

Advantages of PMO

By following a clear project management process within an organization, it is possible to take advantage of the functionality of a PMO without starting with a full-blown, staffed office. This can be accomplished, to a certain extent, when management and staff follow the methodology and practices of the process. Having the common language, tools, and training to implement the methodology is key. This is especially important when evaluating the success of project management efforts. The remainder of this book will outline the language, tools, and methodology to effectively evaluate and calculate the return on investment of project management improvement efforts.

FINAL THOUGHTS

This chapter examined ways to solve project management challenges and also discussed the issue of creating an effective project management culture within an organization. Effective project management involves three different solutions: process, tools, and training. All three are vital to success. These solutions should provide a common methodology throughout the organization, ensure that projects are tied to organizational strategies, provide tools and training to aid in the application of the process, and focus on effective ROI practices.

Another key to success is understanding that project management effectiveness occurs at four levels: personal, interpersonal, managerial, and organizational. To provide lasting solutions throughout the organization's culture, the project management process must be supported at all four levels.

Many organizations benefit from a Project Management Office whose task is to support the organization's mission, vision, values, and strategic initiatives through the effective implementation of the "right" projects.

REFERENCES

Block, Thomas R. and J. Davidson Frame. *The Project Office*. Crisp Publications, Inc. 1998.

CHAPTER 4

The Project Management Scorecard

The number of organizations using project managers has increased, especially in the technology industry. Perhaps the increased use of project managers in the technology industry is because technology often requires the expertise of many people—many people who have to work in harmony to accomplish the same goal—versus the genius of one person going it alone. This team-based approach to managing technology often necessitates a project manager.

However, the technology industry is not the only industry in need of more highly skilled project managers. In general, many professionals across a number of industries are managing projects even though project management is not their major job responsibility. For all of these project managers—whether the project is restructuring, implementing systems, developing staff, changing procedures, buying new companies, or bringing out new products and services—accountability for results is increasing. Companies are fervently seeking project managers who can multi-task, deliver results, and improve business. Unfortunately, clients are often disappointed when projects fail to deliver the anticipated results, leaving both the client and the company's project manager frustrated over the outcome of the project.

While some have regarded the project management profession as a highly desirable occupation, others have characterized it by numerous project failures. The problems facing project managers, although varying with the industry and the type of project, generally fall into the following categories:

- ☐ Lack of accountability
- ☐ Tarnished image
- ☐ Excessive costs
- ☐ An inconsistent process
- ☐ A lack of common toolsets
- ☐ Poor training
- ☐ Undefined roles and responsibilities

Each of these places a cloud over the project management industry, causing some to question the contributions of project consultants. The answer is to provide clearly defined objectives at the outset, with measurable checks throughout implementation to ensure that the project is focused on key results.

The following example illustrates the need for measurement from the beginning of the project management process.

A well-known and respected project manager was asked to manage the development of a software program that would enhance the competitive advantage of the organization. Mid-level managers gave the project manager "time to market" as the most important priority for the project; the software needed to be developed quickly. Quality was the next most important priority and costs were said to be a "non-issue." After creating the vision statement for the project and planning the entire project, the project manager proposed a budget. The budget was approved by mid-level managers, but above them, executives of the organization denied the budget request and cancelled the project due to the high costs proposed for funding the project.

One of the flaws that surfaces from this example is the lack of a clear definition of the project up front and a lack of focus on the specific objectives. While many projects do yield clear definitions up front, measurable objectives addressing critical issues by which success will be evaluated are often overlooked. This failure to focus on results often prevents the project from ever getting off the ground.

In this example, performing some type of forecast evaluation to determine the potential success at the end of the interviews with management may have helped to prevent project cancellation by the executives. In fact, measurement and evaluation can be conducted at key points during the management of any project, helping to keep projects on target. *This is the purpose of a project management scorecard.* The project management scorecard identifies the key measures that have to be taken at critical points in the project management process. In general, scorecard measures should be taken at the end of each of the four steps of the project management process.

This book presents the tools and processes needed to (1) implement a project management scorecard; (2) ensure that project solutions are properly initiated (with the end in mind); and (3) place the necessary emphasis on results, including various feedback mechanisms to keep the project clearly on track. When implemented, this scorecard will ensure that a project management solution not only produces results, but also that those results are significant and aligned with stakeholders needs.

WHAT CAN HAPPEN WITHOUT THE SCORECARD?

The following consequences can result from a flawed project management accountability system:

- ☐ **Wasted resources.** Perhaps the most important consequence of a flawed system is that precious funds are wasted on project solutions. Project solutions are usually very expensive, and in larger organizations, the funding for a project can be significant and often grows without accountability.
- ☐ **Wasted time.** Projects eat up precious staff time, as dozens and sometimes hundreds of employees perform tasks and provide information for the project solution. This is often done with the assumption that the current staff can provide the needed information at less cost. If the project goes astray and does not produce results, the experience represents a tremendous waste of internal time—time that could be devoted to important, profit-generating activities.
- ☐ **Demoralized staff.** Connected very closely with the waste of time is the effect the project has on the staff. A failed project solution can create a morale problem for the project team.
- ☐ **Devastated careers.** Project assignments have been known to tarnish the careers of those individuals who advocated or supported faulty projects. When management realizes the company received very little value for the money they spent, the project managers or project teams involved in the process often lose their luster (and

sometimes their jobs). Also, in a highly political environment, those who resist project assignments often suffer career anxieties and disappointments.

Many of the above-mentioned consequences of ineffective project management can be prevented if proper steps are taken to hold project managers accountable from the beginning of the process, and throughout to the end of the assignment. This is the role of the project management scorecard.

POTENTIAL STEPS TO BUILD THE PROJECT MANAGEMENT SCORECARD

Now comes the key question: What can the client do to make sure the project manager focuses on results? Actually, the client is in the driver's seat. The client can demand, require, specify, as well as expect results. How is this done? From a practical basis, this can be done by focusing on several issues—up to and including the following:

☐ Proven results from previous projects
☐ Guaranteed results from the project
☐ Specified project requirements
☐ Apparent focus on results from the outset
☐ Detailed needs assessment including business impact and job performance needs
☐ Forecasted ROI of the project
☐ Establishment of multiple levels of project objectives
☐ Development of a comprehensive evaluation plan
☐ Expectations are clearly understood by all stakeholders
☐ Method to provide feedback throughout the process
☐ Ability to develop project management scorecard
☐ Determined methodology to isolate the effects of the project solution
☐ Plan to monitor long-term effects of the project

All of these issues may not be appropriate for a particular project solution, but they represent important areas to consider in preparing for the project to be developed properly and structured adequately, and to deliver the results needed and promised. The checklist in Table 4-1 will help the client determine the degree to which the project focuses on results.

Table 4-1. How to Make Sure Your Project Manager Focuses on Results

	YES	NO
1. Does your project manager have results from other projects?	☐	☐
2. Will your project manager agree to guarantee results?	☐	☐
3. Has your project manager carefully specified the requirements for the project?	☐	☐
4. Is there a clear focus on results up front in the proposal and in early discussions?	☐	☐
5. Has there been a detailed analysis and needs assessment indicating the specific business impact and job performance needs for the project?	☐	☐
6. Is it possible to forecast the actual ROI of the project?	☐	☐
7. Have multiple levels of objectives been established for the project?	☐	☐
8. Has an evaluation plan been developed?	☐	☐
9. Have expectations been given by all stakeholders?	☐	☐
10. Is there a method to routinely provide feedback to make adjustments?	☐	☐
11. Can the project manager develop the project management scorecard?	☐	☐
12. Can the project manager isolate the effects of the project solution on key results?	☐	☐
13. Is there a plan to monitor the long-term effects of the project?	☐	☐

Shortcut Ways to Hold a Project Manager Accountable

Following the steps previously discussed can be quite a lengthy process, as they are designed to be comprehensive in order to cover many project situations. A simpler process for small projects would not require so many steps, as they might represent over-analysis. The following simplified steps should be considered when time is critical, funds are low, or the projects are small:

☐ Discuss the specific results that are expected in terms of business measures (output, quality, cost, and time) and implementation requirements.

☐ Detail the specific requirements and expectations showing what is required of all parties and the ultimate outcomes.

☐ Discuss the concept of a guarantee or the consequences of a failed project, addressing the issue in some creative way.

☐ Provide a simple mechanism for providing feedback to the appropriate individuals (key stakeholders) to make necessary adjustments as the project is implemented and the results are developed.

☐ When a complete project management scorecard is not possible, measure the success of the project in terms of implementation, impact, and return on investment, if possible. This can provide excellent information for future projects.

While these shortcut steps produce only limited data with regard to a project, they do provide critical information when a more comprehensive approach is not feasible.

PRELIMINARY EVALUATION INFORMATION

As illustrated in Figure 4-1, the project management scorecard model provides a systematic approach to evaluation and the calculation of a project solution's return on investment. A step-by-step approach keeps the process manageable so that users can address one issue at a time. The model also emphasizes that this is a logical, systematic process that flows from one step to another. Also, it is important to understand that both soft data (difficult to quantify) and hard data (easy to quantify) are important to the project management scorecard. Although some people prefer soft data taken directly from the client or customer while others prefer hard data focused on output, quality, costs, and time, the project management scorecard aims to collect both types of data. This balanced approach seems to be the most effective way to evaluate project management.

Applying the model illustrated in Figure 4-1 provides consistency from one project evaluation to another. This chapter briefly describes each step of the project management scorecard model. Table 4-2 shows the sequence of some of the typical events that would take place as a project manager implements the scorecard.

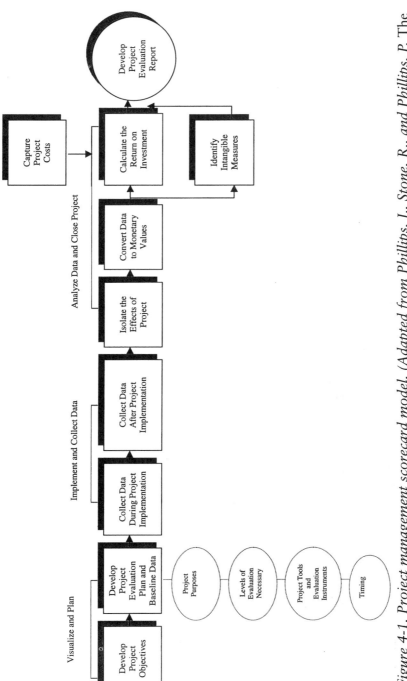

Figure 4-1. Project management scorecard model. (Adapted from Phillips, J., Stone, R., and Phillips, P. The Human Resources Scorecard: Measuring the Return on Investment. Boston: Butterworth-Heinemann, 2001.)

Table 4-2. Typical Sequence of Events in the Implementation of the Project and Scorecard

Visualize and Plan

- ☐ Interview key stakeholders
- ☐ Develop project objectives
- ☐ Write vision statement
- ☐ Ensure that all parties have same vision of end result
- ☐ Answer go/no-go decision

Plan

- ☐ Discuss and prioritize triple constraint
- ☐ Explore and manage hot spots
- ☐ Develop evaluation plans and collect baseline data (data collection plan complete)
- ☐ Break project and evaluation into manageable pieces
- ☐ Enter project and evaluation into chosen project management scheduling tool
- ☐ Determine length of project tasks
- ☐ Determine tasks relationships
- ☐ Determine resources and budget
- ☐ Answer go/no-go decision

Implement and Collect Data

- ☐ Start of project
- ☐ Data collection continues during project implementation
- ☐ Manage the project workload
- ☐ Communicate project milestones
- ☐ Manage changes to project

Close the Project

- ☐ Complete all major tasks of the project
- ☐ Collect data at a predetermined time after project close
- ☐ Isolate the effects of the project solution
- ☐ Convert data to a monetary value
- ☐ Identify intangible measures
- ☐ Capture all costs of project
- ☐ Calculate return on investment
- ☐ Develop project evaluation report
- ☐ Present plan to management

The Purpose of Project Evaluation

Prior to the formal evaluation planning process, four critical issues must be addressed:

1. Evaluation purpose
2. Evaluation levels
3. Data collection instruments
4. Evaluation timing

Several distinct purposes exist for project evaluation. Project evaluation should:

☐ Determine if a project management solution is accomplishing its objectives
☐ Identify the strengths and weaknesses in the project management process
☐ Compare costs to the monetary benefits of the project management solution
☐ Assist in marketing projects in the future
☐ Establish a database of key project measures

Although there are other purposes of evaluation, these are the most important ones (Phillips, *Handbook of Training and Development,* 1997). Evaluation purposes should be considered prior to developing the project evaluation plan because these purposes will often determine the scope of the evaluation, the types of instruments used, and the type of data collected. For example, when an ROI calculation is planned, one of the purposes would be to compare the cost to the benefits of the project. This purpose has implications for the type of data collected, type of data collection method, type of analysis, and the communication medium for results. For most projects, multiple evaluation purposes are pursued. (Specific methods and instruments are discussed later in this chapter.)

Evaluation Levels

Projects should be evaluated on at least five different levels common to the discipline of evaluation. Donald Kirkpatrick is credited for the development of the first four levels and Jack J. Phillips (*Return on Investment,* 1997) is credited for the fifth level of evaluation, of the return on investment, which is a primary focus of this book. It is important that evaluation of project management include plans to collect and analyze data at the first four levels and calculate the ROI (levels) as much as possible. While there is some evidence of correlation between some of the levels, the link may not always exist (Warr, Allan, and Birdi, 1999; Alliger and Tannenbaum, 1997). Therefore, evaluating data at each level will generate the information needed to provide a complete picture of success. The five levels include:

- [ ] Level 1: Measuring Reaction, Satisfaction, and Planned Action with the Project Management Solution
- [ ] Level 2: Measuring Changes in Knowledge and Skills Needed with the Solution
- [ ] Level 3: Assessing Application and Implementation of the Project Management Solution
- [ ] Level 4: Identifying Business Impact from the Project Management Solution
- [ ] Level 5: Calculating Return on Investment (ROI) of the Solution

Data should be collected at Levels 1, 2, 3, and 4 if an ROI analysis is planned. This ensures that the chain of impact occurs as project team members learn new skills and knowledge, apply the skills and knowledge, and influence business results. However, it is important to remember that evaluation typically cannot go to a higher level of evaluation than the level of the objectives that are written for the project. Thus, objectives for each project should be written for all five levels of possible results: how people should react to the project solution and plan to use the skills and knowledge learned (Level 1), all the way through the return on investment (Level 5) expected from implementing the project management solution.

Evaluation Instruments

A variety of instruments are used to collect data about projects. The appropriate instruments should be considered in the early stages of project evaluation planning. The eight most common instruments used to collect data on projects are:

1. Surveys
2. Questionnaires
3. Interviews
4. Focus groups
5. Gantt charts

6. Budget worksheets
7. Performance records
8. Project management software

The instruments best suited to the culture of the organization and most appropriate for the setting and evaluation requirements should be used in the data collection process. Additional information on how instruments are used in a data collection scheme will be covered later.

Evaluation Timing

Another important aspect of the project evaluation plan is the timing of the data collection. In some cases, pre-project measurements are taken to compare with post-project measurements and, in some cases, multiple measurements are taken. In other situations, pre-project measurements are not available and specific follow-ups are still taken after the project. The important issue in this part of the process is to determine the timing for the follow-up evaluation. The timing of the follow-up evaluation should coincide with the completion of the project being managed and the time required for the outcomes of the project to come to fruition.

For example, consider a major change initiative, which impacts not only processes but the paradigms and mindsets of employees within an organization. After the completion of the development of new mission, vision, and value statements, the actual integration within the corporate culture may take several months. The evaluation would not be practical until the change initiative has made some difference. However, it should not be so far past the implementation of the change initiative that the reason for the new corporate culture is forgotten.

On the other hand, changes in practices resulting from a major production project may not take as long to reap as in the example of the change initiative. Change in production practices may become routine within 30 days of completion of the project. Therefore, it would be feasible for the evaluation to take place near the 30-day time frame. These examples illustrate that the timing for follow-up evaluations for projects can vary widely depending on the nature of the projects being managed.

These four elements of evaluation—purposes, levels, instruments, and timing—are all considerations in selecting the data collection methods and developing the data collection plans for evaluating projects.

EVALUATION PLANNING

Planning early is critical in the success of the evaluation process. Appropriate attention up front will save time later when data are actually collected and analyzed, thus improving the accuracy and reducing the cost of the evaluation. It also avoids any confusion surrounding what will be accomplished, by whom, and at what time. Two planning documents are the key to the up-front analysis and should be completed before the project is implemented: the data collection plan and the ROI analysis plan. Each document is described in this section.

Data Collection Plan

Figure 4-2 shows a completed data collection plan containing information for evaluating a project management solution. The project was designed for associates in the engineering department of a major manufacturing organization. Engineers were supposed to be on the manufacturing floor to respond to issues and to troubleshoot production delays that often required major projects to fix. An ROI calculation was planned for a pilot of three groups with project management training as the solution.

This document provides a place for the major elements and issues regarding collecting data for the five evaluation levels. Broad areas for objectives are appropriate for planning. Specific, detailed objectives are developed later, before the project is implemented. The objectives for Level 1 usually include positive reactions to the project and planned actions to be taken by the participants. If it is a new project, as is the example in Figure 4-2, another category, such as suggested project changes, may be included. The responsibility for gathering the reaction data usually belongs to the project manager or a key facilitator in the project implementation.

Level 2 evaluation focuses on the measures of learning. The specific objectives include those areas where project team members are expected to change knowledge, skills, or attitudes. The evaluation method is the specific way in which learning is assessed, whether as a test, simulation, skill, practice, or facilitator assessment. The timing for Level 2 evaluation is usually during or at the end of the project, and the responsibility usually rests with the project manager.

For Level 3 evaluation, the objectives represent broad areas of project implementation, including significant on-the-job activities. The evaluation method includes one of the post-program methods described in a

Program/Project: Manufacturing Production Delays   **Responsibility:** Project Manager   **Date:** _____

Level	Objective(s)	Measures/Data	Data Collection Method/Instruments	Data Sources	Timing	Responsibilities
1	**Reaction/Satisfaction and Planned Action** • Positive Reaction • Recommended Improvements • Action Plan Completed	• 4 out of 5 on response scale	• End of project questionnaire	• Project team • Manufacturing staff • Engineers	• End of first month after project completion	• Project Manager
2	**Learning** • Acquisition of Skills • Understanding of Process	• Satisfactory score of learning assessment	• Learning assessment	• Engineers	• End of first month after project implementation	• Project Manager
3	**Application/Implementation** • Utilize Skills Learned Through Project Implementation	• Frequency of use of skills	• Follow-up questionnaire	• Engineers • Managers	• 3 months after project begins	• Project Manager
4	**Business Impact** • Increase Production Rate	• Weekly production per product line	• Follow-up questionnaire • Performance monitoring	• Engineers • Managers • Company records	• 3 months after project begins	• Project Manager
5	**ROI** • 25% ROI					

Baseline Data: _____

Comments: _____

Figure 4-2. Data collection plan for manufacturing products delays project.

following section and is usually conducted a matter of weeks or months after project completion. Because responsibilities are often shared among several groups, including the project team, division trainers, or local managers, it is important to clarify this issue early in the process.

For Level 4 evaluation, objectives focus on business impact variables that are influenced by the project. The objectives may include the way in which each item is measured. For example, if one of the objectives is to improve quality, a specific measure would indicate how that quality is actually measured, such as defects per thousand units produced. While the preferred evaluation method is performance monitoring or files analysis, other methods such as action planning may be appropriate (methods and instruments are discussed later in this chapter).

The timing for Level 4 evaluations depends on how quickly project team members can generate a sustained business impact. It is usually a matter of months after a project is implemented. The project team itself, supervisors, division training coordinators, or perhaps an external evaluator may be responsible for Level 4 data collection.

For Level 5 evaluation, objectives are written as goals. Projected Level 4 results are compared against the projected costs of implementing a project to set a goal in terms of a percentage. (Or a specified ROI based on the ROI of other investments is used as the Level 5 objective.) The goal represents a percentage of dollars returned from Level 4 results and improvements. Specifically, the goal refers to dollars returned after the costs of the project have been considered. Additional data are not necessarily collected here; however, as explained below, planning for ROI analysis is another critical step in the overall evaluation planning process.

The data collection plan is an important part of the evaluation strategy and should be completed prior to moving forward with the project. For ongoing projects, the plan is completed before pursuing the ROI evaluation solution. The plan provides a clear direction of what type of data will be collected, how they will be collected, when they will be collected, and who will collect them.

ROI ANALYSIS PLAN

Figure 4-3 shows a completed ROI analysis plan for the project described earlier. This planning document is the continuation of the data collection plan presented in Figure 4-2 and captures information on several key items that are necessary to develop the actual ROI calculation. In the first column, important data items are listed, usually Level 4 data items, but in some cases could include Level 3 items. These items will be used in the ROI analysis. The method to isolate the effects of the project management solution is listed next to each data item in the second column. For most cases, the method will be the same for each data item, but there could be variations. The method of converting data to monetary values is included in the third column, using one of the ten strategies outlined in a subsequent chapter of this book. The costs categories that will be captured for the project are outlined in the fourth column. Instructions about how certain costs should be prorated are noted here. The cost categories will be consistent from one project to another, except when a specific cost unique to the project exists. In this case, the additional cost is noted along with the other costs. The intangible benefits expected from this project are outlined in the fifth column. This list is generated from discussions about the project with sponsors, subject matter experts, and other key stakeholders. Intangible benefits are Level 4 measures (those data items listed in the first column) that are not converted to monetary value. Communication targets are listed in the sixth column. Although there could be many groups that should receive the information, four target groups are always recommended:

☐ Senior management group
☐ Supervisors of project team members
☐ Project team members
☐ Training and development staff

All four of these groups need to know about the results of the ROI analysis.

Other issues or events that might influence project implementation are highlighted in the seventh column. Typical items include the capability of project team members, the degree of access to data sources, and unique data analysis issues.

The ROI analysis plan, when combined with the data collection plan, provides detailed information on calculating the ROI, illustrating how the process will develop from beginning to end. When thoroughly completed, these two plans provide the direction necessary for the project management scorecard to be implemented.

Collecting Project Data

Data collection is an absolute for effective implementation of the project management scorecard. In some situations, post-project data are collected and compared to pre-program situations, control group

Program/Project: Manufacturing Production Delays   Responsibility: Project Manager   Date: _____

Data Items (Usually Level 4)	Methods for Isolating the Effects of the Project	Methods of Converting Data to Monetary Values	Project Cost Categories	Intangible Benefits	Communication Targets for Final Report	Other Influences/Issues During Application	Comments
Weekly Production per Product Line	• Control Group • Trend Line Comparing Previous Project to Project Solution Implementation	• Standard Value—Cost per Product per Product Line	• Project Manager Fees • Project Team Fees • Project Materials • Training Fees • Participant Salaries/Benefits • Evaluation Costs	• Customer Satisfaction • Employee Satisfaction • Increased Trust in Production Teams	• Project Team Members • Department Managers • Manufacturing Managers • Senior Executives • Training Staff	• Must Have Job Coverage During Training • No Communication with Control Group • Seasonal Fluctuations Should Be Avoided	

Figure 4-3. ROI analysis for manufacturing products delays project.

differences, and expectations. Both hard data, representing output, quality, cost, and time; and soft data, including work habits, work climate, and attitudes are often collected. Data are collected using a variety of methods, including the following:

☐ *Follow-up surveys* are taken to determine the degree to which project team members have utilized various aspects of the project solution. Surveys administered immediately following the project solution assess project team members' reactions to and satisfaction with the project solution and key learning. Survey responses are often developed on a sliding scale and usually represent attitudinal data. Surveys are especially useful for Level 1–3 data.

☐ *Follow-up questionnaires* are administered to uncover specific applications of skills that the project solution is meant to influence. Project team members provide responses to a variety of open-ended and forced response questions, providing critical data describing the degree to which new skills and knowledge are being applied as well as the consequences of applying the skills and knowledge. Questionnaires can be used to capture Level 1–4 data.

☐ *On-the-job observation* captures actual skill application and use or system performance in the case of projects designed to deploy a new system. Observations are particularly useful on the evaluation of team efforts or project leaders' abilities to inspire and lead others and are more effective when the observer is either invisible or transparent. Observations are appropriate for Level 3 data.

☐ *Post-implementation interviews* are conducted with project team members to determine the extent to which learning has been utilized on the job. Interviews allow for probing to uncover specific applications and are appropriate with Level 3 data. Also, interviews are conducted to determine the project leaders' success in meeting key project stakeholders needs. This is always important data to justify the success and worth of project management efforts.

☐ *Focus groups* are conducted to determine the degree to which a group of project team members have more effectively performed on the job because of the project. Focus groups are appropriate with Level 3 data and to determine if stakeholder needs have been met.

☐ *Project assignments or action plans* are especially useful for simple short-term projects. Project team members complete the assignment or action plan on the job, utilizing skills or knowledge learned in the project training. Completed assignments can often contain both Level 3 and 4 data.

☐ *Performance contracts* are developed by the project team members, the project team members' supervisors, and the project manager. Together, these individuals agree on performance expectations and determine the success of meeting those expectations. Performance contracts are appropriate for both Level 3 and 4 data.

☐ *Follow-up or renewal sessions*, which are utilized to capture evaluation data as well as present additional learning material, are useful for some projects. Often, these follow-up sessions are planned at the point of project milestones and include celebration ceremonies. In the follow-up session, project team members discuss their successes with the project. Follow-up sessions are appropriate for both Level 3 and 4 data.

☐ *Performance monitoring or files analysis* is useful where various performance records and operational data are examined for improvement. This method is particularly useful for Level 4 data. Often, this data can be found within the normal day-to-day operating systems and files of the organization. Thus, it is sometimes referred to as files analysis.

☐ *Gantt charts or project timelines* are visual guides that show the relationships between tasks and time. These charts were created by Henry Gantt around the turn of the nineteenth century to help manage some of the early industrial projects. The charts are easy-to-use tools that provide visual information about the project. They are valuable for keeping everyone involved on the project aware of deadlines and interrelationships and dependencies of tasks. More complex Gantt charts are sometimes called PERT (Program Evaluation Review Technique) charts. The major advantage of such charts is that they provide a visual of the amount of time a project should take. Laying out the entire project on a Gantt chart reveals areas where delays in the project plan can be extremely costly or where changes in resources or techniques can cost time and money. Comparing the planned timelines to the actual timelines serves as a primary measure for the success of the project management applied to the project. Percentages of missed deadlines, increased resources or decreased resources, and overall time spent on each task become important measures of success for managed projects. Many people use software programs such as Microsoft Project to help with this type of project management and measurement.

☐ *Budget worksheets* are columns sometimes included on the project timeline charts (Gantt Charts) or they can be separate worksheets. Typically, the columns in these charts are for the predicted costs of performing each of the major and minor tasks related to a project and the actual costs that are incurred after the tasks are completed. These charts give project managers the opportunity to alter the project to stay within a predetermined cost structure or budget. Often, the actual costs incurred by completing tasks in a project are much greater than the estimated costs outlined in the project plan. Meeting budget requirements is a major measure of success for project management.

Regardless of the methods used to collect data, the important challenge in data collection is to select the method or methods appropriate for the setting and the specific project being managed, and within the time and budget constraints of the organization. Data collection methods are covered in more detail in subsequent chapters.

Isolating the Effects of the Project Management Solution

An often overlooked issue in project evaluations is the process of isolating the effects of the project management solution. In this step of the process, specific strategies are explored, which determine the amount of increased performance directly related to the project management solution. This step is essential because there are many factors that will influence performance data after a project has been implemented. The specific strategies of this step will pinpoint the amount of improvement directly related to the project. The result is increased accuracy and credibility of the ROI calculation. The following strategies have been utilized by organizations to address this important issue:

☐ A control group arrangement is used to isolate the solution impact. With this strategy, one group participates in the project solution, while another similar group does not. The difference in the performance of the two groups is attributed to the project when other factors and conditions are controlled for, making the two groups being compared homogeneous. When properly set up and implemented, the control group arrangement is the most effective way to isolate the effects of the project solution.

☐ Trend lines and forecasts are used to predict the values of specific data points over time, if a solution had not been undertaken. The prediction is compared to the actual data after the project is implemented, and the difference represents the estimate of the impact of the solution. Under certain conditions, this strategy can accurately isolate the impact of the project solution.

☐ Project team members estimate the amount of improvement related to the project solution. With this approach, project team members are provided with the total amount of improvement, on a pre- and post-project basis, and are asked to indicate the percentage of the improvement that is actually related to the project solution.

☐ Supervisors of project team members estimate the impact of the project solution on the output variables. With this approach, supervisors of project team members are presented with the total amount of improvement and are asked to indicate the percent related to the project solution.

☐ Senior management estimates the impact of the project solution. In these cases, managers provide an estimate or "adjustment" to reflect the portion of the improvement related to the project solution. While perhaps inaccurate, there are some advantages of having senior management involved in this process.

☐ Experts provide estimates of the impact of the project solution on the performance variables. Because the estimates are based on previous experience, the experts must be familiar with the type of improvement being implemented and the specific situation.

☐ When feasible, other influencing factors are identified and the impact estimated or calculated, leaving the remaining, unexplained improvement attributed to the project solution. In this case, the influence of all other factors is estimated, and the project solution remains the one variable not accounted for in the analysis. The unexplained portion of the output is then attributed to the project solution.

☐ In some situations, customers provide input on the extent to which the project solution has influenced their decision to use a product or service. Although this strategy has limited applications, it can be quite useful in the evaluation of project management because often the customer is a key stakeholder to the project.

Collectively, these strategies provide a comprehensive set of tools to tackle the important and critical issue of isolating the effects of project solutions.

Converting Data to Monetary Values

To evaluate Level 5, return on investment, the data collected for Level 4 evaluation are converted to monetary values and compared to project solution costs. This requires a value to be placed where possible on each unit of data connected with the project. Ten strategies are available to convert data to monetary values. The specific strategy selected usually depends on the type of data and the project situation:

1. Output data are converted to profit contribution or cost savings. In this strategy, output increases are converted to monetary value based on their unit contribution to profit or the unit of cost reduction. These values are readily available in most organizations.
2. The cost of quality is calculated and quality improvements are directly converted to cost savings. This value is available in many organizations.
3. For programs where employee time is saved, the project team members' wages and benefits are used for the value for time. Because a variety of programs focus on improving the time required to complete projects, processes, or daily activities, the value of time becomes an important and necessary issue to project management.
4. Historical costs are used when they are available for a specific variable. In this case, organizational cost data are utilized to establish the specific value of an improvement.
5. When available, internal and external experts may be employed to estimate a value for an improvement. In this situation, the credibility of the estimate hinges on the expertise and reputation of the individual.
6. External databases are sometimes available to estimate the value or cost of data items. Research, government, and industry databases can provide important information for these values. The difficulty lies in finding a specific database related to the situation.
7. Project team members estimate the value of the data item. For this approach to be effective, project team members must be capable of providing a value for the improvements.
8. Supervisors of project team members provide estimates when they are both willing and capable of assigning values to the improvement. This approach is especially useful when project

team members are not fully capable of providing this input or in situations where supervisors need to confirm or adjust the project team member's estimate.

9. Senior management may provide estimates on the value of an improvement. This approach is particularly helpful to establish values for performance measures that are very important to senior management.

10. HRD staff estimates may be used to determine a value of an output data item. In these cases, it is essential for the estimates to be provided on an unbiased basis.

Converting data to monetary values is very important and absolutely necessary for determining the monetary benefits from a project management solution. The process is challenging, particularly with soft data, but can be methodically accomplished using one or more of the strategies outlined above.

Tabulating Cost of the Project Management Solution

Tabulating the costs involves monitoring or developing all of the related costs of the project solution targeted for the ROI calculation. Among the cost components that should be included are:

- ☐ The cost to design and develop the project solution, possibly prorated over the expected life of the project solution
- ☐ The cost of all project solution materials provided to anyone
- ☐ The cost for the instructor/facilitator who delivers any training related to the project solution, including preparation time as well as delivery time
- ☐ The cost of any special facilities for the project solution
- ☐ The cost of travel, lodging, and meals for the project team, if applicable
- ☐ Salaries, plus employee benefits of the project team members who attend project management meetings and training
- ☐ Administrative and overhead costs of the project management and training function, allocated in some convenient way

In addition, specific costs related to the needs assessment and evaluation should be included, if appropriate. The conservative approach is to include all of these costs so that the total is fully loaded.

Calculating the Return on Investment

The return on investment is calculated using the project solution benefits and solution costs. The benefits/cost ratio is the monetary benefits divided by cost. In formula form it is:

$$BCR = \frac{\text{Project Solution Monetary Benefits}}{\text{Project Solution Costs}}$$

Sometimes this ratio is stated as a cost/benefit ratio, although the formula is the same as BCR.

The return on investment uses the net solution benefits divided by project solution costs. The net benefits are the monetary benefits minus the costs. In formula form, the ROI becomes:

$$ROI\ (\%) = \frac{\text{Net Project Solution Monetary Benefits}}{\text{Project Solution Costs}} \times 100$$

This is the same basic formula used to evaluate other investments where the ROI is traditionally reported as earnings divided by investment.

Identifying Intangible Benefits

In addition to tangible, monetary benefits, most project solutions will have intangible, non-monetary benefits. The ROI calculation is based on converting both hard and soft data to monetary values. Intangible benefits can include items such as:

☐ Increased job satisfaction
☐ Increased organizational commitment
☐ Improved teamwork
☐ Improved customer service
☐ Reduced complaints
☐ Reduced conflicts

During data analysis, every attempt is made to convert all data to monetary values. All hard data such as output, quality, and time are converted to monetary values. The conversion of soft data is attempted for each data item. However, if the process used for conversion is too subjective or inaccurate, and the resulting values lose credibility in the process, then the data is listed as an intangible benefit with the appropriate explanation. For some project solutions, intangible, nonmonetary benefits are extremely valuable, often carrying as much influence as the hard data items.

Implementation Issues

A variety of environmental issues and events will influence the successful implementation of the project management scorecard. These issues must be addressed early to ensure that the project management scorecard process is successful. Specific topics or actions include:

- ☐ A policy statement concerning results-based projects
- ☐ Procedures and guidelines for different elements and techniques of the evaluation process
- ☐ Meetings and formal sessions to develop staff skills with the project management scorecard process
- ☐ Strategies to improve management commitment and support for the project management scorecard
- ☐ Mechanisms to provide technical support for questionnaire design, data analysis, and evaluation strategy
- ☐ Specific techniques to place more attention on results

The project management scorecard process can fail or succeed based on these implementation issues.

FINAL THOUGHTS

This chapter presented the project management scorecard process model for calculating the return on investment for a project solution. The step-by-step process takes the complicated issue of evaluating project effectiveness and calculating ROI and breaks it into simple, manageable tasks and steps. When the process is thoroughly planned, taking into consideration all potential strategies and techniques, the process becomes manageable and achievable.

REFERENCES

Alliger, G., and Tannenbaum, S.I. "A Meta-analysis of the Relations Among Training Criteria." *Personnel Psychology*, 1997;50(2):341–358.

Kirkpatrick, Donald L. *Evaluating Training Programs: The Four Levels*. San Francisco: Berrett-Koehler Publishers, Inc., 1996.

Phillips, J.J. *Handbook of Training Evaluation and Measurement Methods*, 3rd ed. Boston: Butterworth-Heinemann, previously published by Gulf Publishing, 1997.

Phillips, J.J. *Return on Investment in Training and Performance Improvement Programs*. Boston: Butterworth-Heinemann, previously published by Gulf Publishing, 1997.

Warr, P., Allan, C., and Birdi, K. "Predicting Three Levels of Training Outcomes. *Journal of Occupational and Organizational Psychology*, 1999;72:351–375.

PART II

The Seven Measures

CHAPTER 5

How to Measure Reaction and Satisfaction

Reaction and satisfaction measures play an important role in the project management scorecard. These measures define certain thoughts and feelings of reaction and satisfaction with the project as it is planned, explained, and communicated to stakeholders. Project management solutions often go astray and fail to reach full success because of various unmet expectations and unmet levels of satisfaction throughout the steps of the project management cycle. Thus, for any project solution to be successful, various stakeholders must react favorably, or at least not negatively. Also, measures indicating stakeholder planned action after project implementation provide some indication as to the success of application of skills and knowledge learned.

Ideally, the stakeholders should be satisfied with the project, especially since an effective project will offer a win-win situation for each stakeholder. Similarly, an effective project manager will realize the importance of each stakeholder being satisfied. Stakeholders are those who are directly involved with planning, implementing, or utilizing the project. Sometimes, the stakeholders can be the employees whose work will be directly affected by the project or the leaders possessing a vision of how to change the employees' work processes for the better. Given the involvement and support that each stakeholder must provide for a project to be successful, it is important for project managers to understand each stakeholder's reaction to and satisfaction with the project. The following example will serve to illustrate this point.

The CIO of a large pharmaceutical sales team planned to implement a project that would speed up the delivery of information to the field sales representatives. In short, he wanted to install a high-speed Internet line for each field sales representative in order to improve the time sales people spent downloading product information for their sales presentations. The sales representatives were dependent upon the information for each product presentation they gave and the product information was updated nearly daily. The cost to install the system was estimated to be $5,000,000.

The CIO believed that the investment would be a smart decision for several reasons. First, he felt that sales representatives would save time because product information would be downloaded faster to sales representatives' computers. This was a desired outcome of the project and one to which almost all stakeholders reacted favorably. Saving time could lead to increased productivity and sales representatives could use the saved time to increase the number of sales calls. Second, he felt that the technology improvement would increase the sales representatives' level of job satisfaction because they would not be frustrated about the time it takes to download current product information. Positively affecting employee satisfaction was another important desired outcome for the project.

Although the CIO was positive toward the project, two other key stakeholders were not. In fact, the CEO of the organization felt that the estimated $5,000,000 for the project could be spent toward hiring more sales representatives. Also, he felt that an investment in hiring more sales representatives would have a better return on investment than the high-speed Internet line project.

The sales representatives, one of the most important stakeholder groups, reacted entirely differently to the project. They were not concerned about the speed of the Internet line they used to download product information. And they did not feel that a faster line would improve their job satisfaction. The reason they reacted this way was because almost all the sales representatives downloaded the product update files at night, while they were sleeping. In addition, they did not feel that more sales representatives would improve sales because the regions they covered already had too much overlap between sales representatives. They already felt like they were competing among themselves.

This example illustrates several reasons why project managers should consider the stakeholders' perceptions—both prior to and after project implementation. There were three very different reactions to the project: the CIO liked the project, the CEO wanted an alternative to the project, and the sales representatives did not see a need for the project nor the alternative. This situation is a good example of why reaction and satisfaction measures are crucial to an effective project management scorecard. The proposed high-speed Internet line project would ultimately not deliver the value it should because the value was not perceived equally. This example is all too common among projects today. Thus, project managers must understand the importance of measuring stakeholder reaction and satisfaction. These measures, typically called Level 1 measures, should be included as a major component of every project management scorecard.

Projects can go astray quickly, and sometimes a specific project solution is the wrong solution for the specified problem. There are times when a project solution can be mismatched from the beginning, so it is essential to get feedback early in the process so that adjustments can be made. This helps avoid misunderstandings, miscommunications, and, more importantly, misappropriations, as an improperly designed project is altered or changed quickly before more serious problems are created.

SOURCES OF DATA

The concept of continuous process improvement suggests that a project must be adjusted and refined throughout its duration. There must be an important linkage between obtaining feedback and making changes and reporting changes back to the groups who provide the information. This survey-feedback-action loop is critical for any type of project. Data collection must be deliberately pursued in a systematic, logical, rational way. This chapter explores the key issues involved in collecting and using these important measures.

Many of the individuals involved in a project, particularly the project team members, appreciate the opportunity to provide feedback. In too many situations, their input is ignored and their complaints disregarded. They appreciate the project leader asking for input and, more importantly, taking action as a result of that input. Other stakeholders and even clients appreciate the opportunity to provide feedback, not only early in the process but also throughout the process.

Because feedback data are important to the project's success, they are gathered in almost every project. They have become some of the most important data collected. Unfortunately, in some situations, project success is often measured by the reaction feedback. As this book clearly shows, the feedback data are only one part of the project management scorecard and represent only one of the six types of data, yet the importance cannot be understated.

Some organizations collect reaction and satisfaction data from several sources using standard questions, and the data are then compared with data from other project solutions so that norms and standards can be developed. This is particularly helpful at the end of a project as client satisfaction is gauged. These satisfaction data can be used not only to compare the success of the project but also to relate to overall project success and even correlate with other successful measures. Some firms even base part of project manager's compensation on the level of client satisfaction, making reaction and satisfaction data very critical to the success of every project.

When considering the possible data sources that will provide feedback on a project, the categories are easily defined. The categories or sources of data are simply the stakeholder groups. Concerning reaction and satisfaction data, there are several sources of data. Some of the most important sources for reaction and satisfaction data and also other levels of data are described next.

Project Team Members

Project team members are one of the most widely used data sources for project management data. Project team members are frequently asked how they feel about the project. Sometimes they are asked, even before the project is implemented, to explain the worth of the project or to predict the long-term effects of the project. Although project team members cannot always answer every question about a project, they often can discuss how different stakeholders are reacting to the project as well as how they themselves are reacting to the project.

Project team members are a rich source of data for all measures of the project management scorecard, but particularly for reaction and satisfaction measures. They are very credible, since they are the individuals who have been involved with the projects and are often the most knowledgeable of the processes and other influencing factors that are affecting the project. The challenge is to find an effective and efficient way to capture data in a consistent manner between project team members and to decide *when* to capture reaction and satisfaction data from them.

Supervisors of Project Team Members

Another important source of data is those individuals who directly supervise or lead project team members. This group will often have a vested interest in the project management scorecard process, since they give approval for the project team members to be involved in the program. Also, in many situations, they observe the project team members as they attempt to use the knowledge and skills acquired in the project solutions. Consequently, they can report on the successes linked to the project as well as on the difficulties and problems associated with application of project skills. Although supervisor input is usually best for Level 3 (applied project skills data), it can be useful for Level 1 (reaction and satisfaction data), and Level 4 (project organizational results data). It is important, however, for supervisors to maintain objectivity when assessing the project team members' applied project skills (Level 3).

Internal/External Groups

In some situations, internal or external groups, such as the project training and development staff or project consultants, may provide input on the success of the project team members when they attempt to apply the skills and knowledge acquired in the project training. Collecting data from this source has limited uses. Because internal groups may have a vested interest in the outcome of a project, their input may lose credibility. Input from external groups is appropriate for certain types of observations about how different stakeholders are reacting to the project and about how on-the-job performance improves.

DATA COLLECTION METHODS

There are many different methods that can be used to collect reaction and satisfaction data for the project management scorecard. With each method, the data can be collected both quantitatively and qualitatively. Reaction data can be collected using attitude scales and Likert scales, in which the opinion is stated and the respondent indicates his or her level of agreement based on a given scale. These methods are used in conjunction with questionnaires or surveys. Data can also be collected verbally through storytelling or critical incident reviews, although analysis often can be more difficult. Following are the most common methods for collecting reaction and satisfaction data on projects. This type of data collection would be useful for projects of considerable size and expense but not necessary for quick and inexpensive projects that would cost less than the expense to collect reaction and satisfaction data.

Questionnaires and Surveys

Probably the most common form of data collection method is the questionnaire. Ranging from short reaction forms to detailed tools, questionnaires can be used to obtain subjective information about project team members' feelings, as well as to objectively document measurable business results for an ROI analysis. With this versatility and popularity, the questionnaire is the preferred method for capturing much of the information necessary to make a project management scorecard effective.

Surveys represent a specific type of questionnaire and are used in situations where only attitudes, beliefs, and opinions are captured; whereas, a questionnaire has much more flexibility and captures data ranging from attitude data to specific improvement statistics. The principles of survey construction and design are similar to questionnaire design.

TYPES OF QUESTIONNAIRE OR SURVEY QUESTIONS

In addition to the types of data sought, the types of questions distinguish surveys from questionnaires. Surveys can have "yes" or "no" responses when an absolute agreement or disagreement is required, or a range of responses may be used from "strongly disagree" to "strongly agree." A five-point scale is also very common.

A questionnaire may contain any or all of these types of questions:

- ☐ **Open-ended question:** Has an unlimited possibility for an answer. The question is followed by ample blank space for the response.
- ☐ **Checklist:** A list of items where a project team member is asked to check those that apply to the situation.
- ☐ **Two-way question:** Has alternate responses, a "yes/no" or other possibilities.
- ☐ **Multiple-choice question:** Has several choices, and the project team member is asked to select the most correct one.
- ☐ **Ranking scale:** Requires the project team member to rank a list of items.

QUESTIONNAIRE DESIGN STEPS

Questionnaire design is a simple and logical process. When setting up the project management scorecard instruments, there is nothing more confusing, frustrating, and potentially embarrassing than a poorly designed or an improperly worded questionnaire. The following steps can ensure that a valid, reliable, and effective instrument is developed.

Determine the exact information needed. As a first step in questionnaire design, the topics, skills, or attitudes important to the project are reviewed to identify potential items for the questionnaire. It can be helpful to develop this information in outline form so that related questions or items can be grouped.

Involve management in the process. To the extent possible, management should be involved in this process, either as a client, sponsor, supporter, or interested party. If possible, managers most familiar with the project or process should provide information on specific issues and concerns that often frame the actual questions planned for the questionnaire. In some cases, managers want to provide input on specific issues or items. Not only is manager input helpful and useful in the questionnaire design, but it also builds ownership in the measurement and evaluation process.

Select the type(s) of questions. Using the previous five types of questions, the first step in questionnaire design is to select the type(s) that will best result in the specific data needed. The planned data analysis and variety of data to be collected should be considered when deciding which questions to use. Also, specifying the intent for which the data will be used will also help in developing questions.

Develop the questions. The next step is to develop the questions based on the type of questions planned and the information needed. Questions should be simple and straightforward to avoid confusion or lead the project team member to a desired response. A single question should only address one issue. If multiple issues need to be addressed, separate the question into multiple parts, or simply develop a separate question for each issue. Terms or expressions unfamiliar to the project team member should be avoided.

Check the reading level. To ensure that the target audience can easily understand the questionnaire, it is helpful to assess the reading level. Most word processing programs have features that will evaluate the reading difficulty according to grade level. This provides an important check to ensure the perceived reading level of the target audience matches with questionnaire design.

Test the questions. Proposed questions should be tested for understanding. Ideally, the questions should be tested on a sample group of project team members. If this is not feasible, the sample group of employees should be at approximately the same job level as project team members. From this sample group, feedback, critiques, and suggestions are sought to improve questionnaire design.

Address the anonymity issue. Project team members should feel free to respond openly to questions without fear of reprisal. The confidentiality of their responses is of utmost importance, since there is usually a link between survey anonymity and accuracy. Therefore, surveys should be anonymous unless there are specific reasons why individuals have to be identified. In situations where project team members must complete the questionnaire in a captive audience, or submit a completed questionnaire directly to an individual, a neutral third party should collect and process the data, ensuring that the identity is not revealed. In cases where the actual identity must be known (e.g., to compare output data with the previous data or to verify the data), every effort should be made to protect the respondent's identity to those who may be biased in their actions.

Design for ease of tabulation and analysis. Each potential question should be viewed in terms of data tabulation, data summary, and analysis. If possible, the data analysis process should be outlined and reviewed in mock-up form. This step avoids the problems of inadequate, cumbersome, and lengthy data analysis caused by improper wording or design.

Develop the completed questionnaire and prepare a data summary. The questions should be integrated to develop an attractive questionnaire with proper instructions so that it can be administered effectively. In addition, a summary sheet should be developed so that the data can be tabulated quickly for analysis.

QUESTIONNAIRE CONTENT ISSUES

One of the most difficult tasks is to determine the specific issues and content to address on the questionnaire. The following items represent a comprehensive list of questionnaire content possibilities for capturing project reaction and satisfaction information.

PROGRESS WITH PROJECT OBJECTIVES

Sometimes it is helpful to assess progress with the objectives. While this issue is usually assessed during the beginning phases of the project implementation, because it is Level 1 reaction data, it is sometimes helpful to revisit the objectives at the end of the project implementation. Typical areas for satisfaction objectives on a project include:

- ☐ Relevance of the project solution
- ☐ Usefulness of the project solution
- ☐ Economics of the project solution
- ☐ Difficulty in understanding any of the project tools or requirements
- ☐ Difficulty in overcoming any project hot spots
- ☐ Difficulty in implementing any portion of the project solution
- ☐ Difficulty in managing the project solution
- ☐ Perceived support for the project solution
- ☐ Appropriate resources for the project solution
- ☐ Appropriateness of objectives
- ☐ Appropriateness of plans
- ☐ Effectiveness of project leadership
- ☐ Motivation of project team members
- ☐ Cooperation of project team members
- ☐ Capability of project team members
- ☐ Likelihood of project success
- ☐ Perceived value of investing in the project
- ☐ Overall satisfaction with the project

While each of these areas is important, eight are discussed in more detail below.

Relevance of project solution. Although the relevance of the project is often assessed during the beginning of the project implementation, as Level 1 reaction data, it can be helpful to assess the relevance of various aspects of the project after the project has concluded. Often, with today's fast-paced and changing work environments, projects can quickly lose relevance to business needs. Collecting relevance to business needs data helps project designers know which parts of the project were actually useful on the job, providing lasting value.

Use of project tools. If project team members are provided with tools to use as part of the project, then it may be helpful to determine the extent to which these tools have been used. This is particularly helpful when operating manuals, reference books, and job aids have been distributed and explained in the project training programs and are expected to be used on the job.

Knowledge and skills enhancement. Perhaps one of the most important questions for determining how people react to a project is the question pertaining to new knowledge or skills the project brings to individuals, thereby helping employees to be more effective on the job.

Changes with work. Sometimes it is helpful to determine what specific activities or processes have changed about project team members' work as a result of the project. Then, the important question is, how are individuals reacting to those changes? Project team members explore how the project has actually changed work habits, processes, and output and describe the feelings that exist about those changes.

Satisfaction or frustration. Another important issue to add to the questionnaire content list is the issue of satisfaction or frustration. A question that helps project team members rate their satisfaction levels and their frustration levels can help project managers know how the project is progressing.

The project need. Using a questionnaire to determine stakeholders' reactions to the project allows project managers to determine if communication about the purpose and need for the project was effective. Questions about why the project is important or questions asking "if" the project is important can be used for this reason. If most stakeholders rate the importance of the project very low, then perhaps the project deserves serious scrutiny before it should continue. This simple piece of data can be harmless to collect and very helpful for a project manager.

Project management improvement. Managing a project can be extremely difficult. Project managers will be more effective if they seek continuous feedback about the processes and behaviors used to manage projects. The reaction and satisfaction questionnaire should include questions meant to determine how project team members are reacting to the overall management of the project.

Hot spots. Many projects encounter obstacles and challenges not easy to predict or plan for. To identify challenges that surface as a project is implemented, project team members can be asked to share what hot spots have occurred since the implementation of the project. Also, many project team members are aware of the challenges and the possible solutions that can remove those challenges. Thus, a follow-up question that asks project team members to suggest possible solutions to the hot spots can be a wise use of people's insight.

Improving the Response Rate for Questionnaires and Surveys

The content items previously listed represent a small sample of potential issues to explore in a project reaction and satisfaction questionnaire or survey. Obviously, asking many questions could cause the response rate to be reduced considerably. The challenge, therefore, is to tackle questionnaire design and administration for maximum response rate. This is a critical issue when the questionnaire is the primary data collection activity and most of the project management scorecard hinges on the questionnaire results. The following actions can be taken to increase response rate.

Provide advance communication. If appropriate and feasible, project team members should receive advance communications about the requirement for a questionnaire. This minimizes some of the resistance to the process, provides an opportunity to explain in more detail the circumstances surrounding the evaluation, and positions the data collection as an integral part of the project; not an add-on activity that someone initiated three months after the project.

Communicate the purpose. Project team members should understand the reason for the questionnaire, including who or what has initiated this specific project evaluation. Project team members should know if the evaluation is part of a systematic process or a special request for this project.

Explain who will see the data. It is important for project team members to know who will see the data and the results of the questionnaire. If the questionnaire is anonymous, it should clearly be communicated to project team members what steps will be taken to ensure anonymity. If senior executives will see the combined results of the study, project team members should know it.

Describe the data integration process. Project team members should understand how the questionnaire results would be combined with other data, if available. Often the questionnaire is only one of the data collection methods utilized. Project team members should know how the data is weighted and integrated with the final report.

Keep the questionnaire as simple as possible. A simple questionnaire does not always provide the full scope of data necessary for an ROI analysis. However, the simplified approach should always be kept in mind when questions are developed and the total scope of the questionnaire is finalized. Every effort should be made to keep it as simple and brief as possible.

Simplify the response process. To the extent possible, it should be easy to respond to the questionnaire. If appropriate, a self-addressed stamped envelope should be included. Perhaps e-mail could be used for response, if it is easier. In still other situations, a drop box is provided near the workstation.

Utilize local manager support. Management involvement at the local level is critical to response rate success. Managers can distribute the questionnaires themselves, make reference to the questionnaire in staff meetings, follow up to see if questionnaires have been completed, and generally show the support for completing the questionnaire. This direct supervisor support will cause some project team members to respond with usable data.

Consider incentives. A variety of incentives can be offered and they usually fall into three categories. First, an incentive is provided in exchange for the completed questionnaire. For example, if project team members return the questionnaire personally or through the mail, they will receive a small gift, such as a T-shirt or mug. If identity is an issue, a neutral third party can provide the incentive. In the second category, the incentive is provided to make project team members feel guilty about not responding. Examples are a dollar bill clipped to the questionnaire or a pen enclosed in the envelope. Project team members are asked to "take the dollar, buy a cup of coffee, and fill out the questionnaire," or "please use this pen to complete the questionnaire." A third group of incentives is designed to obtain a quick response. This approach is based on the assumption that a quick response will ensure a greater response rate. If an individual puts off completing the questionnaire, the odds of completing it diminish considerably. The initial group of project team members may receive a more expensive gift or they may be part of a drawing for an incentive. For example, in one study, the first twenty-five returned questionnaires were placed in a drawing for a $400 gift certificate. The next twenty-five were added to the first twenty-five in the next drawing. The longer a project team member waits, the lower the odds for winning.

Have an executive sign the introductory letter. Project team members are always interested in who sent the letter with the questionnaire. For maximum effectiveness, a senior executive who is responsible for a major area where the project will have influence should sign the letter. Employees may be more willing to respond to a senior executive when compared to situations where a member of the project team signs a letter.

Use follow-up reminders. A follow-up reminder should be sent a week after the questionnaire is received and another sent two weeks after it is received. Depending on the questionnaire and the situation, these times could be adjusted. In some situations, a third follow-up is recommended. Sometimes the follow-up should be sent in different media. For example, a questionnaire may be sent through regular mail, whereas, the first follow-up reminder is from the immediate supervisor and a second follow-up reminder is sent through e-mail.

Send a copy of the results to the project team members. Even if it is an abbreviated form, project team members should see the results of the questionnaire. More importantly, within the instructions on the questionnaire project team members should learn that they will receive a copy of the results. This promise will often increase the response rate, as some individuals want to see the results of the entire group along with their particular input.

Collectively, these items help boost response rates of questionnaires. Using all of these strategies can result in a 60 to 80 percent response rate, even with lengthy questionnaires that can take 30 minutes to complete.

Timing of Data Collection

The timing of data collection revolves around particular events connected with the project, such as milestones. Any particular activity, implementation issue, or milestone is an appropriate time to collect data, beginning with pre-project data collection and progressing to the implementation. Figure 5-1 shows the timing of feedback on a six-month project. This particular project has pre-project data collection. This is important to make sure that the environment is proper and supportive of the project. A pre-project assessment can be an eye-opening exercise, as particular inhibitors and barriers can be identified that will need adjusting or altering in the project to achieve success. In this particular example, assessment is taken at the beginning of the project as the announcement is made and the project is fully described. Next, a one-month follow-up is taken, followed by a four-month follow-up that is actually three months later. Finally, at the end of the project, the sixth month, an assessment is taken.

Using five time frames for data collection may be too comprehensive for some projects, but is appropriate for major projects. In addition to these data collection opportunities, a six-month follow-up is planned after implementation. Project timing will depend on the resources available, the need to obtain feedback directly from project team members, and the magnitude of events or activities scheduled throughout the project. In addition, they need to make quick adjustments and changes that will also affect the timing. Finally, the need to gain commitment and support and measure the pulse all the way through the process is an important factor in determining the actual timing.

Interviews

Another helpful data collection method is the interview, although it is not used as frequently as questionnaires. The project coordinator, the project training staff, the project team member's supervisor, or an outside third party can conduct interviews. Interviews can secure data not available in performance records, or data difficult to obtain through written responses or observations. Also, interviews can uncover success

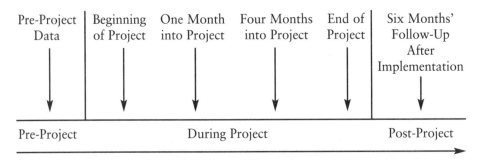

Figure 5-1. Project timetable.

stories that can be useful in communicating evaluation results. Project team members may be reluctant to describe their reactions in a questionnaire but will volunteer the information to a skillful interviewer who uses probing techniques. A major disadvantage of the interview is that it is time-consuming. It also requires training to prepare interviewers and to ensure that the process is consistent.

Types of Interviews

Interviews usually fall into two basic types: structured and unstructured. A structured interview is much like a questionnaire. Specific questions are asked with little room to deviate from the desired responses. The primary advantages of the structured interview over the questionnaire are that the interview process can ensure that the questionnaire is completed and the interviewer understands the responses supplied by the project team member.

The unstructured interview allows probing for additional information. This type of interview uses a few general questions, which can lead into more detailed information, as important data are uncovered. The interviewer must be skilled in the probing process. Table 5-1 gives some typical probing questions.

Interview Guidelines

The design steps for interviews are similar to those of the questionnaire. A brief summary of key issues with interviews is outlined here.

Develop questions to be asked. Once a decision has been made about the type of interview, specific questions need to be developed. Questions should be brief, precise, and designed for easy response.

Try out the interview. The interview should be tested on a small number of project team members. If possible, the interviews should be

Table 5-1. Typical Probing Questions

Can you explain that in more detail?

Can you give me an example of what you are saying?

Can you explain the difficulty that you say you encountered?

conducted as part of the trial run of the project evaluation. The responses should be analyzed and the interview revised, if necessary.

Train the interviewers. The interviewer should have appropriate skills, including active listening, the ability to ask probing questions, and the ability to collect and summarize information into a meaningful form.

Give clear instructions to the project team member. The project team member should understand the purpose of the interview and know what will be done with the information. Expectations, conditions, and rules of the interview should be thoroughly discussed. For example, the project team member should know if statements would be kept confidential. If the project team member is nervous during an interview and develops signs of anxiety, he or she should be made to feel at ease.

Administer the interviews according to a scheduled plan. As with the other evaluation instruments, interviews need to be conducted according to a predetermined plan. The timing of the interview, the person who conducts the interview, and the place of the interview are all issues that become relevant when developing an interview plan. For a large number of project team members, a sampling plan may be necessary to save time and reduce the evaluation cost.

Focus Groups

An extension of the interview, focus groups are particularly helpful when in-depth feedback is needed for the evaluation and when a larger sample size is important. The focus group involves a small group discussion conducted by an experienced facilitator. It is designed to solicit qualitative judgments on a planned topic or issue. Group members are all required to provide their input, as individual input builds on group input.

When compared with questionnaires, surveys, tests, or interviews, the focus group strategy has several advantages. The basic premise of using focus groups is that when quality judgments are subjective, several individual judgments are better than one. The group process, where project team members often motivate one another, is an effective method for generating new ideas and hypotheses. It is inexpensive and can be quickly planned and conducted. Its flexibility makes it possible to explore a project's unexpected outcomes or applications and what individuals' reactions are to those unexpected outcomes.

The focus group is particularly helpful when qualitative information is needed. For example, the focus group can be used in the following situations:

☐ To evaluate the reactions to specific exercises, cases, simulations, or other components of a project
☐ To assess the overall effectiveness of the project as perceived by the project team members immediately following a project milestone
☐ To assess the impact of the project in a follow-up setting after the project is completed

Essentially, focus groups are helpful when evaluation information is needed but cannot be collected adequately with simple, quantitative methods.

GUIDELINES

While there are no set rules on how to use focus groups for evaluation, the following guidelines should be helpful:

Ensure that management supports the focus group process. Because this is a relatively new process for most project managers, it might be unknown to some management groups. Managers need to understand focus groups and their advantages. They need to raise their level of confidence in the information that can be obtained from group sessions.

Plan topics, questions, and strategy carefully. As with any evaluation instrument, planning is the key. The specific topics, questions, and issues to be discussed must be carefully planned and sequenced. This enhances the comparison of results from one group to another and ensures that the group process is effective and stays on track.

Keep the group size small. While there is no magic group size, a range of six to twelve seems to be appropriate for most focus group applications. A group has to be large enough to ensure different points of view, but small enough to give every project team member a chance to talk freely and exchange comments.

Ensure that there is a representative sample of the target population. It is important for groups to be stratified appropriately so that project team members represent the target population. The group should be homogeneous in experience, rank, and influence in the organization.

Insist on facilitators who have appropriate expertise. The success of a focus group rests with the facilitator who must be skilled in the focus group process. Facilitators must know how to control aggressive members of the group and diffuse the input from those who want to dominate the group. Also, facilitators must be able to create an environment in which project team members feel comfortable in offering comments freely and openly. Because of this, some organizations use external facilitators.

In summary, the focus group is an inexpensive and quick way to determine the strengths and weaknesses of projects and project team members' reactions to the project. However, for complete evaluation, focus group information should be combined with data from other instruments because often, focus groups focus only on the issues of the outspoken project team members.

USING REACTION AND SATISFACTION DATA

Sometimes project team member feedback is solicited, tabulated, summarized, and then disregarded. The information must be collected and used for one or more of the purposes of evaluation. Otherwise, the exercise is a waste of the project team members' time. Too often, project evaluators use the material to feed their egos and let it quietly disappear into their files, forgetting the original purposes behind its collection. A few of the more common reasons for gathering reaction and satisfaction data are summarized below.

Monitor Stakeholder Satisfaction

Because this input is the principal measure taken from the project team members, it provides a good indication of their overall reaction to, and satisfaction with, the project. Thus, project managers and owners will know how well satisfied the customers actually are with the project. Data should be reported to clients and others.

Identify Strengths and Weaknesses of the Project

Feedback is extremely helpful in identifying weaknesses as well as strengths of the project. Project team member feedback on weaknesses can often lead to adjustments and changes. Identifying strengths can be helpful in future designs so processes can be replicated.

Develop Norms and Standards

Because reaction and satisfaction evaluation data can be automated and are collected in nearly 100 percent of projects, it becomes relatively easy to develop norms and standards throughout the organization. Target ratings can be set for expectations; particular project results are then compared to those norms and standards.

Evaluate Individual Project Managers

Perhaps one of the most common uses of reaction and satisfaction data is project manager evaluation. If properly constructed and collected, helpful feedback data can be provided to project managers so that adjustments can be made to increase effectiveness. Some caution needs to be taken, though, since project manager evaluations can sometimes be biased, so other evidence may be necessary to provide an overall assessment of performance.

Evaluate Planned Improvements

Feedback data from a questionnaire can provide a profile of planned actions and improvements. These data can be compared with on-the-job actions as a result of the project. This provides a rich source of data in terms of what project team members may be changing or implementing because of what they have learned.

Link with Follow-up Data

If a follow-up evaluation is planned, it may be helpful to link Level 1 data with follow-up data to see if planned improvements became reality. In many cases, planned actions are often inhibited in some way through on-the-job barriers.

Marketing Project Solutions

For some organizations, project team member feedback data provides helpful marketing information. Project team members' quotes and reactions provide information that may be convincing to potential project team members. Project marketing brochures often contain quotes and summaries of feedback data.

SHORTCUT WAYS TO MEASURE
REACTION AND SATISFACTION

The key question for some at this point is what are some shortcut ways to measure reaction and satisfaction? While reaction and satisfaction data must always be collected, there are some shortcuts that can be taken. There are some essential items that must be taken care of for very short, low-profile, inexpensive projects. Unfortunately, omitting Level 1 is not an option because of the critical importance. Three particular issues can be helpful.

Use a Simple Questionnaire

A detailed, comprehensive, 100-item questionnaire is not necessary for every project. A simple ten- to fifteen-item questionnaire using multiple choice, true/false, or even a scale rating will be sufficient for many small-scale projects. Although interviews, focus groups, surveys, and questionnaires are all presented as options, the questionnaire can suffice for most situations.

Collect Data Early and React Quickly

Taking an early pulse is critical. Find out if the project is being accepted and if those involved have concerns. This step is very critical, and the action must be taken quickly. It will ensure that the process is kept on track and that the project enjoys success as planned.

Pay Attention to Project Team Members

The key stakeholders, the project team members, are critical to the process. They can make or break any project, and their feedback is very important. A general rule is to always listen to this group and react to its concerns, issues, and recommendations. Sometimes it will need filtering because of biases. The important thing is to listen and react, when appropriate.

FINAL THOUGHTS

This chapter is the first of four chapters on data collection and represents one of the six measures reported in the project management scorecard. Measuring reaction and satisfaction is included in every study and is a critical part of the success. Although there are many uses for the data, two important uses stand out. The first use is for making adjustments and changes throughout the project as problems or barriers are uncovered. The second is for reporting the level of satisfaction with the project and having it included as one of the six key types of data. There are several ways to collect satisfaction and reaction data, including questionnaires, surveys, interviews, and focus groups. By far the questionnaire is the most common, and sometimes just a simple, one-page reaction questionnaire will be appropriate. Whatever the method used, the important point is to collect data, react quickly, make adjustments, and summarize the data for reporting and for use in preparing the project management scorecard.

FURTHER READING

Barlow, Janelle and Claus Moller. *A Complaint Is a Gift: Using Customer Feedback as a Strategic Tool*. San Francisco: Berrett-Koehler Publishers, 1996.

Gummesson, Evert. *Qualitative Methods in Management Research*, revised ed. Newbury Park, CA: Sage Publications, 1991.

Hronec, Steven M./Arthur Andersen & Co. *Vital Signs: Using Quality, Time, and Cost Performance Measurements to Chart Your Company's Future*. New York: Amacom/American Management Association, 1993.

Krueger, Richard A. *Focus Groups: A Practical Guide for Applied Research*, 2nd ed. Thousand Oaks, CA: Sage Publications, 1994.

Kvale, Steinar. *InterViews: An Introduction to Qualitative Research Interviewing*. Thousand Oaks, CA: Sage Publications, 1996.

Naumann, Earl and Kathleen Giel. *Customer Satisfaction Measurement and Management: Using the Voice of the Customer*. Boise: Thomson Executive Press, 1995.

Rea, Louis M. and Richard A. Parker. *Designing and Conducting Survey Research: A Comprehensive Guide*, 2nd ed. San Francisco: Jossey-Bass Publishers, 1997.

Renzetti, Claire M. and Raymond M. Lee (Eds). *Researching Sensitive Topics*. Newbury Park, CA: Sage Publications, 1993.

Schwartz, Norbert and Seymour Sudman (Eds). *Answering Questions: Methodology for Determining Cognitive and Communicative Processes in Survey Research*. San Francisco: Jossey-Bass Publishers, 1996.

CHAPTER 6

How to Measure Skill and Knowledge Changes During the Project

It may seem unnecessary to measure learning with some projects. After all, when application and implementation are measured, the actual progress made in the workplace is measured; then ultimately, when business impact variables are monitored, the success of the project becomes quite clear. However, it is critical to understand the extent to which learning has occurred, particularly with project solutions where there is a significant amount of job changes, procedure changes, new tools, new processes, and new technology. The extent to which the project team members involved in a project solution actually learn their new tools and new processes may be one of the biggest determinants of the success of the project. This chapter focuses on very simple techniques for measuring learning. Many of them have been used for years to measure learning in many different settings, in terms of formal testing and skill practices. Others are less formal in structure and can suffice when time is a concern or when costs need to be minimized.

There are four key areas that demonstrate why learning is an important measure for the project management scorecard:

1. The issue of transferring learning to project implementation
2. The importance of knowledge, expertise, and competencies
3. The importance of learning with most projects
4. Finding out what went wrong when there is a problem.

Each of these, individually, will probably justify the need to measure learning. Collectively, they provide a major thrust for measuring the amount of skills, knowledge, or change during a project.

The Transfer of Learning

A significant problem that has plagued projects for many years is the lack of transfer of what is actually learned by project team members. In many situations, the learning is not transferred to the actual project. During a project to implement a new technology, project team members may be involved in several learning activities with new project solutions. It is critical to make sure this knowledge transfers to the project itself. The result of the transfer is actually measured on the job during Level 3 evaluation, where application and implementation is measured.

Importance of Knowledge, Expertise, and Competencies

Today, many organizations are focusing more on knowledge, expertise, and competencies than in the past. Many large projects involve developing expertise with employees using tools and techniques not previously used. Some projects focus directly on core competencies and building important skills, knowledge, and behaviors into the organization. With a continuous focus on knowledge management, it is important for knowledge-based employees to understand and acquire a vast array of information, assimilate it, and use it in a productive way. This emphasis on employee knowledge and skills makes it critical to measure learning in almost all projects.

The Importance of Learning in Most Projects

Learning is becoming a large part of projects because of the variety of tools, techniques, processes, and technology that are being applied in most projects today. Gone are the days where the simple tasks and procedures are built into work or automated within the process. Instead, there are complex environments, processes, and tools that must be used in an intelligent way to reap the benefits from the project solution. Employees must learn in a variety of ways, not just in a formal classroom environment but also through technology-based learning and on-the-job facilitation with job aids and other tools. Also, the project team leaders and managers often serve as coaches or mentors in some project implementations.

Finding Out What Went Wrong When There Is a Problem

When the application and implementation of a project solution does not go smoothly, the most important questions become: "What went wrong?" "What areas need to be adjusted?" "What needs to be altered?" When learning is measured, it is easy to see the degree to which the lack of learning is actually a problem or, in some cases, to eliminate the learning deficiency as a problem. In other words, without the learning measurement, the project manager may not know why employees are not performing the way they should or why particular parts of the project are not being managed the way they should.

These key issues illustrate why measuring learning is an important ingredient in most project management scorecards.

MEASURING LEARNING WITH FORMAL TESTS

Testing is important for measuring learning. An improvement in test scores shows the change in skill, knowledge, or attitude of the project team member attributed to the project solution. The principles of test development are similar to those for the design and development of questionnaires and attitude surveys presented in a previous chapter.

The types of tests used in projects can be classified in three ways. The first is based on the medium used for administering the test. The most common media for tests are written or keyboard tests; performance tests, using simulated tools or the actual equipment; and computer-based tests, using computers and video displays. Knowledge and skills tests are usually written, because performance tests are more costly to develop and administer. Computer-based tests and those using interactive video are gaining popularity. In these tests, a computer monitor or video screen presents the questions or situations, and project team members respond by typing on a keyboard or touching the screen. Interactive videos have a strong element of realism because the person being tested can react to images—often moving pictures and video vignettes that reproduce the real job situation.

The second way to classify tests is by purpose and content. In this context, tests can be divided into aptitude tests or achievement tests. Aptitude tests measure basic skills or acquired capacity to learn a job. An achievement test assesses a person's knowledge or competence in a particular subject.

A third way to classify tests is by test design. The most common are objective tests, norm-referenced tests, criterion-referenced tests, essay tests, oral examinations, and performance tests. Objective tests have answers that are specific and precise, based on the objectives of a program. Attitudes, feelings, creativity, problem-solving processes, and other intangible skills and abilities cannot be measured accurately with objective tests. Oral examinations and essay tests have limited use in project evaluations; they are probably more useful in academic settings. The last two types of tests listed above are more common in project settings: criterion-referenced tests and performance testing evaluation. Both are described in more detail below.

Criterion-Referenced Test

The criterion-referenced test (CRT) is an objective test with a predetermined cutoff score. The CRT is a measure against carefully written objectives for the learning components of the project. In a CRT, the interest lies in whether or not a project team member meets the desired minimum standards, not how that project team member ranks with others. The primary concern is to measure, report, and analyze project team member performance as it relates to the learning objectives for the project.

Table 6-1 examines a reporting format based on criterion-referenced testing. This format helps explain how a CRT is applied to an evaluation effort. Four project team members have completed a learning component with three measurable objectives that correspond to each of the modules. Actual test scores are reported, and the minimum standard is shown. For example, on the first objective, Project Team Member 4 received a pass rating for a test that has no numerical value and that is simply rated pass or fail. The same project team member met Objective 2 with a score of 14 (10 was listed as the minimum passing score). The project team member scored 88 on Objective 3 but failed it because the standard was 90. Overall, Project Team Member 4 satisfactorily completed the learning component. The column on the far right shows that the minimum passing standard for the project is at least two of the three objectives. Project Team Member 4 achieved two objectives, the required minimum.

Criterion-referenced testing is not a popular measurement tool with most projects today. This is because many project managers fail to realize the connection between learning and overall project success. Project managers should recognize that the approach of criterion-reference testing is helpful when it is necessary for a group of employees to learn new systems, procedures, or technology as part of a project. Its use can become widespread. Criterion-referenced testing is frequently computer-based, which makes testing more convenient. It has the advantage of being objectives-based, precise, and relatively easy to

Table 6-1. Reporting Format for Criterion Referenced Test Data

| | Objective 1 | Objective 2 | | | Objective 3 | | | Total Objectives | | Overall |
	P/F	Raw Score	Std	P/F	Raw Score	Std	P/F	Passed	Minimum Standard	Score
Project Team Member 1	P	4	10	F	87	90	F	1	2 of 3	Fail
Project Team Member 2	F	12	10	P	110	90	P	2	2 of 3	Pass
Project Team Member 3	P	10	19	P	100	90	P	3	2 of 3	Pass
Project Team Member 4	P	14	10	P	88	90	F	2	2 of 3	Pass
Totals 4	3 Pass 1 Fail			3 Pass 1 Fail			2 Pass 2 Fail	8 Pass 4 Fail		3 Pass 1 Fail

administer. It requires clearly defined objectives that can be measured by tests, which is another reason why this evaluation technique has limited use in many projects today.

Performance Testing

Performance testing allows the project team member to exhibit a skill (and occasionally knowledge or attitudes) that has been learned in a project. The skill can be manual, verbal, or analytical, or a combination of the three. In some improvement-related projects, performance testing comes in the form of skill practices or role-playing. Project team members are asked to demonstrate discussion or problem-solving skills they have acquired as an adequate reflection of the skills learned from the project.

For a performance test to be effective, the following steps are recommended in the design and administration of the test:

1. The test should be a representative sample of the work/task related to the project. The test should allow the project team member to demonstrate as many skills taught in the project as possible. This increases the validity of the test and makes it more meaningful to the project team member.
2. The test should be thoroughly planned. Every phase of the test should be planned—the timing, the preparation of the project team member, the collection of necessary materials and tools, and the evaluation of results.
3. Thorough and consistent instructions are necessary. As with other tests, the quality of the instructions can influence the outcome of a performance test. All project team members should be given the same instructions. They should be clear, concise, and to the point. Charts, diagrams, blueprints, and other supporting information should be provided if they are normally provided in the work setting. If appropriate and feasible, the test should be demonstrated by the appropriate project team member so that project team members observe how the skill is practiced.
4. Procedures should be developed for objective evaluation, and acceptable standards must be developed for a performance test. Standards are sometimes difficult to develop because varying degrees of speed, skill, and quality are associated with individual outcomes. Predetermined standards must be developed so that employees know in advance what has to be accomplished and what will be considered satisfactory and acceptable for test completion.

5. Information that may bias project team member performance should not be included. The learning module is included to develop a particular skill. Project team members should not be led in this direction unless they face the same obstacles in the job environment.

With these general guidelines, performance tests can be utilized as effective tools for a measure of learning for the project management scorecard. Although more costly than written tests, performance tests are essential in situations where a high degree of fidelity is required between work and test conditions.

MEASURING LEARNING WITH SIMULATION

Another technique for measuring learning is job simulation. This method involves the construction and application of a procedure or task that simulates or models the work involved in the project. The simulation is designed to represent, as closely as possible, the actual job situation. Project team members try out their performance in the simulated activity and have it evaluated based on how well the task is accomplished. Simulations may be used during the project training.

There are several simulation techniques used to evaluate learning. They are used in conjunction with project training to develop operational and diagnostic skills. One technique uses software to simulate real-life situations. Another approach involves a project team member's performance in a simulated task representing a part of the project solution. Still another less-effective but popular technique of simulation is a case study.

MEASURING LEARNING WITH
LESS STRUCTURED ACTIVITIES

In many project solution evaluations, it is sufficient to have an informal check of learning to provide some assurance that project team members have acquired the skills and knowledge related to the project, or perhaps to determine if there have been some changes in attitudes. This approach is appropriate when other levels of evaluation are pursued. For example, if a Level 3 application and implementation evaluation is planned, it might not be so critical to conduct a comprehensive Level 2 evaluation. An informal assessment of learning can be sufficient if what project team members do is more important than what project team members know. After all, the resources are scarce, and a comprehensive evaluation at all levels becomes quite expensive. The following are some alternative approaches to measuring learning when inexpensive, low-key, informal assessments are needed.

Exercises/Activities

Many projects involve activities, exercises, or problems that must be explored, developed, or solved during the learning components of the project. Some of these are constructed in terms of involvement exercises, while others require individual problem-solving skills. When these tools are integrated into the learning activity, there are several specific ways in which to measure learning:

☐ The results of the exercise can be submitted for review and for possible scoring by the project manager or project trainer. This becomes part of the overall score for the project and becomes a measure of learning.

☐ The results can be discussed in a group, with a comparison of the various approaches and solutions, and the group can reach an assessment of how much each individual has learned. This may not be practical in many settings, but can work in a few narrowly focused applications.

☐ The solutions to the problem or exercises can be shared with the group, and the project team member can provide a self-assessment indicating the degree to which the skills and/or knowledge have been obtained from the exercise. This also serves as reinforcement in that project team members quickly see the correct solution.

☐ The project manager or project trainer can review the individual progress of each project team member to determine the relative success. This is appropriate for small groups but can be very cumbersome and time-consuming in larger groups.

While this approach to measuring learning lends itself to greater subjectivity than approaches previously mentioned, exercises and activities are a good way to reinforce learning as well as measure the level to which learning has been acquired.

Self-Assessment

In many project situations, self-assessment may be appropriate. Project team members are provided an opportunity to assess their acquisition of skills and knowledge. This is particularly applicable in cases where higher-level evaluations are planned and it is important to know if actual learning is taking place. A few techniques can ensure that the process is effective:

☐ The self-assessment should be made anonymously so that project team members feel free to express realistic and accurate assessments of what they have learned.

☐ The purpose of the self-assessment should be explained, along with the plans for the data. Specifically, if there are implications for project design or individual re-testing, this should be discussed.

☐ If there has been no improvement or the self-assessment is unsatisfactory, there should be some explanation as to what that means and what the implications will be. This will help ensure that accurate and credible information is provided and that project team members feel accountable for their learning.

Some are concerned that self-assessment does not provide an accurate indication of learning acquired. However, the self-assessment does provide some evidence as to whether the individual feels comfortable with the new skills and knowledge. This evidence may be all that is necessary for a particular project, if a higher evaluation is being pursued.

Project Manager or Project Trainer Assessment

A final technique is for the project manager or project trainer to provide an assessment of the learning that has taken place. Although this approach is very subjective, it may be appropriate when a higher-level evaluation is planned. One of the most effective ways to accomplish this is to provide a checklist of the specific skills that need to be acquired. Project managers can then check off the assessment of the skills individually. Also, if there is a particular body of knowledge that needs to be acquired, a checklist of the categories should be developed for assuring that the individual has a good understanding of those items. This could create a problem if the project team members have not had the appropriate time and opportunity to demonstrate skills or knowledge acquisition, and the project manager may have a difficult time in providing appropriate responses. There is also the question of what to do if there is no evidence of learning. The specific consequences need to be considered and addressed before the method is used.

Administrative Issues

There are several administrative issues that need to be addressed for measuring learning. Each is briefly discussed below and should be part of the overall plan for administering a Level 2 evaluation, an important part of the project management scorecard.

Consistency

It is extremely important that different tests, exercises, or processes for measuring learning are administered consistently from one group to another. This includes issues such as the time required to respond, the actual learning conditions in which the project team members complete the process, the resources available to them, and the assistance from other members of the group. These issues can easily be addressed in the instructions.

Monitoring

In some situations, it is important for project team members to be monitored as they are completing the test or other measurement processes. This ensures that each individual is working independently and also that someone is there to provide assistance or answer questions as needed. This may not be an issue in all situations but needs to be addressed in the overall plan.

Scoring

The scoring instructions need to be developed for the measurement process so that the person evaluating the responses will be objective in the process and provide consistent scores. Ideally, the potential bias from the individual scoring the instrument should be completely removed through proper scoring instructions and other information necessary to provide an objective evaluation.

Reporting

A final issue is reporting the results. In some situations, the project team members are provided with the results immediately, particularly with self-scoring tests or with group-based scoring mechanisms. In other situations, the actual results may not be known until later. In these situations, a mechanism for providing scoring data should be built into the evaluation plan unless it has been predetermined that project team members will not know the scores. The worst-case scenario is to promise test scores and deliver them late or not at all.

USING LEARNING DATA

Although there can be several uses for learning data, the following uses are most common:

Providing individual feedback to build confidence. Learning data, when provided directly to project team members, provides reinforcement for correct answers and enhances learning for the solutions. This reinforces the learning process and provides much-needed feedback to project team members.

Ensure that learning has been acquired. Sometimes it is essential to show the extent and scope of learning. Measuring learning, even if informally, will provide input on this issue.

Improving projects. Perhaps the most important use of learning data is to improve the project. Consistently low responses for certain learning measures may indicate that inadequate project training has been provided on that topic. Consistently low scores with all project team members may indicate that the objectives and scope of coverage are too ambitious or misdirected.

Evaluating project managers or project trainers. Just as reaction and satisfaction data can be used to evaluate project managers and other project team members, learning measures provide additional evidence of the success of the staff. The project manager or project trainer has a significant responsibility to ensure that project team members have learned the new skills and knowledge and that testing is a reflection of the degree to which the skills/knowledge have been acquired and internalized from actual application.

FINAL THOUGHTS

This chapter briefly discusses some of the key issues involved in measuring learning—an important ingredient of most projects. Even if it is accomplished informally, learning must be assessed to determine the extent to which the project team members in a project are learning new skills, techniques, processes, tools, and procedures. Without measuring learning, it is impossible to know what may be wrong should there be an implementation problem later. Also, measuring learning provides an opportunity to make adjustments quickly so that changes can be made to enhance learning. The approach does not have to be so formal, except for major projects. A less-formal, less-structured approach—even if a self-assessment activity—is usually appropriate for most learning situations.

Further Reading

Boyce, Bert R., Charles T. Meadow, and Donald H. Kraft. *Measurement in Information Science*. San Diego: Academic Press, 1994.

Dixon, Nancy M. *Evaluation: A Tool for Improving HRD Quality*. San Diego: University Associates, Inc./American Society for Training and Development, 1990.

Fetterman, David M., Shakeh J. Kaftarian, and Abraham Wandersman (Eds.). *Empowerment Evaluation: Knowledge and Tools for Self-Assessment & Accountability*. Thousand Oaks, CA: Sage Publications, 1996.

Fitz-enz, Jac. *How to Measure Human Resources Management*. New York: McGraw-Hill, Inc., 1995.

Gummesson, Evert. *Qualitative Methods in Management Research,* revised ed. Newbury Park, CA: Sage Publications, 1991.

Kirkpatrick, Donald L. *Evaluating Training Programs: The Four Levels*, 2nd ed. San Francisco: Berrett-Koehler Publishers, 1998.

Phillips, Jack J. *Accountability in Human Resource Management*. Boston: Butterworth-Heinemann, previously published by Gulf Publishing, 1996.

Phillips, Jack J. *Handbook of Training Evaluation and Measurement Methods*, 3rd ed. Boston: Butterworth-Heinemann, previously published by Gulf Publishing, 1997.

Rea, Louis M. and Richard A. Parker. *Designing and Conducting Survey Research: A Comprehensive Guide*, 2nd ed. San Francisco: Jossey-Bass Publishers, 1997.

Schwartz, Norbert and Seymour Sudman (Eds.). *Answering Questions: Methodology for Determining Cognitive and Communicative Process in Survey Research*. San Francisco: Jossey-Bass Publishers, 1996.

Swanson, Richard A. and Elwood F. Holton III. *Results: How to Assess Performance, Learning, and Perceptions in Organizations*. San Francisco: Berrett-Koehler Publishers, Inc., 1999.

CHAPTER 7

How to Measure Implementation, Application, and Progress

Measuring the application and implementation of project management solutions is critical since these steps play a pivotal role in the overall success or failure of the project management process. If new skills and tools are not applied effectively, there will be no change in the success of the project—and no benefit from the project management solution.

While many options are available to measure application and implementation, this chapter explores the most common ways project management solutions are evaluated. The range of possibilities varies from the use of questionnaires to observation and action planning. This chapter explores the issues faced in applying these processes on the job and provides several examples.

WHY MEASURE APPLICATION AND IMPLEMENTATION?

In addition to the obvious reasons for measuring application and implementation, there are several specific reasons why this is one of the most important measures to track in the project management process.

The Value of the Information

The value of the evaluation information increases as progress is made through the chain of impact from Level 1 to Level 5. Thus, information concerning application and implementation at Level 3 is more valuable to the client than reaction/satisfaction (Level 1) and learning (Level 2). This is not meant to discount the importance of these two levels, but rather to emphasize that measuring the extent to which the project management solution is implemented often provides critical data not only about the success of the project but also on the factors that can contribute to greater success as the project management process is fully integrated within the organization.

A Key Transition Issue

The two previous measures, reaction/satisfaction and learning, occur during the early stages of implementing a project management solution where there is more attention and focus on the solution. Level 3, measuring application and implementation, occurs after the solution has been implemented and measures the success of implementation. Essentially, this measure reflects the degree to which the solution is achieving success. Evaluation at this level is a key transition step and is the first measure captured after the project management solution has been fully implemented. Application and implementation is a critical issue, where various measures of success are identified and enhancements to additional success are pinpointed.

The Key Focus of Many Projects

As many project management solutions focus directly on application and implementation, the solution sponsor is often concerned about these measures of success. Major projects designed to transform an organization and build a stronger customer base will have key issues surrounding this level of evaluation. The sponsor will be interested in knowing the extent to which all of the key stakeholders are adjusting to and implementing the desired new behaviors, processes, and procedures, as described in the project management solution. This interest by the client is at the core of application and implementation.

Problems, Obstacles, and Barriers

When a project management solution goes astray, the first question is, "What happened?" More importantly, when it appears that a project management solution is not adding value, the first question should be, "What can we do to change the direction of the project?" In either scenario, it is critical to have information that identifies barriers to success, problems encountered in implementation of the solution, and obstacles to the application of the solution. It is at Level 3, measuring application and implementation, that these problems are addressed, identified, and examined for solutions. In many cases, the key stakeholders directly involved in the implementation of solutions provide important input into the recommendations for making changes or for using a different approach in the future.

Enablers and Enhancers

When there is success, the obvious question is, "How can we repeat this or even improve on this in the future?" The answer to this question is also found at Level 3. Identifying the factors that contribute directly to the success of project management solutions is critical since those same items can be used to replicate the process to enhance results in the future. When key stakeholders identify those issues, it helps make the project solution more successful and provides an important case history of what is necessary for success.

Reward Those Who Are Most Effective

Measuring application and implementation allows the client and project team to reward those who are doing the best job of applying the processes and implementing the project. Measures taken at this level give clear evidence of various efforts and roles, providing an excellent basis for performance review or special recognition. This often has a reinforcing value for keeping the project on track and communicating a strong message for future improvements.

KEY ISSUES

When implementing a process to measure application and implementation of project management solutions, several key issues should be addressed. These are very similar to those issues at Level 1 (reaction/satisfaction). A few issues may differ slightly due to the post-project time frame for this type of data.

Areas of Coverage

To a large degree, the areas of coverage for this process parallel the same areas identified in Chapter 5, How to Measure Reaction and

Satisfaction. However, because this stage of evaluation comes later in the process, additional issues may surface that become opportunities to measure success. In addition, the perspective of the follow-up is changed to post-project rather than the predictive nature of some of the issues in Level 1. The areas of coverage are fully detailed in the section on using questionnaires to measure application and implementation.

Sources

The sources of data mirror those identified in Chapter 5, How to Measure Reaction and Satisfaction. Essentially, all key stakeholders are candidates for sources of data. Perhaps the most important source is those who are actually involved in the application and implementation. It may involve the entire project team, or team leaders charged with the responsibility of implementation.

Timing

The timing of data collection can vary significantly. Since this is a follow-up activity, the key issue is determining the best time for a post-project implementation evaluation. The challenge is to analyze the nature and scope of the application and implementation and determine the earliest time that a trend and pattern will evolve. This occurs when the application of skills/tools becomes routine and the implementation is making significant progress. It is a judgment call. The important point is to go in as early as possible so that potential adjustments can still be made but, at the same time, to wait until significant change in behavior can be observed due to the complete implementation of projects. If projects span a considerable length of time, several measures may be taken at three- to six-month intervals. This well-timed evaluation provides successive input in terms of implementation progress and clearly shows the extent of improvement, as well as identifying the issues that are inhibiting a successful implementation.

Responsibilities

Measuring application and implementation may involve the responsibility and work of several individuals. Because this time period follows the project's completion, an important issue may surface in terms of who is responsible for this follow up. A range of possibilities exists, from project staff to the client staff, as well as the possibility of an external, independent third party. This matter should be addressed in the evaluation planning stage so that there is no misunderstanding as to the distribution of responsibilities. More importantly, those who are responsible should fully understand the nature and scope of their responsibility and what is necessary to collect the data. Additional information on responsibilities is covered in a later chapter.

USING QUESTIONNAIRES TO MEASURE APPLICATION AND IMPLEMENTATION

Questionnaires have become a mainstream data collection tool for measuring application and implementation because of their flexibility, low cost, and ease of administration. The issues involved in questionnaire design discussed in Chapter 5 apply equally to questionnaire development for measuring application and implementation. This section will be limited to the specific content issues of follow-up questionnaires.

Although the content items on a follow-up questionnaire can vary, the following content items are more desirable for capturing application, implementation, and impact information (Level 3 and 4 data). Figure 7-1 presents a questionnaire used in a follow-up evaluation when project management solutions were implemented. The evaluation was designed to capture the return on investment (ROI), with the primary method of data collection being the follow-up questionnaire. This example will be used to illustrate many of the issues involving potential content items for a follow-up questionnaire.

Following a carefully planned growth pattern through acquisitions, National Bank initiated a project to integrate a large acquisition into the bank. The project involved all functional areas of the bank. To improve the project management process, project management training was initiated with the project team. In addition, National Bank established a project management office.

Six months after the project was implemented, an evaluation of the solution was planned using the questionnaire in Figure 7-1. Most of the data from the questionnaire covered application and implementation, while some involved impact measures. Some of the items on the questionnaire were left blank. In these situations, the questionnaire items depend on the specific solution. This type of feedback helps the project team know which parts of the intervention are most effective and useful.

Project Management at National Bank
Follow-up Questionnaire

1. Listed below are the objectives of the project. After reflecting on this project, please indicate the degree of success in meeting the objectives. Use the following scale:

   1. No success at all
   2. Limited success
   3. Moderate success
   4. Generally successful
   5. Very successful

As a result of this project	1	2	3	4	5
a.	☐	☐	☐	☐	☐
b.	☐	☐	☐	☐	☐
c.	☐	☐	☐	☐	☐
d.	☐	☐	☐	☐	☐
e.	☐	☐	☐	☐	☐

2. Did you develop and implement an on-the-job action plan for this project?
   Yes ☐   No ☐

   If yes, please describe the nature and outcome of the plan. If not, explain why. _____
   _____
   _____
   _____

Figure 7-1. Sample follow-up questionnaire.

3. Please rate the relevance to your job of each of the following major tasks and components of the project using the following scale:
   1. No relevance
   2. Limited relevance
   3. Moderate relevance
   4. Generally relevant
   5. Very relevant in every way

	1	2	3	4	5
	☐	☐	☐	☐	☐
	☐	☐	☐	☐	☐
	☐	☐	☐	☐	☐
	☐	☐	☐	☐	☐
	☐	☐	☐	☐	☐
	☐	☐	☐	☐	☐
	☐	☐	☐	☐	☐

4. Have you used the project management tools related to implementing this project?
   Yes ☐   No ☐

   Please explain. _____
   _____
   _____
   _____
   _____

5. Please indicate the change in your application of knowledge and skills as a result of your participation in the project. Use the following scale:

   1. No change
   2. Limited change
   3. Moderate change
   4. Much change
   5. Very much change

Figure 7-1. Continued.

	1	2	3	4	5	No Opportunity to Use Skill
a.	☐	☐	☐	☐	☐	☐
b.	☐	☐	☐	☐	☐	☐
c.	☐	☐	☐	☐	☐	☐
d.	☐	☐	☐	☐	☐	☐
e.	☐	☐	☐	☐	☐	☐
f.	☐	☐	☐	☐	☐	☐
g.	☐	☐	☐	☐	☐	☐

6. What has changed about your work or the project team as a result of this project? _____

_____

_____

_____

7. Please identify any specific accomplishments/improvements that can be linked to this project. _____

_____

_____

_____

8. What specific value, in U.S. dollars, can be attributed to the above accomplishments/improvements? Use first-year values only. While this is a difficult question, try to think of specific ways in which the above project improvements can be converted to monetary units. Along with the monetary values, please indicate the basis of your calculation.

$_____

Basis _____

_____

_____

_____

Figure 7-1. Continued.

$_____

Basis _____

_____

_____

_____

Comments?

9. Other factors often influence improvements in project results. Please indicate the percentage of the aforementioned improvements related directly
to this project (and not to some other factor). _____%

10. What level of confidence do you place in the above estimations? (0% = No
Confidence, 100% = Certainty) _____%

Please explain. _____

_____

_____

_____

11. Do you think the project represented a good investment for National
Bank?
Yes ☐   No ☐

Please explain. _____

_____

_____

_____

12. Indicate the extent to which you think this project has influenced each of
these measures. Use the following scale:

1. No influence
2. Limited influence
3. Moderate influence
4. Significant influence
5. Very significant influence

Figure 7-1. Continued.

	1	2	3	4	5
a. Productivity	☐	☐	☐	☐	☐
b. Sales	☐	☐	☐	☐	☐
c. Quality	☐	☐	☐	☐	☐
d. Cost Control	☐	☐	☐	☐	☐
e. Employee Satisfaction	☐	☐	☐	☐	☐
f. Customer Satisfaction	☐	☐	☐	☐	☐
g. Other _____	☐	☐	☐	☐	☐

13. Please rate the success of the immediate project team and the quality of the team's leadership. Use the following scale:

    1. No success
    2. Limited success
    3. Moderate success
    4. Generally successful
    5. Very successful

Team Characteristic	1	2	3	4	5
Capability	☐	☐	☐	☐	☐
Motivation	☐	☐	☐	☐	☐
Cooperation	☐	☐	☐	☐	☐
Communication	☐	☐	☐	☐	☐

Leadership Issue	1	2	3	4	5
Leadership Style	☐	☐	☐	☐	☐
Organization	☐	☐	☐	☐	☐
Communication	☐	☐	☐	☐	☐
Support for team	☐	☐	☐	☐	☐
Training for team	☐	☐	☐	☐	☐

Figure 7-1. Continued.

14. What barriers, if any, have you encountered that prevented this project from being successful. Please explain, if possible._____

_____

_____

_____

15. What has helped this project be successful? Please explain.

_____

_____

_____

_____

_____

16. Which of the following statements best describes the level of management support this project received?
    ☐ There was no management support for this project.
    ☐ There was limited management support for this project.
    ☐ There was a moderate amount of management support for this project.
    ☐ There was a tremendous amount of management support for this project.

17. What other solutions (besides this project) could have been effective in meeting the business need(s) and business goals of this project?

    Are there other solutions that would have delivered comparable results?
    Yes ☐   No ☐

    Please explain. _____

    _____

    _____

18. What specific suggestions do you have for improving this project?

    _____

    _____

    _____

    _____

    _____

19. Other comments about this project?_____

    _____

    _____

    _____

    _____

Figure 7-1. Continued.

Progress with Objectives

Sometimes it is helpful to assess progress made with the objectives of the solution in the follow-up evaluation as illustrated by Question 1 in Figure 7-1. While this issue is usually assessed during the early stages of the evaluation process, it is sometimes helpful to revisit the objectives after the team has had an opportunity to implement the solution.

Action-Plan Implementation

If an action plan is required in the solution, the questionnaire should reference the plan and determine the extent to which it has been implemented. If the action-plan requirement is very low-key, perhaps only one question on the follow-up questionnaire will be devoted to the action plan, as illustrated in Question 2 in Figure 7-1. If the action plan is quite comprehensive and contains an abundance of Levels 3 and 4 data, then the questionnaire takes a secondary role, and most of the data collection process will focus directly on the status of the completed action plan. The action-planning process is described later in the chapter.

Relevance of Project Management Solutions

Although the relevance of the project management solution is often assessed during the initiation of the project with Level 1 data, it is helpful to assess the relevance to various aspects of the solution after application and implementation (see Question 3). Level 1 data provide information on the perceived relevance immediately following the solution. Level 3 data provide information regarding relevance after skills, knowledge, processes, and tools have actually been put to use. This input adds credibility to the perceived relevance and compares it to the situation during implementation.

Use of Materials

If project team members are provided tools, job aids, and references to use with project management, then it may be helpful to determine the extent to which these materials have been used. This is particularly helpful when operation manuals, reference books, and job aids have been distributed and explained with the project management solution and are expected to be used with the project. Question 4 in Figure 7-1 focuses on this issue.

Knowledge/Skills Use

Another important issue on the follow-up questionnaire is the application of skills and knowledge. Most project management solutions require learning skills and knowledge. As Question 5 in Figure 7-1 shows, the specific skills and knowledge areas are listed, with the question framed around the amount of change since the project management solution was implemented. This is the recommended approach when there are no pre-project data. If pre-data have been collected, it is more appropriate to compare post-project assessments with pre-project assessments using the same type of question. Sometimes it is helpful to determine the most frequently used skills that are directly linked to the solution. A more detailed variation of this question is to list each skill and indicate the frequency of use. For many skills, it is important to experience frequent use quickly after the skills are acquired so that the skills become internalized.

Changes with Project Work

Sometimes it is helpful to determine what specific features have changed about the project team's work that can be connected to the solution. As Question 6 in Figure 7-1 illustrates, the participant explores how the skill application has actually changed the work of the project team.

Improvements/Accomplishments

Question 7 in Figure 7-1 begins a series of four impact questions that are appropriate for most follow-up questionnaires. The first question in the series seeks specific accomplishments and improvements that are directly linked to the project management solution. This question focuses on specific, measurable successes that can be easily identified by the project team members. Since this is an open-ended question, it can be helpful to seek examples that indicate the nature and range of responses requested. However, examples can also limit the responses.

Monetary Impact

Perhaps the most difficult question, Question 8 in Figure 7-1, asks team members to provide monetary values for the improvements identified in Question 7. Although these are business impact data, it may be helpful to collect them here. Only the first-year improvement is sought. Team members are asked to specify net improvements so that the actual monetary values will represent gains from the solution implementation. An important part of the question is the basis for calculation, where team members specify the steps taken to develop the annual net value and the assumptions made in the analysis. It is very important for the basis to be completed with enough detail to understand the process.

Improvements Linked with the Solution

Next in the series of impact questions, Number 9 in Figure 7-1, isolates the effects of the solution. Project team members indicate the percentage of the improvement that is directly related to the solution. As an alternative, the various factors that have influenced the results may be listed. Project team members are asked to allocate a percentage to each factor.

Confidence Level

To adjust for the uncertainty of the data provided in the impact questions, project team members are asked to provide a level of confidence for each estimation given. This confidence factor is expressed as a percentage with a range of 0–100 percent, as shown in Question 10 in Figure 7-1. This input adjusts the participant estimates to account for their uncertainty. This conservative approach adds credibility to the estimation process.

Investment Perception

The project team members' perception of the value of the solution is useful information. As illustrated in Question 11 in Figure 7-1, team members are asked if they believe the solution to be a good investment. An option for this question is to present the actual cost of the solution to enable team members to respond more accurately. Also, the question can be divided into two parts: one reflecting the investment of money by the organization and the other an investment in the team member's time devoted to the solution. The perceived value is an indicator that the solution is being implemented.

Linkage with Output Measures

Sometimes it is helpful to determine the degree to which the solution has influenced certain output measures. As shown in Question 12 in Figure 7-1, team members are often asked to indicate the degree to which they think certain measures have been influenced by the solution. However, when this issue is uncertain, listing potential business performance measures that are known to have been influenced, and asking team members to indicate which measures they believe to have been influenced, will identify the measures most affected by the solution.

Success of Project Team

It is helpful at times to solicit input about the working relationships in the project team. Also, large-scale projects rely on the quality of the project leadership team. Question 13 in Figure 7-1 asks members to indicate the degree to which the project team is successful and the quality of project leadership. This information is helpful in making adjustments in future project/management solutions.

Barriers

Several barriers can influence the successful application of a project solution. Question 14 in Figure 7-1 identifies these barriers. As an alternative, the perceived barriers are listed and project team members check all that apply. Still another variation is to list the barriers with a range of responses, indicating the extent to which the barrier inhibited results.

Enablers

Just as important as barriers are the enablers—those issues, events, or situations that have enabled the project solution to be successful. The same options are available with this question as with the question on barriers. Question 15 in Figure 7-1 addresses this issue.

Management Support

Management support is critical to the successful application of newly acquired project management solutions. At least one question should be included in the questionnaire on the degree of management support. Sometimes this question is structured so that various descriptions of management support are detailed and team members check the one that applies to their situation. Question 16 in Figure 7-1 is such an example.

Appropriateness of Solution

The specific project management solution is usually only one of many potential solutions to a project performance problem. If the initial analysis and needs assessment is faulty or if there are alternative approaches to meeting the desired business need, another solution may achieve the same or greater success. Project management team members are asked to identify alternative solutions that could have been effective in obtaining the same or similar results. Question 17 in Figure 7-1 represents this type of question. The project team can use this information to help improve processes and understand the use of alternative approaches.

Suggestions for Improvement

Project team members are asked to provide suggestions for improving any part of the solution. As illustrated in Question 18 in Figure 7-1, the open-ended structure is intended to solicit qualitative responses to be used in making improvements.

Other Comments

A final step is to seek other comments concerning a project solution. This provides an opportunity to offer additional intangible benefits, present concerns, or suggest issues that need to be addressed in the future. Question 19 in Figure 7-1 is a typical question.

USING INTERVIEWS AND FOCUS GROUPS TO MEASURE IMPLEMENTATION AND APPLICATION

Interviews and focus groups can be used on a follow-up basis to collect data on implementation and application. However, the steps needed to design and administer these instruments are the same as the ones presented in Chapter 5 and will not be repeated here.

OBSERVING PROJECT TEAM MEMBERS ON THE JOB TO MEASURE IMPLEMENTATION AND APPLICATION

Another potentially useful data collection method is observing team members on the job and recording any changes in behavior and specific actions taken. This technique is particularly useful when it is important to know precisely how the team members are using new skills, knowledge, tasks, procedures, or systems. Team member observation is often used when significant skill development is a primary part of the project management solution. The observer may be the project leader, a member of a peer group, or an external resource. The most common observer, and probably the most practical, is the project leader.

Guidelines for Effective Observation

Observation is often misused or misapplied to evaluation situations, forcing some to abandon the process. The effectiveness of observation can be improved with the following guidelines.

OBSERVERS MUST BE FULLY PREPARED

Observers must fully understand what information is needed and what skills are covered in the solution. They must be prepared for the assignment and provided a chance to practice observation skills.

THE OBSERVATIONS SHOULD BE SYSTEMATIC

The observation process must be planned so that it is executed effectively without any surprises. The individual team members should be notified about the observation in advance as well as why they are being observed. If the observation is planned to be invisible, the individuals are monitored unknowingly. The timing should also be a part of the plan. There are right times to observe a participant, and there are wrong times. If a participant is observed when work situations are not normal (i.e., in a crisis), the data collected may be useless.

Planning a systematic observation is important. Several steps are necessary for success:

1. Determine what behavior will be observed.
2. Prepare the forms for the observer's use.

3. Select the observers.
4. Prepare a schedule of observations.
5. Prepare observers to observe properly.
7. Inform project team members of the planned observation, providing explanations.
8. Conduct the observations.
9. Summarize the observation data.

As in previous steps in the measurement and evaluation process, planning the work and working the plan will help ensure the success of the various steps. This includes gathering Level 3 data through observation.

The Observers Should Know How to Interpret and Report What They See

Observations involve judgment decisions. The observer must analyze which behaviors are being displayed and what actions the team members are taking. Observers should know how to summarize behavior and report results in a meaningful manner.

The Observer's Influence Should Be Minimized

Except for "mystery" or "planted" observers and electronic observations, it is impossible to completely isolate the overall effect of an observer. Project team members will display the behavior they think is appropriate, performing at their best. The presence of the observer must be minimized. To the extent possible, the observer should blend into the work environment.

Select Observers Carefully

Observers are usually independent of the project team members. They are typically the project leader or a third party observer. The independent observer is usually more skilled at recording behavior and making interpretations of behavior and is usually unbiased in these interpretations. Using an independent observer reduces the need for preparation of observers and relieves the project leader of the responsibility. On the other hand, the independent observer has the appearance of an outsider and team members may resent this kind of intrusion. Sometimes it is more feasible to recruit observers from outside the organization. Another advantage is the ability to neutralize the prejudicial feelings entering the decisions.

Observation Methods

Five methods of observation are suggested and appropriate depending on the circumstances surrounding the type of information needed. Each method is briefly described below.

BEHAVIOR CHECKLIST AND CODES

A behavior checklist is useful for recording the presence, absence, frequency, or duration of a project team's behavior as it occurs. A checklist does not provide information on the quality, intensity, or possible circumstances surrounding the behavior observed. The checklist is useful, though, since an observer can identify exactly which behaviors should or should not occur. Measuring the duration of a behavior may be more difficult and requires a stopwatch and a place on the form to record time intervals. This factor is usually not as important when compared to whether or not a particular behavior was observed and how often. The number of behaviors listed in the checklist should be small and listed logically if they normally occur in a sequence. A variation of this approach involves coding behaviors on a form. While this method is useful when there are many behaviors, it is more time-consuming because a code is entered that identifies a specific behavior instead of checking an item.

DELAYED REPORT METHOD

With a delayed report method, the observer does not use any forms or written materials during the process. The information is either recorded upon completion or at particular time intervals during an observation. The observer tries to reconstruct what has been witnessed during the observation period. The advantage of this approach is that the observer is not as noticeable, and there are no forms being completed or notes being taken during the observation. The observer becomes more a part of the situation and less of a distraction. An obvious disadvantage is that the information written may not be as accurate and reliable as the information collected at the time it occurred. A variation of this approach is the 360-degree feedback process in which surveys are completed on other individuals based on observations given within a specific time frame.

Video Recording

A video camera records behavior in every detail. However, this intrusion can be awkward and cumbersome, causing the team members to be unnecessarily nervous or self-conscious while they are being videotaped. If the camera is concealed, the privacy of the team member may be invaded. Because of this, video recording of on-the-job behavior is not frequently used.

Audio Monitoring

Monitoring conversations of team members who are using the skills taught in the solution is an effective observation technique. While this approach may stir some controversy, it is an effective way to determine if skills are being applied consistently and effectively. To work smoothly, it must be fully explained and the rules clearly communicated.

Computer Monitoring

Where applicable, computer monitoring is becoming an effective way to "observe" team members as they perform job tasks. The computer monitors frequency, sequence of steps, use of routines, and other activities to determine if the team member is performing the work according to the guidelines of the project management solution. As technology continues to be a significant part of the workplace, computer monitoring holds much promise. This is particularly helpful for application and implementation data.

Using Action Plans and Follow-up Assignments to Measure Implementation and Application

In some cases, follow-up assignments can develop implementation and application data. In a typical follow-up assignment, the project team member is asked to meet a goal or complete a particular task or project by a set date. A summary of the results of the completed assignments provides further evidence of the success of the solution and of actual implementation of new skills and knowledge gained.

The action plan is the most common type of follow-up assignment process and is fully described in this section. With this approach, team members are required to develop action plans as part of the solution.

Action plans contain detailed steps to accomplish specific objectives. The process is one of the most effective ways to enhance support for a project solution and build the ownership needed for the successful application and implementation of the solution.

The plan is typically prepared on a printed form, such as the one shown in Figure 7-2. The action plan shows what is to be done, by whom, and when the objectives should be accomplished. The action-plan approach is a straightforward, easy-to-use method for determining how team members will change their behavior on the job and achieve success with the project management solution. The approach produces data answering such questions as:

- [ ] What on-the-job improvements have been realized since the solution was implemented?
- [ ] Are the improvements linked to the solution?
- [ ] What may have prevented team members from accomplishing specific action items?

With this information, project team leaders can decide if the project should be modified and in what ways, if it is not too late. The project manager can then assess the findings to evaluate the success of the solution.

Developing the Action Plan

The development of the action plan requires two major tasks: determining the areas for action and writing the action items. Both tasks should be completed during the solution implementation and, at the same time, related to on-the-job activities. A list of areas for action can be developed with the help of the project leader. The list may include an area needing improvement or representing an opportunity for increased performance. Examples of typical questions that should be answered before determining the areas for action are listed below:

- [ ] How much time will this action require?
- [ ] Are the skills for accomplishing this action item available?
- [ ] Who has the authority to implement the action plan?
- [ ] Will this action have an effect on other individuals?
- [ ] Are there any organizational constraints for accomplishing this action item?

ACTION PLAN

Name _____ Project Leader Signature _____ Follow-Up Date _____

Objective _____ Evaluation Period _____ to _____

Action Steps	Expected Consequences	Target Date	Responsibility
1.			
2.			
3.			
4.			
5.			
6.			
7.			
8.			

Comments: _____

Figure 7-2. *Typical action plan.*

Usually, it is more difficult to write specific action items than it is to identify the action areas. The most important characteristic of an action item is that it is written so that everyone involved will know when it occurs. One way to help achieve this goal is to use specific action verbs and set deadlines for completion of each action item. Some examples of action items are:

- ☐ Implement the new customer contract software by (date).
- ☐ Handle every piece of paper only once to improve my personal time management by (date).
- ☐ Probe my customers directly about a particular problem by (date).

If appropriate, each action item should indicate other individuals or resources necessary for completion of the action item. Planned behavior changes should be observable. It should be obvious to the team member and others when the change takes place. Action plans, as used in this context, do not require the prior approval or input from the project leader although, as in any case, his or her support may be helpful.

Using Action Plans Successfully

The action-plan process can be an integral part of the consulting intervention and is not necessarily considered an add-on or optional activity. To gain maximum effectiveness from action plans to collect data for evaluation, the following steps should be implemented.

COMMUNICATE THE ACTION-PLAN REQUIREMENT EARLY

One of the most negative reactions to action plans is the surprise factor often inherent in the way the process is introduced. When team members realize they must develop a detailed action plan, there is often immediate, built-in resistance. Communicating to team members in advance, when the process is shown to be an integral part of the solution, will often minimize resistance. When team members fully realize the benefits before they become involved in the solution, they take the process more seriously and usually perform extra steps to ensure its success.

Describe the Action Planning Process at the Outset of the Project

At the first meeting, action plan requirements are discussed, including an outline of the purpose of the process, why it is necessary, and the basic requirements during and after the project management solution implementation. Some team leaders furnish a separate notepad for team members to collect ideas and useful techniques for their action plans. This is a productive way to focus more attention on the process.

Teach the Action Planning Process

An important prerequisite for action planning success is an understanding of how it works and how specific action plans are developed. A portion of the project solution time is allocated to teaching team members how to develop plans. In this session, the requirements are outlined, special forms and procedures are discussed, and a positive example is distributed and reviewed. Sometimes an entire half-day module is allocated to this process so that team members will fully understand and use it. Any available support tools, such as key measures, charts, graphs, suggested topics, and sample calculations, should be used in this session to help facilitate the plan's development.

Allow Time to Develop the Plan

When action plans are used to collect data for project solution evaluation, it is important to allow team members to develop plans during the project management solution implementation. Sometimes it is helpful to have members work in teams so they can share ideas as they develop specific plans. In these sessions, project managers often monitor the progress of individuals or teams to keep the process on track and answer any questions that arise.

Have the Project Leader Approve Action Plans

It is essential for the action plan to be related to project management solution objectives and, at the same time, represent an important accomplishment for the organization when it is completed. It is easy for the team members to stray from the intent and purpose of action planning and not give it the attention it deserves. Consequently, it is helpful to have the project members actually sign off on the action plan, ensuring that the plan reflects all the requirements necessary to thoroughly implement the solution.

ASK PROJECT TEAM MEMBERS TO ISOLATE THE EFFECTS OF THE PROJECT MANAGEMENT SOLUTION

Although the action plan is initiated because of the project management solution, the actual improvements reported on the plan may be influenced by other factors. Thus, the action planning process should not take full credit for the improvement. For example, a plan to reduce product defects may take only partial credit for an improvement because of the other variables that will usually affect the defect rate. While there are several ways to isolate the effects of a project management solution, team member estimation is usually more appropriate in the action-planning process. Consequently, the team members are asked to estimate the percentage of the improvement actually related to a particular solution. This question can be asked on the action plan form or on a follow-up questionnaire.

REQUIRE ACTION PLANS TO BE PRESENTED TO THE GROUP, IF POSSIBLE

There is no better way to secure commitment and ownership of the action-planning process than to have team members describe their action plans in front of fellow team members. Presenting the action plan helps ensure that the process is thoroughly developed and will be implemented on the job. If the number of project team members is too large for individual presentations, perhaps the group can be divided into teams, and one team member can be selected as a spokesperson. Under these circumstances, the team will usually select the best action plan for presentation to the group.

EXPLAIN THE FOLLOW-UP MECHANISM

Project team members must have a clear understanding of the timing, implementation, and follow up of the action plan. The method in which data will be collected, analyzed, and reported should be openly discussed. Five options are common:

1. The group is convened to discuss progress on the plans.
2. Project team members meet with their immediate managers to

discuss the success of the plan. A copy is forwarded to the team leaders.
3. A meeting is held with the evaluator, the team member, and the project leader to discuss the plan and the information it contains.
4. Team members send the plan to the evaluator and it is discussed in a conference call.
5. Team members send the plan directly to the project leader or evaluator with no meetings or discussions. This is the most common option.

While there are other ways to collect the data, it is important to select a mechanism that fits the culture and constraints of the organization.

Collect Action Plans at Predetermined Follow-up Times

Because it is critical to have an excellent response rate, several steps may be necessary to ensure that action plans are completed and the data returned to the appropriate individual or group for analysis. Some organizations use follow-up reminders by mail or e-mail. Others call project team members to check progress. Still others offer assistance in developing the final plan. These steps may require additional resources, which must be weighed against the importance of having more data. When the action plan process is implemented, as outlined in this chapter, the response rates will normally be very high—in the 50–80 percent range. Usually, team members will see the importance of the process and develop their plans in detail during the project management solution.

Summarize and Report the Data

If developed properly, each action plan should result in improvements. Also, each individual has indicated the percentage of improvement directly related to the project management solution, either on the action plan or the questionnaire. The data must be tabulated, summarized, and reported in a way that shows success with application and implementation.

Advantages/Disadvantages of Action Plans

Although there are many advantages to using action plans, there are at least two concerns:

1. The process relies on direct input from the project team member, usually with no assurance of anonymity. As such, the information can sometimes be biased and unreliable.
2. Action plans can be time-consuming for the team member. If the project leader is not involved in the process, there is a chance the team member may not complete the assignment.

As this section has illustrated, the action plan approach has many inherent advantages. Action plans are simple and easy to administer; are easily understood by project team members; are suitable for a wide variety of project management solutions; are appropriate for all types of data; are able to measure reaction, learning, behavior changes, and results; and may be used with or without other evaluation methods.

Because of the tremendous flexibility and versatility of the process and the conservative adjustments that can be made in analysis, action plans have become important data collection tools for evaluating project management solutions.

USING PERFORMANCE CONTRACTS TO MEASURE IMPLEMENTATION AND APPLICATION

The performance contract is essentially a slight variation of the action planning process. Based on the principle of mutual goal setting, a performance contract is a written agreement between a project team member and the project leader. The team member agrees to improve performance in an area of mutual concern related to the project management solution. The agreement is in the form of a project to be completed or a goal to be accomplished soon after the solution is implemented. The agreement spells out what is to be accomplished, at what time, and with what results.

Although the steps can vary according to the specific kind of contract and the organization, a common sequence of events follows:

1. The project team member becomes involved in the project management solution.
2. The team member and project leader mutually agree on a subject for improvement related to the project management solution (i.e., "What's in it for me?").
3. Specific, measurable goals are set.
4. The team member is involved in the solution when the contract is discussed, and plans are developed to accomplish the goals.

5. After implementation of the project management solution, the team member works on the contract against a specific deadline.
6. The team member reports the results of the effort to the project manager.
7. The manager and team member document the results and forward a copy to the project evaluator along with the appropriate comments.
8. The individuals mutually select the subject or action to be taken or performance to be improved prior to the solution.

The process of selecting the area for improvement is similar to that used in the action planning process. The topic can cover one or more of the following areas:

☐ Routine performance—includes specific improvements in routine performance measures, such as production, efficiency, and error rates.
☐ Problem solving—focuses on specific problems, such as an unexpected increase in accidents, a decrease in efficiency, or a loss of morale.
☐ Innovative or creative applications—includes initiating changes or improvements in work practices, methods, procedures, techniques, and processes.
☐ Personal development—involves learning new information or acquiring new skills to increase individual effectiveness.

The topic selected should be stated in terms of one or more objectives. The objectives should state what is to be accomplished when the contract is complete. The objectives should be:

☐ Written
☐ Understandable by all involved
☐ Challenging (requiring an unusual effort to achieve)
☐ Achievable (something that can be accomplished)
☐ Largely under the control of the project team member
☐ Measurable and dated

The details required to accomplish the contract objectives are developed following the guidelines for action plans presented earlier. Also, the methods for analyzing data and reporting progress are essentially the same, as with the action-planning process.

SHORTCUT WAYS TO MEASURE APPLICATION AND IMPLEMENTATION

Measuring application and implementation is a critical issue for most project management solutions. It is hard to understand the success of the solution unless there is some indication as to how well the stakeholders are using the process. While this chapter presented a variety of techniques to measure application and implementation, ranging from questionnaires to observation to action plans, a simplified approach for low-key, inexpensive solutions is to use a simple questionnaire. The questionnaire presented in Figure 7-1 is very detailed around a complex solution. A much more simplified questionnaire addressing five or six key issues is sufficient for small-scale solutions. The areas that should be targeted are actual changes in:

☐ Work and skills applied
☐ Specific implementation issues
☐ Degree of success of implementation
☐ Problems encountered in implementation
☐ Issues that supported the project

These are the core issues that must be addressed.

Another option is to combine the data collected on reaction and satisfaction with the data on application and implementation. These are related issues, and a questionnaire combining the key issues on topics presented in this chapter and in Chapter 5 may be sufficient. The important point is to collect data in the simplest way to see how well the project solution worked.

FINAL THOUGHTS

This chapter outlines techniques for measuring application and implementation—a critical issue in determining the success of the project management solution. This essential measure determines not only the success achieved, but areas where improvement is needed and areas where the success can be replicated in the future. A variety of techniques are available, ranging from observation to questionnaires to action plans, but the method chosen must match the scope of the project solution. Complicated solutions require a comprehensive approach that measures all issues involved in application and implementation. Simple projects can take a less formal approach and collect data only from a questionnaire.

Further Reading

Boyce, Bert R., Charles T. Meadow, and Donald H. Kraft. *Measurement in Information Science*. San Diego: Academic Press, 1994.

Gummesson, Evert. *Qualitative Methods in Management Research*, revised ed. Newbury Park, CA: Sage Publications, 1991.

Krueger, Richard A. *Focus Groups: A Practical Guide for Applied Research*, 2nd ed. Thousand Oaks, CA: Sage Publications, 1994.

Kvale, Steinar. *InterViews: An Introduction to Qualitative Research Interviewing*. Thousand Oaks, CA: Sage Publications, 1997.

Langdon, Danny, G. *The New Language of Work*. Amherst, MA: HRD Press, Inc., 1995.

McClelland, Samuel B. *Organizational Needs Assessments: Design, Facilitation, and Analysis*. Westport, CT: Quorum Books, 1995.

Phillips, Jack J., Ron D. Stone, Patricia P. Phillips. *The Human Resources Scorecard: Measuring the Return on Investment*. Boston: Butterworth-Heinemann, 2001.

Phillips, Jack J. *The Consultant's Scorecard*. New York: McGraw Hill, 2000.

Rea, Louis M. and Richard A. Parker. *Designing and Conducting Survey Research: A Comprehensive Guide*, 2nd ed. San Francisco: Jossey-Bass Publishers, 1997.

Renzetti, Claire M. and Raymond M. Lee (Eds.). *Researching Sensitive Topics*. Newbury Park, CA: Sage Publications, 1993.

Schwartz, Norbert and Seymour Sudman (Eds.). *Answering Questions: Methodology for Determining Cognitive and Communicative Processes in Survey Research*. San Francisco: Jossey-Bass Publishers, 1997.

CHAPTER 8

How to Capture Business Impact Data

WHY MEASURE BUSINESS IMPACT?

Although there are several obvious reasons for measuring impact, three particular issues support the rationale for collecting business impact data related to the implementation of project solutions.

Higher-Level Needs

Many project management solutions are created because project results need improvement. Many projects are conceived based on Level 4 needs, driven by the application and implementation of a project. They often represent the bottom-line measures that are positively influenced when a project is successful. If the business needs defined by business measures are the drivers for a project, then the key measure for evaluating the project is the business impact. The extent to which measures actually have changed is the key determinant of the success of the project management solution.

Payoff with Stakeholders

Business impact data often reflect key payoff measures from the perspective of the stakeholders. These are the measures most often desired by the stakeholders and that the stakeholders want to see changed or improved. They often represent hard, indisputable facts that reflect performance critical to the business and operational units of the organization.

Easy to Measure

One unique feature about business impact data is that the data are often very easy to measure. Hard and soft data measures at this level often reflect key measures that are found throughout most organizations. It is not unusual for organizations to have hundreds or even thousands of measures reflecting specific business impact items. The challenge is to connect the project objectives to the appropriate business measures. This is more easily accomplished at the beginning of the project, since connecting the project objectives to desired organizational business results after the project would be too late for remedial purposes.

TYPES OF DATA

The fundamental premise for evaluating a project is to collect data directly related to the objectives of the project. Project managers are sometimes concerned that appropriate data are unavailable in the organization. Fortunately, this is often not the case. The data needed to evaluate most projects at a business impact level are already collected in a vast majority of settings. The confusion sometimes stems from the types of outcomes planned for projects.

Often, the project focuses on skill and behavioral outcomes reflecting what project team members will be able to do after the project is completed. The outcomes of some solutions are easy to observe and evaluate. It is easy to measure the speed and quality of a new team-based assembly line, for instance. However, behavioral outcomes associated with change management are not nearly as obvious or measurable. Demonstrating that a manager is an effective change agent is much more difficult than demonstrating that an assembly line operation is maintaining quality and quantity standards.

To help project managers focus on desired business impact measures, a distinction is made between two general categories of data: hard data and soft data. Hard data are the primary measurement of improvement, presented through rational, undisputed facts that are easily gathered. They are the most desirable type of data to collect. The ultimate criteria for measuring the effectiveness of management rest on hard data items, such as productivity, profitability, cost control, and quality control.

Hard data are:

- [ ] Easy to measure and quantify
- [ ] Relatively easy to convert to monetary values
- [ ] Objectively based
- [ ] A common measure of organizational performance
- [ ] Credible with management

Because changes in these data may lag behind changes in the organization by many months, it is highly recommended to supplement these measures with interim assessments of measures of soft data, such as attitude, motivation, satisfaction, and skill usage. Although a project designed to enhance competencies or manage change should have an ultimate impact on hard data items, it may be more efficiently measured by soft data items. Soft data are more difficult to collect and analyze but are used when hard data are unavailable.

Soft data are:

- [ ] Sometimes difficult to measure or quantify directly
- [ ] Difficult to convert to monetary values
- [ ] Subjectively based, in many cases
- [ ] Less credible as a performance measurement
- [ ] Usually behaviorally oriented

Hard Data

Hard data can be grouped into four categories (or subdivisions) as shown in Figure 8-1. These categories—output, quality, cost, and time—are typical performance measures in almost every organization. When they are unavailable, the basic approach is to convert soft data to one of the four basic categories.

OUTPUT

Probably the most visible hard data results achieved from many projects are those involving improvements in the output of a work unit. Every organization, regardless of type, has basic measurements of work output, appearing in various forms as outlined in Table 8-1. Since these factors are monitored by organizations, changes can be easily measured by comparing before-and-after work output.

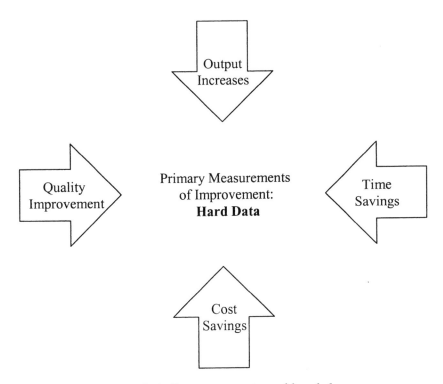

Figure 8-1. Four categories of hard data.

QUALITY

One of the most important hard data results used as a business impact measure on the project management scorecard is quality. Every organization is concerned with quality, and processes are usually in place to measure and monitor quality. Many projects are designed to improve quality, and the results can be easily documented using a variety of quality improvement measurements as illustrated in Table 8-1.

COST

Another major hard data result area is improvement in costs. Many projects that produce a direct cost savings can easily show a bottom-line contribution. A few examples of the types of costs are shown in Table 8-1. There can be as many cost items as there are accounts in a cost-accounting system. In addition, costs can be combined to develop any number of combinations needed for evaluation purposes. Cost

Table 8-1. Examples of Hard Data

Output	Time	Costs	Quality
Units produced	Cycle time	Budget variances	Scrap
Tons manufactured	Response time for complaint	Unit costs	Waste
Items assembled	Equipment downtime	Cost by account	Rejects
Items sold	Overtime	Variable costs	Error rates
Sales	Average delay time	Fixed costs	Rework
Forms processed	Time to project completion	Overhead costs	Shortages
Loans approved	Processing time	Operating costs	Product defects
Inventory turnover	Supervisory time	Delay costs	Deviation from standard
Patients visited	Training time	Penalties/fines	Product failures
Applications processed	Meeting time	Project cost savings	Inventory adjustments
Students graduated	Repair time	Accident costs	Percentage of tasks completed properly
Tasks completed	Efficiency (time-based)	Program costs	Number of accidents
Productivity	Work stoppages	Sales expense	Customer complaints
Work backlog	Order response time	Administrative costs	
Incentive bonus	Late reporting	Average cost reduction	
Shipments	Lost time days		
New accounts generated			

reductions are almost always a key measure on the project management scorecard.

TIME

The fourth hard data category area is time. Easy to measure and just as critical as cost and quality, time savings may mean a project is completed faster than planned, a new product is introduced earlier, or the time to complete a sale is reduced. The savings translate into additional output or lower operating costs. Examples of time savings generated by projects are shown in Table 8-1.

Although these four hard data categories make it easier for a project manager to predict the business impact of project solutions, the distinction between these four groups of hard data is sometimes unclear, since there are overlap factors to consider. For example, accident costs may be listed under the cost category, the number of accidents listed under quality, and the work days lost due to an accident listed under the time category. The rationale? Accidents represent a cost that can easily be determined. Accidents are usually caused by someone making a mistake and are often a reflection of the quality of employee efforts. Days lost on the job represent time lost to the organization. An incentive bonus may be listed as output, since the amount of bonus is usually tied directly to the output of an employee or group of employees. However, the bonus is usually presented in cash, which represents a cost to the organization. The distinction between the different subdivisions is not as important as the awareness of the vast number of measurements in these four areas.

Soft Data

There are times when hard, rational numbers just do not exist. When this is the case, soft data may be meaningful in evaluating projects. Table 8-2 shows common types of soft data, categorized or subdivided into five areas: work habits, climate/satisfaction, customer service, employee development, and initiative. There may be other ways to divide soft data into categories. Due to the many types of soft data, the possibilities are almost limitless.

WORK HABITS

Employee work habits are critical to the success of a work group. Dysfunctional work habits can lead to an unproductive and ineffective

Table 8-2. Examples of Soft Data

Work Habits

Absenteeism

Tardiness

Visits to the dispensary

First-aid treatments

Violations of safety rules

Number of communication
  breakdowns

Excessive breaks

Work Climate/Satisfaction

Number of grievances

Number of discrimination charges

Employee complaints

Litigation

Job satisfaction

Organizational commitment

Employee turnover

Employee Development

Number of promotions

Number of pay increases

Number of training programs
  attended

Requests for transfer

Performance appraisal ratings

Increases in job effectiveness

Customer Service

Customer complaints

Customer satisfaction

Customer dissatisfaction

Customer impressions

Customer loyalty

Customer retention

Customer value

Lost customers

Initiative/Innovation

Implementation of new ideas

Successful completion of projects

Number of suggestions implemented

Setting goals and objectives

New products and services
  developed

New patents and copyrights

work group, while productive work habits can boost the output and morale of the group. The most common and easily documented unproductive work habits include absenteeism and tardiness. These can be tied to cost much easier than other types of soft data. Some projects, such as an absenteeism reduction intervention, are designed to improve the work habits of employees. In most organizations, measurement systems are in place to record employee work habit problems such as absenteeism and tardiness. In other situations, the work habits may have to be documented by the employee's supervisor.

Work Climate/Satisfaction

The climate of the work group is important for team effectiveness. Grievances, discrimination charges, complaints, and job dissatisfaction are often linked to the work climate. The result: less efficiency, less output, unionization drives, and possibly employee resignations. Many projects are designed to improve work climate.

Projects are also frequently designed to improve satisfaction with work, environment, or customers. Reactions to these measures provide additional evidence of success.

Customer Service

One of the most important soft data areas is the customer service category. Measuring the extent of customer satisfaction and dissatisfaction is critical to developing the desired customer loyalty and retention. This business impact soft data category can be extremely important to projects that include customers as a key stakeholder.

Employee Development

Another important type of soft data is employee development. Promotions, transfers, pay increases, and performance ratings are typical data that indicate improvement in this area. In the case of managers/supervisors, measures focus on the extent to which the project helps them provide developmental opportunities for their employees.

Initiative and Innovation

The final category of soft data is initiative. In some projects, project team members are encouraged to try new ideas and techniques. The extent to which employees accomplish their goals is additional evidence of the success of the project. Also, the employees' initiative to generate ideas and submit suggestions is further indication that improvement has occurred. New product and service developments and new inventions, patents, and copyrights are important innovation measures.

As with hard data, these subdivisions have some overlap. Some items listed under one category could appropriately be listed in another. For instance, consider employee loyalty. This measure is related both to the feelings and attitudes of an employee as well as work habits. An employee exhibits loyalty through attitudes and feelings in the following situations:

- ☐ Balancing the organization's goals with personal goals
- ☐ Purchasing the company's products rather than those of a competitor

On the other hand, loyalty may surface in these work habits if an employee:

- ☐ Returns to work promptly after break
- ☐ Studies job information on his or her own time
- ☐ Takes work home when necessary to finish the job

Soft Data Versus Hard Data

The preference by project managers for hard data for the project management scorecard does not dilute the value of soft data. Soft data are essential for a complete evaluation of a project. In fact, a project's total success may rest on soft data measurements. For example, for a project to reduce turnover at a fast-food restaurant, four key measures of success were identified: employee turnover, interview-to-hire ratios, project team members' performance evaluations, and reduced litigation.

Most interventions use a combination of hard and soft data items in the evaluation. A comprehensive evaluation uses several hard data and soft data measurements. For example, a maintenance improvement project had the following measures of success:

- ☐ Reduction of costs associated with specific maintenance activities
- ☐ Improvement in production equipment and processes
- ☐ Changes in maintenance responsibilities and procedures

☐ Improvement in intervention of maintenance employees
☐ Changes in organization and personnel

These changes included both hard data (production and costs) and soft data (increased intervention, changes in procedures, and changes in the organization).

Soft data are typically best used when evaluating behavior and skill outcomes. For example, in building core competencies, which has proven to be a very effective strategy for many organizations, the evaluation of behavioral and skill outcomes relies almost entirely on soft data.

The important point is that there is a place for both hard- and soft-data project evaluation. A comprehensive approach to the project management scorecard will use both types of data. Some projects will rely on soft data as primary measures, while others will rely on hard data as primary measures. Hard data are preferred because of their distinct advantages and level of credibility.

Other Data Categories

In addition to classifying data as hard and soft, it is sometimes helpful to explain other ways to classify or categorize data. As shown in Figure 8-2, data can be categorized at several different levels. As the figure illustrates, some data are considered strategic and are linked to the corporate level of an organization. Other data are more operational at the business unit level. Still other types are considered more tactical in nature and scope and are utilized at the operating level.

Examples of data categorized at the strategic level include financial, people-oriented, or internal versus external. At the business unit level, classifications such as output, quality, time, cost, job satisfaction, and customer satisfaction are critical categories. At the tactical level, the categories include items such as productivity, efficiency, cost control, quality, time, attitudes, and individual and team performance. The important point is not the concern about the classification of data but to be aware of the vast array of data available. Regardless of what they are called, these data types are a consequence of applying and implementing skills, knowledge, tools, and processes and serve as an important measure of success. These measures are captured throughout an organization and used for a variety of purposes. The challenge is to find the data items connected directly to the project. Ideally, this would be accomplished on the front end of the process so that the data are linked

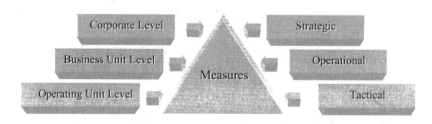

Figure 8-2. Data categories at different organizational levels.

with the initial analysis. If not, it would be a process of trying to identify the appropriate measures for the output of the project management process.

MONITORING BUSINESS PERFORMANCE DATA

Data are available in every organization to measure business performance. Monitoring performance data enables management to measure performance in terms of output, quality, costs, time, job satisfaction, and customer satisfaction. In determining the source of data to be used for the project management scorecard, the first consideration should be existing databases and reports. In most organizations, performance data suitable for measuring improvement resulting from a project are available. If not, additional record-keeping systems will have to be developed for measurement and analysis. At this point, the question of economics surfaces. Is it economical to develop the record-keeping systems necessary to evaluate a project? If the costs are greater than the expected return for the entire project, then it is pointless to develop those systems.

Using Current Measures

If existing performance measures are available, specific guidelines are recommended to ensure that the measurement system is easily developed and easily implemented into the project management scorecard.

IDENTIFY APPROPRIATE MEASURES

Existing performance measures should be thoroughly researched to identify those related to the proposed objectives of the project. Frequently, an organization will have several performance measures related to the same project goal. For example, the efficiency of a production unit can be measured in several ways, some of which are outlined below:

- ☐ The number of units produced per hour
- ☐ The number of on-schedule production units
- ☐ The percentage of utilization of the equipment
- ☐ The percentage of equipment downtime
- ☐ The labor cost per unit of production
- ☐ The overtime required per unit of production
- ☐ The total unit cost

Each of these, in its own way, measures the efficiency of the production unit. All related measures should be reviewed to determine those most relevant to the project goals and most understood and accepted by stakeholders.

CONVERT CURRENT MEASURES TO USABLE ONES

Occasionally, existing performance measures are integrated with other data, and it may be difficult to keep them isolated from unrelated data. In this situation, all existing related measures should be extracted and tabulated again to be more appropriate for use in the project management scorecard.

At times, conversion factors may be necessary. For example, the average number of new sales orders per month may be presented regularly in the performance measures for the sales department. In addition, the sales costs per sales representative are also presented. However, in the evaluation of a project, the average cost per new sale is needed. Thus, the average number of new sales orders and the sales lost per sales representative are required to develop the data necessary for comparison. In this case, the data must be converted in order to be useful.

Developing New Measures

In some cases, data are not available for the information needed to measure the effectiveness of a project. The project team must work with the organization to develop record-keeping systems, if economically feasible. For example, in one organization, a retention project for new professional staff involved several measures including early turnover defined as the percentage of employees who left the company in the first six months of employment. Initially, this measure was not available. Once the project was implemented, the organization began collecting early turnover figures for comparison. Several questions regarding this issue should be addressed:

- ☐   Which department will develop the measurement system?
- ☐   Who will record and monitor the data?
- ☐   Where will it be recorded?
- ☐   Will forms be used?

These questions will usually involve other departments or a management decision that extends beyond the scope of the project manager's responsibilities. Often the administration department, operations, or the information technology unit will be instrumental in helping determine whether new measures are needed and, if so, how they will be developed.

USING ACTION PLANS TO DEVELOP BUSINESS IMPACT DATA

The action plan can be a very useful tool for capturing business impact data. The basic design principles and the issues involved in developing and administering action plans are the same for business impact data as they are for application and implementation data. However, a few issues unique to business impact and return on investment (ROI) are presented here. The following steps are recommended when an action plan is developed and implemented to capture business impact data and convert the data to monetary values.

Have Each Project Team Member Set Goals and Targets

As shown in Figure 8-3, an action plan can be developed with a direct focus on business impact data. The plan presented in this figure requires project team members to develop an overall objective for the plan, which is usually the primary objective of the project or for their phase of the project. In some cases, there may be more than one objective, which requires additional action plans. In addition to the objective, the improvement measure and the current levels of performance are identified. This information requires the project team member to anticipate the application and implementation of the project and set goals for specific performances that can be realized.

Name _____ Project Manager Signature _____ Follow-Up Date _____

Objective _____ Evaluation Period _____ to _____

Improvement Measure _____ Current Performance _____ Target Performance _____

Action Steps	Analysis
1. _____	A. What is the unit of measure? _____
2. _____	B. What is the value (cost) of one unit? $ _____
3. _____	C. How did you arrive at this value? _____
4. _____	_____
5. _____	_____
6. _____	_____
7. _____	D. How much did the measure change during the evaluation period? (monthly value) _____
	E. What percent of this change was actually caused by this project? _____ %
Intangible Benefits:	F. What level of confidence do you place on the above information? (100% = Certainty and 0% = No Confidence) _____ %

Comments: _____

Figure 8-3. Action plan.

The action plan is completed during the project, often with the input, assistance, and facilitation of the project team. The project manager actually approves the plan, indicating that it meets the particular requirements of being Specific, Measurable, Achievable, Realistic, and Time-based (SMART). The plan can be developed in a one- to two-hour time frame and often begins with action steps related to the implementation of the project. These action steps are actually Level 3 activities that detail the application and implementation of the project. All of these steps build support for, and are linked to, business impact measures.

Define the Unit of Measure

The next important issue is to define the actual unit of measure. In some cases, more than one measure may be used and will subsequently be contained in additional action plans. The unit of measure is necessary to break down the process into the simplest steps so that the ultimate value of the project can be determined. The unit can be output data, such as an additional unit manufactured or additional hotel room rented, or it can be sales and marketing data, such as additional sales units, dollars earned, or a 1 percent increase in market share. In terms of quality, the unit can be one reject, error, or defect. Time-based units are usually measured in minutes, hours, days, or weeks. Other units are specific to their particular type of data, such as one grievance, complaint, or absence. The important point is to break them down into the simplest terms possible.

Require Project Team Members to Assign
Monetary Values for Each Improvement

During implementation, project team members are asked to determine, calculate, or estimate the monetary value for each improvement outlined in the project plan. The unit value is determined using standard values, expert input, external databases, or estimates. The process used in arriving at the value is described in the action plan. When the actual improvement occurs, project team members will use these values to capture the annual monetary benefits of carrying out the action plan. For this step to be effective, it is helpful to see examples of common ways in which values can be assigned to the actual data.

Project Team Members Implement the Action Plan

Project team members implement the action plan during the project, which often lasts for weeks or months following the project kick-off point. Upon completion, a major portion, if not all, of the project is slated for implementation. The project team members implement action-plan steps and the subsequent results are achieved.

Project Team Members Estimate Improvements

At the end of the specified follow-up period—usually three months, six months, nine months, or one year—the project team members indicate the specific improvements made, sometimes expressed as a monthly amount. This determines the actual amount of change that has been observed, measured, or recorded. It is important for the project team members to understand the necessity for accuracy of the data that are recorded. In most cases only the changes are recorded, as those amounts are needed to calculate the actual value of the intervention. In other cases, before and after data may be recorded, allowing the research to calculate the actual differences.

Ask Project Team Members to Isolate the Effects of the Project Management Solution

Although the action plan is initiated because of the project solution, the actual improvements reported on the action plan may be influenced by other factors. Thus, the action-planning process initiated within the project should not be given full credit for the improvement. For example, an action plan to reduce employee turnover in a division could take only partial credit for an improvement because of the other variables that affect the turnover rate. While there are several ways to isolate the effects of a project management solution, project team member estimation is usually most appropriate in the action-planning process. Consequently, project team members are asked to estimate the percentage of the improvement actually related to this particular project solution. This question can be asked on the action plan form or in a follow-up questionnaire.

Ask Project Team Members to Provide a Confidence Level for Estimates

Since the process to convert data to monetary values may not be exact and the amount of the improvement actually related to the project may not be precise, project team members are asked to indicate their level of confidence in those two values, collectively. On a scale of 0–100 percent, where zero percent means the values are completely false and 100 percent means the estimates represent certainty, this value provides project team members a mechanism for expressing their uneasiness with their ability to be exact with the estimate concerning the amount of credit the project deserves.

Collect Action Plans at Specified Time Intervals

As mentioned previously, it is essential that the action plans are completed and returned. Using the steps suggested in the previous chapter, follow-up reminders, progress checks, and the offer of assistance will help ensure an appropriate response rate.

Summarize the Data and Calculate the ROI

If developed properly, each action plan should have annualized monetary values associated with improvements. Also, each individual should have indicated the percentage of the improvement directly related to the project solution. Finally, project team members should have provided confidence percentages to reflect their uncertainty with the estimate process and the subjective nature of some of the data that may be provided.

Because this process involves estimates, it may not appear to be accurate. Several adjustments during the analysis make the process very credible and more accurate. The following adjustments are made:

Step 1: For those project team members who do not provide data, it is assumed that they had no improvement to report. This is a very conservative approach.

Step 2: Each value is checked for realism, usability, and feasibility. Extreme values are discarded and omitted from the analysis.

Step 3: Because the improvement is annualized, it is assumed the project solution had no improvement after the first year for short-term projects. Some projects add value in years two and three.

Step 4: The improvement from Step 3 is then adjusted with the confidence level, multiplying it by the confidence percentage. The confidence level is actually an error percentage suggested by the project team members. For example, a project team member indicating 80 percent confidence with the process is reflecting a 20 percent error possibility. In a $10,000 estimate with an 80 percent confidence factor, the project team member is suggesting that the value can be in the range of $8,000 to $12,000. To be conservative, the lower number is used. Thus, the confidence factor is multiplied times the amount of improvement.

Step 5: The new values are then adjusted by the percentage of the improvement related directly to the project, using straight multiplication. This isolates the effects of the solution.

The monetary values determined in these five steps are totaled to arrive at a total project benefit. Since these values are already annualized, the total of these benefits becomes the annual benefits for the solution. This value is placed in the numerator of the ROI formula to calculate the ROI.

USING QUESTIONNAIRES TO COLLECT BUSINESS IMPACT MEASURES

As described in the previous chapters, the questionnaire is one of the most versatile data collection tools and can be appropriate for Level 1, 2, 3, and 4 data. Some of the issues discussed in earlier chapters apply equally in collecting business impact data. Essentially, the design principles and the content issues are the same except that questionnaires developed for a business impact evaluation will contain additional questions to capture particular business impact data.

Key Impact Questions

Figure 8-4 shows a series of key impact questions that can be added to a questionnaire to capture business impact data. While there are a variety of ways to collect this category of data, these simple questions can be very powerful if project team members are committed to providing this type of information.

To ensure an appropriate response, strategies for improving the response rate for questionnaires and surveys apply equally to follow-up questionnaires where business impact data is collected. These questions must be thoroughly explained and if possible even reviewed prior to actually achieving the accomplishments outlined in the questionnaire. The first impact question provides project team members with the opportunity to detail specifically what has changed about their work as a result of the project. This is in fact application data, but it sets the stage for collecting the business impact data.

1. What has changed about you or your work as a result of your participation in this project? (Specific behavior change, action items, new projects, etc.)

    _____

    _____

    _____

2. Please identify any specific accomplishments/improvements that you can link to the project (job performance, project completion, response times, etc.).

    _____

    _____

    _____

3. What specific annualized value in U.S. dollars can be attributed to the above accomplishments/improvements? Use first-year values only. While this is a difficult question, try to think of specific ways in which the above improvements can be converted to monetary units. Along with the monetary value, please indicate the basis of your calculation.
    $_____ Basis:

    _____

    _____

    _____

4. Other factors often influence improvements in performance. Please indicate the percentage of the above improvement that is related directly to this project. _____% Please explain.

    _____

    _____

    _____

5. Do you think this project represented a good investment for the company?
    Yes ☐ No ☐ Please explain.

    _____

    _____

6. What level of confidence do you place on the above estimations?
    (0% = No Confidence, 100% = Certainty) _____%

    _____

    _____

    _____

Figure 8-4. Key impact questions.

Question 2 focuses directly on business impact data but is expressed in general terms to allow flexibility for project team member responses. If the responses need to follow a narrowly focused set of possibilities, the question can be more narrowly worded.

Question 3 focuses on the actual monetary values. While this may only be necessary if an ROI analysis is planned, it is sometimes helpful to see the impact of the particular change in business measures expressed in monetary terms. Project team members are asked not only to supply the values, but also to provide an annual improvement as well. Most importantly, they are asked to provide an explanation of how they arrived at these values. This brings additional credibility to the responses and is important in making the decision to use the data.

Question 4 focuses on isolating the effects of the project solution on business impact measures. In almost every setting, other factors will influence the output measures, so it is important to try to determine how much of the improvement is actually related to the specific project management solution. This question attempts to do that by asking project team members to provide a percentage of the improvement related to the project solution.

Question 5 simply asks project team members their opinion as to whether or not the project solution was a good investment for the company. While this information cannot be used in the analysis, it provides supporting evidence of success—or the lack thereof.

Finally, in Question 6, the level of confidence is captured using the scale of 0–100 percent. This confidence is spread over all of the questions and can be used to provide additional supporting evidence around the data gathered in the previous question. Also, the confidence value can be used to adjust the data. This will be explored later.

These simple questions can make the data collection instrument very powerful and identify significant improvements in the business impact area.

There are different approaches and different ways to explore the issues surrounding data collection. The most important issue is that the proper climate be established for project team members to provide the data.

ROI Analysis

While there are several approaches to data analysis, the recommended steps to calculate the ROI are briefly described here. The calculations are based on the responses from the series of impact questions.

The following five adjustments are made to the data to ensure that they are credible and accurate:

1. The project team members who do not complete the questionnaire or provide usable data on the impact questions are assumed to have no improvement.
2. Extreme and unrealistic data items are omitted.
3. Only annualized values are used, as requested in the responses.
4. The values are adjusted to reflect the confidence level of project team members.
5. The values are adjusted for the amount of the improvement related directly to the project solution.

These five adjustments create a very credible value that is usually considered to be an understatement of the benefits.

SELECTING THE APPROPRIATE METHOD FOR EACH LEVEL

By now you have realized that there are several methods for collecting data. Eight specific issues, which are discussed next, should be considered when deciding which method is appropriate for a situation. These should be considered when selecting data collection methods for all areas of the project management scorecard.

Type of Data

Perhaps one of the most important issues to consider when selecting the method is the type of data to be collected. Some methods are more appropriate for Level 4, while others are best for Level 3. Table 8-3 shows the most appropriate types of data for specific methods of Level 3 and 4 data collection. Follow-up surveys, observations, interviews, and focus groups are best suited for Level 3 data, sometimes exclusively. Performance monitoring, action planning, and questionnaires can easily capture Level 4 data.

Project Team Members' Time for Data Input

Another important factor in selecting the data collection method is the amount of time project team members must spend with data collection and evaluation systems. Time requirements should always be min-

Table 8-3. Choosing Your Method to Collect Level 3 and 4 Data

Data-Collection Method	Level 3	Level 4
Follow-up surveys	✓	
Follow-up questionnaires	✓	✓
Observation on the job	✓	
Interviews with participants	✓	
Follow-up focus groups	✓	
Action planning	✓	✓
Performance contracting	✓	✓
Business performance monitoring		✓

imized, and the method should be positioned so that it is a value-added activity (i.e., the project team members understand that this activity is something valuable so they will not resist). This requirement often means that sampling is used to keep the total project team member time to a minimum. Some methods, such as performance monitoring, require no project team member time, while others, such as interviews and focus groups, require a significant investment in time.

Supervisory Time for Data Input

The time that a project team member's direct supervisor must allocate to data collection is another important issue in the method selection. This time requirement should always be minimized. Some methods, such as performance contracting, may require much involvement from the supervisor before and after the project. Other methods, such as questionnaires administered directly to project team members, may not require any supervisor time.

Cost of Method

Cost is always a consideration when selecting the method. Some data collection methods are more expensive than others. For example, interviews and observations are very expensive. Surveys, questionnaires, and performance monitoring are usually inexpensive.

Disruption of Normal Work Activities

Another key issue in selecting the appropriate method—and perhaps the one that generates the most concern with managers—is the amount of disruption the data collection will create. Routine work processes should be disrupted as little as possible. Some data collection techniques, such as performance monitoring, require very little time and distraction from normal activities.

Questionnaires generally do not disrupt the work environment and can often be completed in only a few minutes, or even after normal work hours. On the other extreme, some items such as observations and interviews may be too disruptive to the work unit.

Accuracy of Method

The accuracy of the technique is another factor to consider when selecting the method. Some data collection methods are more accurate than others. For example, performance monitoring is usually very accurate, whereas questionnaires can be distorted and unreliable. If actual on-the-job behavior must be captured, observation is clearly one of the most accurate methods.

Utility of an Additional Method

Because there are many different methods to collect data, it is tempting to use too many data collection methods. Multiple data collection methods add to the time and costs of the evaluation and may result in very little additional value. *Utility* refers to the added value of the use of an additional data collection method. As more than one method is used, this question should always be addressed. Does the value obtained from the additional data warrant the extra time and expense of the method? If the answer is "no," the additional method should not be implemented.

Cultural Bias for Data Collection Method

The culture or philosophy of the organization can dictate which data collection methods are used. For example, some organizations are accustomed to using questionnaires and find the process fits in well with their culture. Some organizations will not use observation because their culture does not support the potential invasion of privacy often associated with it.

How the Credibility of Data Is Influenced

When impact data are collected and presented to selected target audiences, credibility will be an issue. The degree to which the target audience will believe the data is influenced by the following eight factors.

Reputation of the Data Source

The actual source of the data represents the first credibility issue. How credible is the individual or groups providing the data? Do they understand the issues? Are they knowledgeable of all the processes? The target audience will often place more credibility on data obtained from those who are closest to the source of the actual improvement or change.

Reputation of the Source of the Study

The target audience scrutinizes the reputation of the individual, group, or organization presenting the data. Do they have a history of providing accurate reports? Are they unbiased in their analyses? Are they fair in their presentations? Answers to these and other questions will form an impression about the reputations behind the report.

Motives of the Evaluators

The motives of the individuals providing the data must also be considered. Do the individuals presenting the data have an ax to grind? Do they have a personal interest in creating a favorable or unfavorable result? These issues will cause the target audience to closely examine the motives of those who conducted the study.

The perspective of the target audience can make a difference as well. If they are biased for or against a particular project, they may react favorably or unfavorably based on their predisposition, attitude, or previous knowledge of the issue. Consequently, the expected bias of the target audience is identified as the data are prepared, and the counter argument is fully explained, so as to dilute the audience's predetermined position.

Methodology of the Impact Study

The target audience will want to know specifically how the research was conducted. How were the calculations made? What steps were followed? What processes were used? A lack of information on the methodology will cause the audience to become wary and suspicious of the results.

Assumptions Made in the Analysis

In many impact studies, calculations and conclusions are based on certain assumptions made. What are the assumptions? Are they standard? How do they compare with other assumptions in other studies? When assumptions are omitted, the audience will substitute its own, often unfavorable, assumptions.

Realism of Outcome Data

Impressive values and high ROI numbers could cause problems. When outcomes appear to be unrealistic, it may be difficult for the target audience to believe them. Huge claims often fall on deaf ears, causing reports to be thrown away before they are reviewed.

Type of Data

The target audience usually has a preference for hard data, as it is seeking business performance data tied to output, quality, costs, and time. These measures are usually easily understood and closely related to organizational performance. Conversely, soft data are sometimes viewed suspiciously from the outset, as many senior executives are concerned about their soft nature and the limitations this may impose on the analysis.

Scope of Analysis

Is the scope of the analysis very narrow? Does it involve just one group, or all of the employees in the organization? Limiting the study to a small group of employees or a series of groups makes the process more accurate.

Collectively, these factors will influence the credibility of the project management scorecard and provide a framework within which the final report may be developed. Thus, when considering each of the issues, the following key points are suggested for an impact study:

- ☐ Use the most credible and reliable source for estimates.
- ☐ Present the material in an unbiased, objective way.

☐ Fully explain the methodology used throughout the process, preferably on a step-by-step basis.

☐ Define the assumptions made in the analysis and compare them to assumptions made in similar studies.

☐ Consider factoring or adjusting output values when they appear to be unrealistic.

☐ Use hard data whenever possible and combine with soft data if available.

☐ Keep the scope of the analysis very narrow. Conduct the impact study with one or more groups of project team members in the program, instead of all project team members or all employees.

Losing credibility at the outset can be devastating to future evaluation attempts. Addressing each of the previously mentioned issues will enhance the credibility of the process as perceived not only by others, but also by those on the project team.

Shortcut Ways to Capture Business Impact Data

While this chapter has explored several different ways to capture business impact data, there are some ways the process can be simplified when the projects are small in scope or inexpensive to develop and deliver.

Revisit Initial Needs

In the ideal situation, the business needs are the drivers for the project and project management solution. If possible, the initial needs will be revisited to see which specific measures have to change as a result of the project. These are the measures that should be examined for changes. This can be an extremely simple process if the project management solution is developed appropriately. If not, other approaches may be necessary.

Monitor Business Performance Measures

For most projects, even those small in scope, it is possible to monitor the business measures that are linked or perceived to be linked to the projects. These are usually well known, discussed in conjunction with the project, and readily available in operating units and business units throughout the organization. Only those measures perceived to be directly linked to the project should be examined, and some caution should be taken not to overextend the project by examining measures that may be only casually linked to the project.

Build It into the Process

As described in one of the examples in this chapter, it is a relatively easy task to build data collection and part of the analysis into the project. With this approach, the project team members provide the data, isolate the effects of the solution on those data, and convert the data to monetary values. The remaining steps for a project management scorecard process are simply the additional steps for capturing the costs, detailing the intangibles, actually developing the ROI calculations, and, of course, presenting the entire report. By building data collection and some analysis into the process and gaining the necessary commitments from project team members, it is possible for a project team to generate the required business data that are directly connected to the project with very little cost and effort.

If Questionnaires Are Used, Consider Business Impact Data

If a detailed follow-up questionnaire is used to capture data for application and implementation, a few additional questions can be added to capture business impact. The key impact questions contained in Figure 8-4 are very simple questions that can usually be addressed by many professional employees. They can be included in the questionnaire with little additional effort, and the analysis is not very time-consuming. The results can be very interesting and far-reaching data that not only show value, but also identify several issues pertinent to the project solution. Collectively, these are shortcut ways to ensure that business impact data are collected with minimum effort. It is important and almost essential that business data be collected if they are to be are linked to the project. After all, this is the type of data that most clients desire and are expecting from the project.

FINAL THOUGHTS

After describing the types of data that reflect business impact, this chapter provides an overview of several data collection approaches that can be used to capture business data. A variety of options are available.

Some methods are gaining more acceptance for use in developing ROI calculations. In addition to performance monitoring, follow-up questionnaires and action plans are used regularly to collect data for the project management scorecard. The credibility of data will always be an issue when this level of data is collected and analyzed. Several strategies are offered to enhance the credibility of data analysis.

FURTHER READING

Brown, Mark Graham. *Keeping Score: Using the Right Metrics to Drive World-Class Performance.* New York: Quality Resources, 1996.

Campanella, Jack. *Principles of Quality Costs: Principles, Implementation, and Use,* 3rd ed. Milwaukee: ASQ Quality Press, 1999.

Lynch, Richard L. and Kelvin F. Cross. *Measure Up! Yardsticks for Continuous Improvement.* Cambridge, MA: Blackwell Business, 1991.

Naumann, Earl and Kathleen Giel. *Customer Satisfaction Measurement and Management: Using the Voice of the Customer.* Cincinnati, OH: Thomson Executive Press, 1995.

Price Waterhouse Financial & Cost Management Team. *CFO: Architect of the Corporation's Future.* New York: John Wiley & Sons, 1997.

CHAPTER 9

How to Calculate and Interpret ROI

This chapter explores the various techniques, processes, and issues involved in calculating the return on investment. As discussed in earlier parts of the book, the return on investment (ROI) is becoming a critical measure demanded by many stakeholders, including clients and senior executives. It is the ultimate level of evaluation for showing the actual payoff of the project management solution. The ROI is expressed as a percentage and based on the same formula as ROI evaluation for other types of investments. Because of its perceived value and familiarity with senior management, it is now becoming a common requirement for most project management solutions, and in some cases, the most important measure on the project management scorecard. When ROI is required or needed, it must be planned for and developed.

BASIC ISSUES

Before presenting the formulas for calculating the ROI, a few basic issues are described and explored. An adequate understanding of these issues is necessary to complete this major step in the project management scorecard.

"ROI" Defined

The term "return on investment" is occasionally misused, sometimes intentionally. In these situations, a very broad definition for ROI is offered to include any benefit from the project. ROI is thus defined as a vague concept in which even subjective data linked to a project are included in the concept. In this book, the return on investment is more precise and is meant to represent an actual value by comparing project costs to benefits. The two most common measures are the benefit/cost ratio and the ROI formula. Both are presented along with other approaches to calculate the return or payback.

Recently, project managers have sought to calculate the actual return on investment for project management solutions. If the project solution is considered an investment, not an expense, then it is appropriate to place the project solution in the same funding process as other investments, such as the investment in equipment and facilities. Although the other investments are quite different, they are often viewed by management in the same way. Thus, it is critical to the success of the project and the project management solution to develop specific values that reflect the return on investment.

Annualized Values—A Fundamental Concept

All of the formulas presented in this chapter use annualized values so that the first-year impact of the project management solution investment can be calculated. Using annualized values are becoming a generally accepted practice for developing the ROI for many organizations. This approach is a conservative way to develop the ROI, since many short-term projects have added value in the second or third year. For long-term project solutions, first-year values are inappropriate and longer time frames need to be used.

When selecting the approach to measure ROI, it is important to communicate to the target audience the formula used and the assumptions made in arriving at the decision to use it. This helps avoid misunderstandings and confusion surrounding how the ROI value was actually developed. Although several approaches are described in this chapter, two stand out as the preferred methods: the benefit/cost ratio and the basic ROI formula. These two approaches are described next, along with brief coverage of the other approaches.

Benefit/Cost Ratio

One of the earliest methods used for evaluating project solutions is cost-benefit analysis, which produces a benefit/cost ratio (BCR). This method compares the benefits of the project management solution to the costs, using a ratio. In formula form, the ratio is:

$$BCR = \frac{Project\ Solution\ Benefits}{Project\ Solution\ Costs}$$

In simple terms, the BCR compares the annual economic benefits of the project solution to the cost of the project solution: a BCR of 1 means that the benefits equal the costs. A BCR of 2, usually written as 2:1, indicates that for each dollar spent on the project solution, two dollars are returned in benefits.

For example, a project solution was implemented at an electric and gas utility, yielding a first-year payoff for the project of $1,077,750. The total fully loaded solution implementation cost was $215,500. Thus, the ratio was:

$$BCR = \frac{\$1,077,750}{\$215,500} = 5:1$$

For every dollar invested in the project, five dollars in benefits were returned.

The principal advantage of using this approach is that it avoids traditional financial measures so there is no confusion when comparing the project investments with other investments in the company. Investments in plants, equipment, or subsidiaries, for example, are not usually evaluated by the benefit/cost formula. Some firm executives prefer not to use the same method to compare the return on project investments with the return on other investments. In these situations, the ROI for projects stands alone as a unique type of evaluation.

Unfortunately, there are no standards that constitute an acceptable benefit/cost ratio from the stakeholders' perspective. A standard should be established within the organization, perhaps even for a specific type of project. However, a 1:1 ratio (break-even status) is unacceptable for many projects. In others, a minimum 1.25:1 ratio is required, where the benefits are 1.25 times the cost of the project.

ROI FORMULA

Perhaps the most appropriate formula for evaluating project investments is net project solution benefits divided by solution cost. The ratio is usually expressed as a percentage when the fractional values are multiplied by 100. In formula form, the ROI becomes:

$$ROI\ (\%) = \frac{Net\ Project\ Solutions\ Benefits}{Project\ Solution\ Costs} \times 100$$

Net benefits are project solution benefits minus costs. The ROI value is related to the BCR by a factor of one. For example, a BCR of 2.45 is the same as an ROI value of 145 percent (1.45 × 100 percent). This formula is essentially the same as the ROI in other types of investments. For example, when a firm builds a new plant, the ROI is developed by dividing annual earnings by the investment. The annual earnings are comparable to net benefits (annual benefits minus the cost). The investment is comparable to fully loaded project costs, which represent the investment in the project.

An ROI on a project of 50 percent means that the costs are recovered and an additional 50 percent of the costs are reported as "earnings." A 150 percent ROI indicates that the costs have been recovered and an additional 1.5 times the costs is captured as "earnings." For example, a project solution at an electronics company yielded an annual value of $321,600. The total fully loaded costs for the project were $38,233. Thus, the return on investment becomes:

$$ROI\ (\%) = \frac{\$321,600 - \$38,233}{\$38,233} \times 100 = 741\%$$

For each dollar invested, the company received $7.40 in return after the costs of the project had been recovered.

Using the ROI formula essentially places project management investments on a level playing field with other investments using the same formula and similar concepts. The ROI calculation is easily understood by key management and financial executives who regularly use ROI calculations with other investments.

While there are no generally accepted standards, some organizations establish a minimum requirement or hurdle rate for the ROI. This rate is based on the expected ROI for other investments, which is determined by the cost of capital and other factors. An ROI minimum of 25 percent is set by many organizations. In North America, Western Europe, and the Asia Pacific regions, this target value is usually greater than the percentage required for other types of investments. The rationale? The project management scorecard is still relatively new and sometimes involves subjective input, including estimations. Because of that, a higher standard is required or suggested, with 25 percent being the desired figure for most organizations.

OTHER ROI MEASURES

In addition to the traditional ROI formula previously described, several other measures are occasionally used under the general heading of return on investment. These measures are designed primarily for evaluating other types of financial measures but sometimes work their way into project evaluations.

Payback Period

The payback period is another common method for evaluating capital expenditures. With this approach, the annual cash proceeds (savings) produced by an investment are equated to the original cash outlay required by the investment to arrive at some multiple of cash proceeds equal to the original investment. Measurement is usually in terms of years and months. For example, if the cost savings generated from a project are constant each year, the payback period is determined by dividing the total original cash investment (e.g., development costs, expenses, etc.) by the amount of the expected annual or actual savings. The savings represent the net savings after the project expenses are subtracted.

To illustrate this calculation, assume that an initial project cost is $100,000 with a three-year useful life. The annual net savings from the project is expected to be $40,000. Thus, the payback period becomes:

$$\text{Payback period} = \frac{\text{Total Investment}}{\text{Annual Savings}} = \frac{\$100,000}{\$40,000} = 2.5 \text{ years}$$

The project will "pay back" the original investment in 2.5 years.

The payback period is simple to use but has the limitation of ignoring the time value of money. It has not enjoyed widespread use in evaluating project investments.

Discounted Cash Flow

Discounted cash flow is a method of evaluating investment opportunities in which certain values are assigned to the timing of the proceeds from the investment. The assumption, based on interest rates, is that a dollar earned today is more valuable than a dollar earned a year from now.

There are several ways of using the discounted cash flow concept to evaluate the project investment. The most common approach is the net present value of an investment. This approach compares the savings, year by year, with the outflow of cash required by the investment. The expected savings received each year is discounted by selected interest rates. The outflow of cash is also discounted by the same interest rate. If the present value of the savings exceeds the present value of the outlays after discounting at a common interest rate, the investment is usually considered acceptable by management. The discounted cash flow method has the advantage of ranking investments, but it becomes difficult to calculate.

Internal Rate of Return

The internal rate of return (IRR) method determines the interest rate required to make the present value of the cash flow equal to zero. It represents the maximum rate of interest that could be paid if all project funds were borrowed and the organization had to break even on the projects. The IRR considers the time value of money and is unaffected by the scale of the project. It can be used to rank alternatives and can be used to accept/reject decisions when a minimum rate of return is specified. A major weakness of the IRR method is that it assumes all returns are reinvested at the same internal rate of return. This can make an investment alternative with a high rate of return look even better than it really is and a project with a low rate of return look even worse. In practice, the IRR is rarely used to evaluate project management solutions.

Consequences of Not Engaging in Project Management Solutions

For some organizations, the consequences of not engaging in a project can be very serious. A company's inability to perform adequately in a particular area might mean that it is unable to take on additional business or that it may lose existing business because of a persistent problem or missed opportunity. Also, a project can help avoid serious operational problems (such as production efficiencies) or non-compliance issues (such as EEOC violations). This method of calculating the return on project management solutions has received recent attention and involves the following six steps:

1. Establish that there is a potential problem, loss, or opportunity.
2. Isolate the problems created by this situation, such as non-compliance issues, loss of business, or the inability to take on additional business.
3. Develop an estimate of the potential value of the problem, loss, or opportunity.
4. If other factors are involved, determine the impact of each factor on the loss of income or costs.
5. Estimate the total cost of the project management solution using the techniques outlined in Chapter 11.
6. Compare benefits with costs.

This approach has some disadvantages. Because estimates are used, the potential loss of income can be highly subjective and difficult to measure. Also, it may be difficult to isolate the factors involved and to determine their weight relative to lost income. Because of these concerns, this approach to evaluating the return on investing in project management solutions is limited to certain types of projects and situations.

Scorecard Issues

The project management scorecard can become quite complex, raising several issues that will need additional coverage. The most important issues are covered next.

Benefits of ROI in the Project Management Scorecard

Although the benefits of adopting ROI into the project management scorecard may appear to be obvious, the following distinct and important benefits can be derived from the implementation of ROI for project management solutions. They represent a brief summary of the advantages of including ROI in the project management scorecard.

Measures the Contribution

The project staff will know the contribution of a specific project. The ROI will show how the benefits, expressed in monetary values, overshadow the costs. It will determine if the project made a contribution to the organization and if it was indeed a good investment.

Develops Priorities for Project Solution

Calculating the ROI for different types of project solutions will determine which projects contribute the most to the organization, allowing priorities to be established for high-impact project solutions.

Improves the Project Management Process

As with any evaluation technique, a scorecard for project managers provides a variety of data to make adjustments and changes to the project process. Because different types of data are collected at different levels, from different sources, the opportunity for improvement is significant. This allows for a complete analysis of project effectiveness.

Focuses on Results

The project management scorecard is a results-based process that focuses on results for all projects, even for those not targeted for an ROI calculation. The process requires project managers and support groups to concentrate on measurable objectives (i.e., what the project is attempting to accomplish). Thus, this process has the added benefit of improving the effectiveness of all projects.

Builds Management Support for the Project Management Process

The project management scorecard, when applied consistently and comprehensively, can convince the management group that the project is an investment and not an expense. Managers will see the project as making a viable contribution to their objectives, thus increasing the respect and support for the process. ROI development is an important step in building a partnership with management and increasing the commitment to the project.

Alters Perceptions of the Project Management Solution

Routine ROI impact data, when communicated to a variety of target audiences, will alter perceptions of the project management solution. The project team members, their leaders, and other stakeholders will view the project management solution as a legitimate function in the organization, adding value to work units, departments, and divisions.

They will have a better understanding of the connection between the project and results.

These key benefits, inherent with almost any type of impact evaluation process, make the project management scorecard an attractive and necessary challenge for the project management field.

SIMPLIFIES A COMPLEX ISSUE

Developing the return on investment for a project management solution should not be a complex issue. The approach presented in this book is to take a complex process and simplify it by breaking it into small steps so it is understandable and acceptable to a variety of audiences.

Potential Shortcuts to Using the Project Management Solution

Because of the possible complexity and sensitivity of the project management solution, caution is needed when developing, calculating, and communicating the return on investment. The scorecard process is a very important issue and achieving a positive ROI is the goal of many projects. A few issues, described next, should be addressed to keep the process from going astray.

ENSURE NEEDS ASSESSMENT AND ANALYSIS HAVE BEEN CONDUCTED

The project management scorecard should be developed for project solutions where a needs assessment and analysis have been conducted. Because of the evaluation problems that can develop when there is not a clear needs assessment, it is recommended that the ROI be conducted only for projects in which a comprehensive needs assessment, preferably with Level 3 and 4 data, has been conducted. However, practical considerations and management requests may prohibit this suggested requirement.

ISOLATE THE EFFECTS OF THE PROJECT MANAGEMENT SOLUTION

The ROI analysis should always include one or more strategies for isolating the effects of the project solution. Because of the importance of accounting for the influence of other factors, this step in the process must not be ignored. Too often, an excellent study, from what appears to be a very successful project solution, is considered to be worthless because there was no attempt to account for other factors. Omission of this step seriously diminishes the credibility of the study.

Use Credible Sources after Estimating Values

When making estimates, use the most reliable and credible sources. Because estimates are critical to any type of analysis, they will usually be an important part of the scorecard process. When they are used, they should be developed properly and obtained from the most reliable and credible sources, the individuals who best understand the overall situation and who can provide the most accurate estimation.

Be Conservative

Take a conservative approach when developing both benefits and costs. Conservatism in ROI analysis builds accuracy and credibility. What matters most is how the target audience perceives the value of the data. A conservative approach is always recommended for both the numerator of the ROI formula (benefits) and the denominator (project costs).

Ensure That a Clear Understanding of the ROI Calculation Exists

There are many ways to calculate the return on funds invested or assets employed. The ROI is just one of them. Although the calculation for ROI for a project uses the same basic formula as in other investment evaluations, it may not be fully understood by the target group. Its calculation method and its meaning should be clearly communicated. More importantly, it should be an item accepted by management as an appropriate measure for a project evaluation.

Involve Management in Setting ROI Targets

Involve management in developing the ROI targets. Management ultimately makes the decision if an ROI value is acceptable. To the extent possible, management should be involved in setting the parameters for calculations and establishing targets by which projects are considered acceptable within the organization.

Be Cautious of Sensitive Issues

Occasionally, sensitive and controversial issues will be generated when discussing an ROI value. It is best to avoid debates over what is measurable and what is not measurable unless there is clear evidence of the issue in question. Also, some projects are so fundamental to the survival of the organization that any attempt to measure them is unnecessary. For example, a project designed to improve customer service in a customer-focused company may escape the scrutiny of an evaluation using the project management scorecard process, on the assumption that if the project is well designed, it will improve customer service.

TEACH THE PROCESS TO OTHERS

Teach others the methods for calculating the return on investment of project management solutions. Each time an ROI is calculated, the appropriate executive should use this opportunity to educate other managers and colleagues in the organization. Even if it is not in their area of responsibility, they will be able to see the value of this approach to the project and evaluation. Also, when possible, each project should serve as a case study to educate the project staff on specific techniques and methods.

DO NOT BOAST ABOUT A HIGH ROI

It is not unusual to generate what appears to be a very high return on investment for a project. Several examples in this book have illustrated the possibilities. A project manager who boasts about a high rate of return will be open to potential criticism from others unless there are indisputable facts on which the calculation is based.

BE SELECTIVE IN USING ROI

Do not try to use ROI on every project management solution. Some projects are difficult to quantify, and an ROI calculation may not be feasible. Other methods of presenting the benefits may be more appropriate. Project managers are encouraged to set targets for the percent of projects in which the ROI is developed. Also, specific criteria should be established that select projects for ROI analysis.

FINAL THOUGHTS

After the benefits are collected and converted to monetary values and the project costs are tabulated, the ROI calculation becomes a very easy step. It is just a matter of plugging the values into the appropriate formula. This chapter presented the two basic approaches for calculating the ROI: the ROI formula and the benefit/cost ratio. Each has its own advantages and disadvantages. Alternatives to ROI development were briefly discussed. Several examples were presented along with key issues that must be addressed in ROI calculations.

Further Reading

Dauphinais, G. William and Colin Price (Eds.). *Straight from the CEO: The World's Top Business Leaders Reveal Ideas that Every Manager Can Use.* London: Nicholas Brealey Publishing, 1998.

Epstein, Marc J. and Bill Birchard. *Counting What Counts: Turning Corporate Accountability to Competitive Advantage.* Reading, MA: Perseus Books, 1999.

Friedlob, George T. and Franklin J. Plewa, Jr. *Understanding Return on Investment.* New York: John Wiley & Sons, Inc., 1991.

Gates, Bill with Collins Hemingway. *Business @ the Speed of Thought: Using a Digital Nervous System.* New York: Warner Books, 1999.

Hiebeler, Robert, Thomas B. Kelly, and Charles Ketteman. *Best Practices: Building Your Business with Customer-Focused Solutions.* New York: Arthur Andersen/Simon & Schuster, 1998.

Mitchell, Donald, Carol Coles, and Robert Metz. *The 2,000 Percent Solution: Free Your Organization From "Stalled" Thinking to Achieve Exponential Success.* New York: Amacom/American Management Association, 1999.

Phillips, Jack J. *The Consultant's Scorecard.* New York: McGraw-Hill, 2000.

Phillips, Jack J. *Return on Investment in Training and Performance Improvement Programs.* Boston: Butterworth-Heinemann, previously published by Gulf Publishing, 1997.

Phillips, Jack J., Ron D. Stone, and Patricia Pulliam Phillips. *The Human Resources Scorecard.* Boston: Butterworth-Heinemann, 2001.

Price Waterhouse Financial & Cost Management Team. *CFO: Architect of the Corporation's Future.* New York: John Wiley & Sons, 1997.

Weddle, Peter D. *ROI: A Tale of American Business.* McLean, VA: ProAction Press, 1989.

CHAPTER 10

Identifying Intangible Measures of a Project Management Solution

The results generated by a project management solution include both tangible and intangible measures. By definition, intangible measures are the benefits or detriments linked to a project management solution that cannot or should not be converted to monetary values. These measures are often monitored after the project has been completed. Intangible measures often appear in the business unit where project management has been improved. As shown in Figure 10-1, improved project management should drive several business unit measures, including intangibles. Although not converted to monetary values, these measures are still an important part of the evaluation process. The range of intangible measures is varied, however, this chapter describes some common variables linked with project management solutions.

Table 10-1 lists common examples of these measures. This listing is not meant to imply that these measures cannot be converted to monetary values. In one study or another, each item has been monetarily quantified. However, in typical project management evaluation studies, these variables are considered intangible benefits.

WHY IDENTIFY INTANGIBLES?

Again, not all measures can or should be converted to monetary values. By design, some are captured and reported as intangibles. Although they may not be perceived as being as valuable as the quantifiable measures, intangibles are critical to the overall evaluation process. In some project management solutions, team development, job satisfaction, communications, and customer satisfaction are more important than monetary measures. Consequently, these measures should be monitored

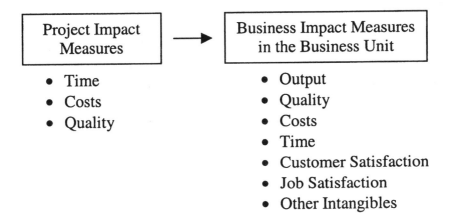

Figure 10-1. Business unit improvement linked to a solution.

Table 10-1. Common Intangible Variables Linked with Project Management Solutions

☐ Knowledge base	☐ Customer satisfaction/dissatisfaction
☐ Job satisfaction	☐ Community image
☐ Organizational commitment	☐ Investor image
☐ Work climate	☐ Customer complaints
☐ Employee complaints	☐ Customer response time
☐ Employee grievances	☐ Customer loyalty
☐ Employee stress reduction	☐ Teamwork
☐ Employee absenteeism	☐ Cooperation
☐ Employee turnover/retention	☐ Conflict
☐ Innovation	☐ Decisiveness
☐ Request for transfers	☐ Communication

and reported as part of the overall evaluation. In practice, every solution, regardless of its nature, scope, and content, will produce intangible measures. The challenge is to identify them effectively and report them appropriately.

Where Do They Come From?

Intangible measures can be taken from different sources and at different times in the process, as depicted in Figure 10-2. They can be uncovered early in the process, during the initial analysis, and planned for collection as part of the overall data collection strategy. For example, one project management solution has several hard data measures linked to the solution. An intangible measure, customer satisfaction, is identified and monitored with no plans to convert it to a monetary value. Thus, from the beginning, this measure is destined to be a nonmonetary benefit reported along with the ROI results.

A second opportunity to identify intangible benefits is to discuss the issue with clients or sponsors of the project management solution. Clients can usually identify the intangible measures they expect to be influenced by the solution. For example, a project management solution in a large multi-national company was conducted, and an ROI analysis was planned. Project team members, project managers, and senior executives identified potential intangible measures that were perceived to be influenced by the project management solution.

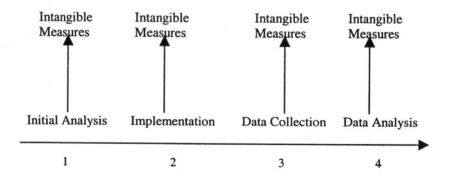

Figure 10-2. Project phases that influence intangible measures.

The third opportunity to identify intangible measures presents itself during data collection. Although the measure is not anticipated in the initial project evaluation design, it may surface on a questionnaire, in an interview, or during a focus group. Questions are often asked about other improvements linked to the solution, and project team members usually provide several intangible measures for which there are no plans to assign a value. For example, in the evaluation of a customer service project, project team members were asked to define specifically what had improved about their project work and relationships with customers as a result of the project. Team members provided more than a dozen intangible measures that project managers attributed to the solution.

The fourth opportunity to identify intangible measures is during data analysis and reporting, while attempting to convert data to monetary values. If the conversion loses credibility, the measure should be reported as an intangible benefit. For example, in a sales improvement project, customer satisfaction was identified early in the process as a measure of the success with the project management solution. A conversion to monetary values was attempted, but it lacked accuracy and credibility. Consequently, customer satisfaction was reported as an intangible benefit.

How Are Intangibles Analyzed?

For each intangible measure identified, there must be some evidence of its connection to the project management solution. However, in many cases no specific analysis is planned beyond tabulating responses. Early attempts to quantify intangible data sometimes result in aborting the entire process; thus, no further data analysis is conducted. In some cases, isolating the effects of the project management solution may be undertaken using one or more of the methods outlined in Chapter 12. This step is necessary when there is a need to know the specific amount of change in the intangible measure linked to the solution. Intangible data often reflect improvement. However, neither the precise amount of improvement nor the amount of improvement directly related to the solution is usually identified. Since the value of this data is not included in the ROI calculation, intangible measures are not normally used to justify additional expenditures for solutions or continuing an existing solution. A detailed analysis is not necessary. Intangible benefits are viewed as additional evidence of the solution's success and are presented as supportive qualitative data.

MEASURING EMPLOYEE SATISFACTION

Employee satisfaction is an important intangible measure. Many project management solutions improve job satisfaction if they are perceived by the team members or business unit managers to be successful. A few of the most important employee satisfaction measures are briefly described here.

Job Satisfaction

Many organizations conduct surveys that gauge how satisfied employees are with their organization, job, supervisor, team members, and a host of other issues. Employee job satisfaction is closely correlated with absenteeism and turnover, both of which are sometimes linked with project management solutions. Some survey items focus on issues directly related to projects, such as satisfaction with job-design changes, re-engineered processes, or compensation adjustments. Attitude survey data are usually linked to project management solutions when specific issues in the survey address the solution.

Because attitude surveys are usually taken annually, the results may not be in sync with the timing of the project management solution. When job satisfaction is one of the objectives, some organizations conduct surveys after the project and design the survey instrument around project issues.

Organizational Commitment

Measuring organizational commitment is perhaps a more important measure for understanding employees' motivational state. Similar to attitude surveys, organizational commitment instruments gauge how much employees are aligned with company goals, values, philosophies, and practices. Organizational commitment measures often correlate with productivity and performance; therefore, organizational commitment is an important intangible measure. Changes in organizational commitment in survey data may indicate that a project management solution has been successful if the project is designed to change employee motivation. The difficulty with this intangible measure is that it is not routinely tracked in organizations.

Work Climate

Some organizations conduct climate surveys, which reflect work climate changes in communication, openness, trust, feedback, and other areas. Climate surveys are similar to attitude surveys but are more general and often focus on a range of workplace issues and environmental enablers and inhibitors. Conducting climate surveys before and after the implementation of a management solution helps determine how much the project changed these intangible measures.

Employee Complaints

Some organizations record and report specific complaints made by employees. Because a reduction in employee complaints may be directly related to the project management solution, such as a team-building project, the level of complaints is reported as an intangible and is used to measure the solution's success.

Employee Stress Reduction

Occasionally, interventions reduce work-related stress by focusing on job and technology improvements that allow employees to be more efficient. The reduction in tension and anxiety, and the subsequent reduction in stress, may be directly linked to the intervention.

MEASURING EMPLOYEE WITHDRAWAL

When employee satisfaction deteriorates to the point that employees withdraw from work or the organization, either permanently or temporarily, the results can be disastrous. Several employee withdrawal measures, such as absenteeism, turnover, and requests for transfers, may be linked to project management solutions.

Employee Turnover

Perhaps the most serious employee withdrawal measure is employee turnover. Turnover is an extremely costly variable and, when excessive, can have devastating consequences on organizations. Many projects are designed to reduce employee turnover in specific work units, and turnover is often converted to a monetary value using one of the methods described in Chapter 13. However, because of the multitude of costs and assumptions involved in calculating the value, some organizations prefer not to do so. In these cases, a reduction in turnover is reported as an intangible benefit, reflecting the success of the project.

Employee Absenteeism

Unplanned or unscheduled absenteeism is another costly variable. Excessive absenteeism disrupts customer service and customer contact functions and jeopardizes customer loyalty. Some projects are aimed at reducing absenteeism, and the impact of the project management solution on absenteeism may be pinpointed. Although the cost of absenteeism can be calculated, the conversion process is not credible enough for some audiences. In those situations, absenteeism changes are reported as intangible effects.

Requests for Transfer

Another costly measure of employee withdrawal is requests for transfer. These requests are generally a clear indication of dissatisfaction with the current situation. Requesting transfer from one department to another can cause stress for both the employee making the request and the supervisor or manager, as well as discomfort and loss of productivity within the team. Unlike cases of turnover or absenteeism, the employee still arrives at work every day in anticipation of transfer. The cost of such a measure may be more difficult to calculate than either turnover or absenteeism; therefore, it is usually reported as an intangible measure.

MEASURING CUSTOMER SERVICE

Because of the importance of building and improving customer service, a number of related measures are typically monitored and reported to track the payoff of project management solutions. Several types of customer service projects have a direct influence on these measures, but since it is so difficult to place values on the changes, the outcomes are sometimes reported as intangible benefits. Some of those measures are described below.

Customer Satisfaction/Dissatisfaction/Impression

One of the most important measures is a survey of satisfied or dissatisfied customers. These survey values, reported as absolute data or as an index, represent important data that can be used to determine the success of a customer service project. Techniques to convert survey data to monetary values are available, but in most cases a conversion is not attempted, and improvements are reported as intangible benefits.

Customer Complaints

Most organizations monitor customer complaints. Each complaint is recorded, along with the disposition, the time required to resolve the complaint, and specific costs associated with complaint resolution. Projects are often designed to reduce or prevent an increase in the number of customer complaints. Because it is difficult to assign accurate monetary values to complaints, the measure is usually reported as an important intangible.

Customer Response Time

Providing prompt customer service is a critical issue for most organizations. Therefore, organizations monitor the time it takes to respond to specific customer service requests, orders, or problems. Although reducing response time may be an objective of a project, the measure is not usually converted to a monetary value. Thus, customer response time is reported as an important intangible measure.

Other Customer Responses

Many other types of customer responses can be tracked, such as creativity with customer responses, sensitivity to cost and pricing issues, and customer loyalty. Monitoring these variables can provide more evidence of project results when the solution influences specific variables. Because of the difficulty in assigning values to the items, they are usually reported as intangible measures.

MEASURING TEAM EFFECTIVENESS

To evaluate the success of teams within an organization, several key measures are monitored. Although the output and quality of the teams' work are often measured as hard data and converted to monetary values, other interpersonal measures may be tracked and reported separately. A few of these measures are represented here.

Teamwork

Cross-functional, high-performance, and virtual teams are important assets for organizations striving to improve performance. Sometimes, team members are surveyed before and after a project to see if the level of teamwork has increased. The monetary value of increased teamwork is rarely developed as a measure; rather, it is usually reported as an intangible benefit.

Cooperation/Conflict

The success of a team often depends on the cooperative spirit of team members. Some instruments measure the level of cooperation before and after a project, but since it is so difficult to convert the findings to a monetary value, the measure is always reported as an intangible.

In some team environments, the level of conflict is measured. A decrease in conflict may reflect the success of a project management solution. In most situations, a monetary value is not placed on such a reduction, and it is reported as an intangible benefit.

Decisiveness/Decision Making

Teams make decisions, and the expedience and quality of the decision-making process often become important issues. Decisiveness is usually measured by how quickly decisions are made. Survey measures may reflect the perception of the team or, in some cases, monitor precisely how quickly decisions are made. The quality of the decisions reflects value as well. Some projects are expected to influence this process, with improvements usually reported as intangible benefits.

Team Communication

Communication is critical for every team. Several instruments are available to qualify and quantify communication among a team. Positive changes in communication skills or perceptions of skills driven by a project are not usually converted to monetary values but, rather, are reported as intangible benefits.

FINAL THOUGHTS

Intangible measures are crucial to reflecting the success of a project management solution. The intangible benefits are the sixth measure used to develop the project management scorecard described in this book. While they may not carry the weight of the actual ROI calculation or the hard business impact data, they are nevertheless an important part of the overall project solution evaluation. Intangible measures should be identified, explored, examined, and monitored for changes linked to the project management solution. Collectively, they add a unique dimension to the project management scorecard because most, if not all, projects result in intangible benefits. Although some of the most common intangible measures are explored in this chapter, the coverage is not meant to be complete. The range of intangible measures is practically limitless.

FURTHER READING

Bacon, Frank R., Jr. and Thomas W. Butler, Jr. *Achieving Planned Innovation: A Proven System for Creating Successful New Products and Services.* New York: The Free Press, 1998.

Campanella, Jack, ed. *Principles of Quality Costs: Principles, Implementation and Use.* Milwaukee: ASQ Quality Press, 1999.

Denton, Keith D. *Quality Service: How America's Top Companies Are Competing in the Customer-Service Revolution . . . and How You Can Too.* Houston: Gulf Publishing, 1989.

Heskett, James L., W. Earl Sasser, Jr., and Leonard A. Schlesinger. *The Service Profit Chain: How Leading Companies Link Profit and Growth to Loyalty, Satisfaction, and Value.* New York: The Free Press, 1997.

Howe, Roger J., Dee Gaeddert, and Maynard A. Howe. *Quality on Trial: Bringing Bottom-Line Accountability to the Quality Effort,* 2nd ed. New York: McGraw-Hill, 1995.

Keen, Peter G.W. *The Process Edge: Creating Value Where It Counts.* Boston: Harvard Business School Press, 1997.

Naumann, Earl and Kathleen Giel. *Customer Satisfaction Measurement and Management: Using the Voice of the Customer.* Cincinnati: Thomson Executive Press, 1995.

Silverman, Lori L. and Annabeth L. Propst. *Critical Shift: The Future of Quality in Organizational Performance.* Milwaukee: ASQ Quality Press, 1999.

Slaikeu, Karl A. and Ralph H. Hasson. *Controlling the Costs of Conflict: How to Design a System for Your Organization.* San Francisco: Jossey-Bass, 1998.

CHAPTER 11

Monitoring the True Costs of the Project Solution

This chapter explores cost accumulation and tabulation steps, outlining the specific project solution costs that must be captured in order to calculate return on investment. One of the important challenges addressed in this chapter is deciding which costs should be included in the project solution cost calculation. For some projects, certain costs are hidden and never included in the cost calculation. Yet, the conservative philosophy presented here is to account for all costs, direct and indirect. Several checklists and guidelines are also included in the chapter to aid in this effort.

WHY MONITOR PROJECT SOLUTION COSTS?

Monitoring the project costs is an essential step in developing the ROI calculation since it represents the denominator in the ROI formula. It is just as important to pay attention to costs as it is to project results and benefits. In practice, however, costs are often more easily captured than project benefits.

Costs should be monitored in an ongoing effort to control expenditures and keep the project within budget. Monitoring cost activities not only reveals the status of expenditures, but also gives visibility to expenditures and influences the entire project team to spend wisely. And of course, monitoring costs in an ongoing fashion is much easier, more accurate, and more efficient than trying to reconstruct events to capture costs retrospectively.

HOW TO DEVELOP COSTS

The first step in monitoring costs is to define and discuss several issues about a cost-control system. The key issues are presented here.

Costs Are Critical

Capturing costs is challenging because the figures must be accurate, reliable, and realistic. Although most organizations develop costs with much more ease than the monetary value of the benefits, the true cost of the project can be an elusive figure even with some of the easiest projects. While the direct charges are usually easily developed, it is more difficult to determine the indirect costs of a project. Fortunately, for most projects, the major costs are known up front and are often documented in the project proposal. However, the hidden and indirect costs that are linked to the project are not usually detailed. To develop a realistic ROI, costs must be accurate, complete, and credible. Otherwise, the painstaking difficulty and attention to the monetary benefits of the project will be wasted because of inadequate or inaccurate costs.

Fully Loaded Costs

When using a conservative approach to calculating ROI, it is recommended that project solution costs be fully loaded. With this approach, all costs that can be identified and linked to a particular project solution are included. The philosophy is simple: For the denominator, when in doubt, include it (i.e., if it is questionable whether a cost be included, it is recommended that it be included, even if the cost guidelines for the organization do not require it). When an ROI is calculated and reported to target audiences, the process should withstand even the closest scrutiny in terms of its accuracy and credibility. The only way to meet this test is to ensure that all costs are included. Of course, from a realistic viewpoint, if the controller or chief financial officer insists on not using certain costs, then it is best to leave them out.

The Danger of Reporting Costs Without the Benefits

It is dangerous to communicate the costs of a project management solution without presenting the benefits of the project. Unfortunately, many organizations have fallen into this trap for years. For example, project management training costs can easily be collected and presented to management. While these costs may be helpful, it may be troublesome to present them without showing benefits. When most executives review project management training costs, a logical question comes to mind: What benefit was received from the training? This is a typical management reaction, particularly when costs are perceived to be very high. Because of this, some organizations have developed a policy of not communicating project cost data unless the benefits can be captured and presented along with the costs. Even if the benefits are subjective and intangible, they are included with the cost data. This helps to maintain a balance between the two issues.

Developing and Using Cost Guidelines

For most project teams, it may be helpful to detail a policy on costs in guidelines for the project managers or others who monitor and report costs. Cost guidelines detail specifically which cost categories are included with projects and how the data are captured, analyzed, and reported. Standards, unit cost guiding principles, and generally accepted values are included in the guidelines. Cost guidelines can range from a one-page brief to a hundred-page document for some large, complex organizations. The simpler the approach is, the better.

When fully developed, cost guidelines should be reviewed and approved by the finance and accounting staff. The final document serves as the guiding force in collecting, monitoring, and reporting costs. When the ROI is calculated and reported, costs are included in a summary form or table, and the cost guidelines are referenced in a footnote or attached as an appendix.

COST-TRACKING ISSUES

The most important task is to define which specific costs are included in project management solutions. This task involves decisions that will be made by the project team and usually approved by the client. If appropriate, the client's finance and accounting staff may need to approve the list.

Sources of Costs

It is sometimes helpful to first consider the sources of costs for project solutions. There are three major categories of sources as illustrated in Table 11-1. The charges and expenses from the project management firm will represent the greatest segment of costs and are transferred directly to the client for payment. These are often placed in categories under fees and expenses. The second major cost category is those expenses born by the client organization—both direct and indirect. In many projects, these costs are not identified but nevertheless reflect the cost of the project. The third cost is the cost of payments made to other organizations as a result of the project. These include payments made directly to suppliers for equipment and services prescribed by the project. The finance and accounting records should be able to track and reflect the costs from these three different sources, and the process presented in this chapter has the capability of tracking these costs as well.

Prorated Versus Direct Costs

Usually, all costs related to a project solution are captured and expensed to that project. However, some costs are prorated over a longer period of time. Equipment purchases, software development and acquisition, and the development of training programs are all significant costs with a useful life that may extend beyond the project. Consequently, a portion of these costs should be prorated to the project.

Using a conservative approach, the expected life of the project solution is fixed. Some organizations will consider one year of operation for a simple project solution. Others may consider three to five years. If there is some question about the specific time period to be used in the

Table 11-1. Sources of Costs

Source of Costs		Cost Reporting Issues	
1.	Project management organization: fees and expenses	A	Costs are usually accurate.
		B	Variable expenses may be underestimated.
2.	Client expenses: direct and indirect	A	Direct expenses are usually not fully loaded.
		B	Indirect expenses are rarely included in costs.
3.	Other expenses: equipment and services	A	Sometimes understated
		B	May lack accountability

prorated formula, the finance and accounting staff should be consulted, or appropriate guidelines should be developed and followed.

A brief example will illustrate the prorated development costs. In a large telecommunications company, a project management training program cost $98,000. It was anticipated that the training would have a three-year life cycle before it would need a major revision. The revision costs at the end of the three years were estimated to be about half of the original development costs, or $49,000. A three-year payback period was used with an ROI calculation. Since the project management training will have half of its residual value at the end of three years, only half of the costs should be written off for this three-year period. Thus, the $49,000, representing half of the original development, is used for the development costs in the ROI calculation.

Employee Benefits Factor

Employee time is valuable, and when time is required on a project solution, the costs must be fully loaded (i.e., representing total compensation, including perks and benefits). This number is usually well known in the organization and is used in other costing formulas. It represents the cost of all employee benefits expressed as a percentage of payroll. For some organizations, this value is as high as 50–60 percent. In others, it may be as low as 25–30 percent. The average in the United States is 38 percent (*Nation's Business*, 1999).

MAJOR COST CATEGORIES

Table 11-2 shows the recommended cost categories for a fully loaded, conservative approach to estimating costs. Each category is described below.

Initial Analysis and Assessment

One of the most underestimated items is the cost of conducting the initial analysis and assessment to determine the appropriate project management solution. In a comprehensive project, this involves data collection, problem solving, assessment, and analysis. In some project solutions, this cost is near zero because the project is conducted without an appropriate assessment. However, as more project managers place increased attention on needs assessment and analysis, this item will become a significant cost in the future.

Table 11-2. Projected Cost Categories—Prorated or Expensed

	Cost Item	Prorated	Expensed
A	Initial analysis and assessment		✓
B	Development of solutions		✓
C	Acquisition of solutions		✓
D	Implementation and application		
	Salaries/benefits for project members' time		✓
	Salaries/benefits for coordination time		✓
	Salaries/benefits for project members' time		✓
	Project materials		✓
	Hardware/software	✓	
	Travel/lodging/meals		✓
	Use of facilities		✓
	Capital expenditures	✓	
E	Maintenance and monitoring		✓
F	Administrative support and overhead	✓	
G	Evaluation and reporting		✓

All costs associated with the analysis and assessment should be captured to the fullest extent possible. These costs include project time, direct expenses, and internal services and supplies used in the analysis. The total costs are usually allocated over the life of the project.

Development of Solutions

One of the more significant items is the cost of designing and developing the solutions for a project. These costs include project time in both design and development and the purchase of supplies, technology, and other materials directly related to the solutions. As with needs assessment costs, design and development costs are usually fully charged to the project. However, in some situations, the major expenditures may be prorated over several projects.

Acquisition Costs

In lieu of development costs, many organizations purchase solutions from other sources to use as is or in a modified format. The acquisition costs for these projects include the purchase price, support materials, and licensing agreements. Many projects have both acquisition costs and solution-development costs.

Application and Implementation Costs

Usually, the largest cost segment in a project solution is associated with implementation and delivery. Eight major categories of implementation costs are reviewed below:

1. **Salaries and benefits for the project team members' time.** This includes all of the charges for project team leaders assigned directly to the project. This cost represents their specific fees for the time they are involved with the project. These are direct charges only and are usually charges allocated directly from the project organization or tracked on a time-log for internal project staff.

2. **Salaries and benefits for coordinators and organizers.** The salaries of those who implement the project solution should be included. These are usually individuals from different business units of the organization who play a coordination role, but are not necessarily project team members. If a coordinator is involved in more than one project, the time should be allocated to the specific project under review. If external facilitators are used, all expenses should be included in the project management solution. The important issue is to capture all of the time of internal employees or external providers who work directly with the project management solution. The benefits factor should be included each time direct labor costs are involved. This factor is a widely accepted value, usually generated by the finance and accounting staff and is in the 30–50 percent range.

3. **Project team members' salaries and benefits.** The salaries plus employee benefits of project team members represent an expense that should be included. These costs can be estimated using average or midpoint values for salaries in typical job classifications. When a project is targeted for an ROI calculation, project team members can provide their salaries directly (in a confidential manner).

4. **Project materials and software.** Project materials such as field journals, instructions, reference guides, case studies, surveys, and project team member workbooks should be included in the delivery costs, along with license fees, user fees, and royalty payments. Supporting software, CD-ROMs, and videos are also included in this category.

5. **Hardware.** This includes all equipment purchased directly for this project assignment. If this hardware is used in other projects, then prorating per allocation over different projects may be appropriate.

6. **Travel, lodging, and meals.** Direct travel costs for project team members, facilitators, coordinators, and originators are included. Lodging and meals during travel and during the intervention are included. Entertainment and refreshments during the intervention are included as well.

7. **Facilities.** The direct cost for the use of facilities for the project solution should be included. For external meetings, this is the direct charge from the conference center, hotel, or motel. If the meetings are conducted in-house, the conference room represents a cost for the organization, and the cost should be estimated and included—even if it is uncommon to include facilities costs in other reports. A commonsense approach should be taken with this issue. Charging excessively for space or charging for small intervals may reflect an unreasonable approach, underscoring the need for formal guidelines.

8. **Capital expenditures.** For expenses that represent significant investment, such as in a major remodeling of facilities, the purchase of a building, and purchases of major equipment, the expenses should be recorded as capital expenditures and allocated over a period of time. If the equipment, building, or facility is used for other projects, then the costs should be allocated over the different projects and only a portion captured for a particular assignment.

All of these costs should be considered in developing the project management solution cost profile.

Maintenance and Monitoring

Maintenance and monitoring involves routine expenses to maintain and operate the solution implemented in the project. These represent ongoing expenses to make the new solution continue to work. These expenses may involve staff member salaries and benefits, additional equipment and repair expenses, and follow-up processes, and may be significant for some projects.

Support and Overhead

Another charge is the cost of support and overhead. The overhead category represents any project cost not considered in the above calculations. Typical items include the cost of clerical support, telecommunication expenses, office expenses, salaries of client managers, and other fixed costs. Some organizations obtain an estimate for allocation by estimating the total number of project days for the year and then estimating the overhead and support needed each day. This becomes a standard value to use in calculations.

Evaluation and Reporting

Usually the total evaluation cost is included in project solution costs to compute the fully loaded cost. ROI costs include the cost of developing the evaluation strategy, designing instruments, collecting and analyzing data, preparing and distributing reports, and communicating results. Cost categories include time, materials, purchased instruments, or surveys. A case can be made to prorate the evaluation costs over several projects instead of charging the total amount as an expense to one project. For example, if similar projects are conducted over a three-year period and the next project is selected for an ROI calculation, then some of the ROI costs could logically be prorated over the multiple projects. The initial ROI analysis should reflect some of the costs for the projects (e.g., instructional design and evaluation strategy).

COST ACCUMULATION AND ESTIMATION

There are two basic ways to classify project costs. One is with a description of the expenditure such as labor, materials, supplies, travel, and so forth. These are expense-account classifications. The other is with categories in the project process or function, such as initial analysis and assessment, development of solutions, and implementation and application.

An effective system monitors costs by account categories according to the description of those accounts, but also includes a method for accumulating costs in the process/functional category. Many systems stop short of this second step. While the first grouping sufficiently gives the total solution cost, it does not allow for a useful comparison with other programs, processes, and solutions to provide information on areas where costs might be excessive by relative comparisons.

Cost Classification Matrix

Costs are accumulated under both of the above classifications. The two classifications are obviously related, and the relationship depends on the organization. For instance, the specific costs that comprise the initial analysis and assessment phase of a project management solution may vary substantially with the organization.

An important part of the classification process is to define the types of costs in the account classification system that normally applies to the process/functional categories. Table 11-3 is a matrix that represents the categories for accumulating all project costs in the organization. Those costs that normally are a part of a process/functional category are checked in the matrix. Each member of the client staff should know how to charge expenses properly (e.g., equipment that is rented to use in the implementation of a project). Should all or part of the cost be charged to implementation? Or should the cost be charged to maintenance and monitoring? More than likely, the cost will be allocated in proportion to the extent to which the item was used for each category.

Cost Accumulation

With expense account classifications clearly defined and the process/functional categories determined, it is easy to track costs for individual projects. This is accomplished by using special account numbers and project numbers. An example illustrates the use of these numbers.

A project number is a three-digit number representing a specific project. For example:

Re-engineering of sales division	112
New team leader job design	315
Statistical quality control project	218
Culture audit	491

Table 11-3. Cost Classification Matrix

Expense Account Classification	Process / Functional Categories					
	Initial Analysis and Assessment	Development of Solutions	Acquisition Costs	Implementation and Application	Maintenance and Monitoring	Evaluation and Reporting
01 Salaries and Benefits – Project Leaders	X	X	X	X	X	X
02 Salaries and Benefits – Project Staff	X	X			X	X
03 Meals, Travel, and Incidentals – Project Leaders	X	X	X	X	X	X
04 Meals, Travel, and Accommodations – Project Staff		X		X	X	
05 Office Supplies and Materials	X	X		X	X	X
06 Project Materials and Supplies		X	X	X	X	
07 Printing and Copying	X	X	X	X	X	X
08 Software and Electronic Materials	X		X	X	X	
09 External Services	X	X	X	X	X	X
10 Hardware/Equipment Expense Allocation	X	X	X	X	X	
11 Hardware/Equipment – Rental		X	X	X	X	
12 Hardware/Equipment – Maintenance				X	X	
13 Fees, Licenses, and Royalties				X	X	
14 Facilities Expense Allocation				X	X	
15 Facilities Rental				X	X	
16 General Overhead Allocation	X	X	X	X	X	X
17 Other Miscellaneous Expenses	X	X	X	X	X	X

Numbers are assigned to the process/functional breakdowns. Using the example presented earlier, the following numbers are assigned:

Initial analysis and assessment	1
Development of solutions	2
Acquisition of solutions	3
Implementation and application	4
Maintenance and monitoring	5
Evaluation and reporting	6

Using the two-digit numbers assigned to account classifications in Table 11-3, an accounting system is complete. For example, if CD-ROMs are produced for the re-engineering project to be used during implementation, the appropriate charge number is 08-4-112. The first two digits denote the account classification, the next digit the process/functional category, and the last three digits the project number. This system enables rapid accumulation and monitoring of project costs. Total costs can be presented:

☐ By project
☐ By process/functional categories (implementation)
☐ By expense-account classification (software and electronic materials)

The important point is to devise a system that provides easy determination of all project management solution costs.

Cost Estimation

The previous section offered procedures for classifying and monitoring costs related to project solutions. It is important to monitor and compare ongoing costs with the budget or with projected costs. However, an important reason for tracking costs is to predict the cost of future projects. Usually, this goal is accomplished through a formal cost-estimation method unique to the organization.

Cost-estimating worksheets are sometimes helpful in determining the total cost for a proposed project. Table 11-4 shows an example of a cost-estimating worksheet that captures costs by project functional areas, such as implementation. The worksheets contain a few formulas that make it easier to estimate the cost. In addition to these worksheets, current charge rates for services, supplies, and salaries are available. These data become outdated quickly and are usually prepared periodically as a supplement.

Table 11-4. Example of a Cost-Estimating Worksheet

	Project Firm	Client Firm
Initial Analysis and Assessment Costs		
Salaries & Employee Benefits – Project Leaders (No. of Project Leaders × Avg. Salary × Employee Benefits Factor × No. of Hours on Project)	_____	_____
Salaries and Benefits – Project Staff	_____	_____
Meals, Travel, and Incidentals – Project Leaders	_____	_____
Office Supplies and Materials	_____	_____
Printing and Copying	_____	_____
Software, Electronic Materials	_____	_____
External Services	_____	_____
Hardware/Equipment Expense Allocation	_____	_____
General Overhead Allocation	_____	_____
Other Miscellaneous Expenses	_____	_____
Total Initial Analysis and Assessment Cost	_____	_____
Development of Solutions		
Salaries & Employee Benefits – Project Leaders (No. of People × Avg. Salary × Employee Benefits Factor × No. of Hours on Project)	_____	_____
Salaries and Benefits – Project Staff	_____	_____
Meals, Travel, and Incidentals – Project Leaders	_____	_____
Meals, Travel, and Incidentals – Project Staff	_____	_____

Table 11-4. Continued

	Project Firm	Client Firm
Office Supplies and Materials		
Project Materials and Supplies		
Printing and Copying		
External Services		
Hardware/Equipment Expense Allocation		
Hardware/Equipment – Rental		
General Overhead Allocation		
Other Miscellaneous Expenses		
Total Development of Solutions		

Acquisition Costs

	Project Firm	Client Firm
Salaries & Employee Benefits – Project Leaders (No. of People × Avg. Salary × Employee Benefits Factor × No. of Hours on Project)		
Meals, Travel, and Incidentals – Project Leaders		
Project Materials and Supplies		
Printing and Copying		
Software and Electronic Materials		
External Services		
Hardware/Equipment Expense Allocation		
Hardware/Equipment – Rental		
General Overhead Allocation		
Other Miscellaneous Expenses		
Total Acquisition Costs		

Table 11-4. Continued

	Project Firm	Client Firm
Implementation and Application		
Salaries & Employee Benefits – Project Leaders (No. of People × Avg. Salary × Employee Benefits Factor × No. of Hours on Project)	_____	_____
Meals, Travel, and Incidentals – Project Leaders	_____	_____
Meals, Travel, and Incidentals – Project Staff	_____	_____
Office Supplies and Materials	_____	_____
Project Materials and Supplies	_____	_____
Printing and Copying	_____	_____
Software and Electronic Materials	_____	_____
External Services	_____	_____
Hardware/Equipment Expense Allocation	_____	_____
Hardware/Equipment – Rental	_____	_____
Fees, Licenses, and Royalties	_____	_____
Facilities Expense Allocation	_____	_____
Facilities Rental	_____	_____
General Overhead Allocation	_____	_____
Other Miscellaneous Expenses	_____	_____
Total Delivery Costs	===========	===========
Maintenance and Monitoring		
Salaries & Employee Benefits – Project Leaders (No. of People × Avg. Salary × Employee Benefits Factor × No. of Hours on Project)	_____	_____
Salaries and Benefits – Project Staff	_____	_____
Meals, Travel, and Incidentals – Project Leaders	_____	_____
Meals, Travel, and Incidentals – Project Staff	_____	_____

Table 11-4. Continued

	Project Firm	Client Firm
Office Supplies and Materials		
Project Materials and Supplies		
Printing and Copying		
Software and Electronic Materials		
External Services		
Hardware/Equipment Expense Allocation		
Hardware/Equipment – Rental		
Hardware/Equipment – Maintenance		
Fees, Licenses, and Royalties		
Facilities Expense Allocation		
Facilities Rental		
General Overhead Allocation		
Other Miscellaneous Expenses		
Total Maintenance and Monitoring		

Evaluation and Reporting Costs

	Project Firm	Client Firm
Salaries & Employee Benefits – Project Leaders (No. of People × Avg. Salary × Employee Benefits Factor × No. of Hours on Project)		
Salaries and Benefits – Project Staff		
Meals, Travel, and Incidentals – Consultants		
Office Supplies and Materials		
Printing and Copying		
External Services		
General Overhead Allocation		
Other Miscellaneous Expenses		
Total Evaluation Costs		
TOTAL PROJECT COSTS		

The most appropriate basis for predicting costs is to analyze the previous costs by tracking the actual costs incurred in all phases of the project, from initial analysis to evaluation and reporting. This way, it is possible to see how much is spent on the total project and how much is being spent in the different categories. Until adequate cost data are available, it may be necessary to use the detailed analysis in the worksheets for cost estimation.

Final Thoughts

Costs are important and should be fully loaded in the ROI calculation. From a practical standpoint, some costs may be optional based on the organization's guidelines and philosophy. However, because of the scrutiny involved in ROI calculations, it is recommended that all costs be included, even if this goes beyond the requirements of the policy.

Reference

Annual Employee Benefits Report, *Nation's Business*, January 1999.

Further Reading

Cascio, Wayne F. *Costing Human Resources: The Financial Impact of Behavior in Organizations.* Kent Human Resource Management Series. New York: Van Nostrand Reinhold Company, Richard W. Beatty (Ed.), 1982.

Donovan, John, Richard Tully, and Brent Wortman. *The Value Enterprise: Strategies for Building a Value-Based Organization.* Toronto: McGraw-Hill/Ryerson, 1998.

Epstein, Marc J. and Bill Birchard. *Counting What Counts: Turning Corporate Accountability to Competitive Advantage.* Reading, MA: Perseus Books, 1999.

Friedlob, George T. and Franklin J. Plewa, Jr. *Understanding Return on Investment.* New York: John Wiley & Sons, 1991.

Fuller, Jim. *Managing Performance Improvement Projects: Preparing, Planning, and Implementing.* San Francisco: Pfeiffer, 1997.

Hronec, Steven M., Arthur Andersen & Co. *Vital Signs: Using Quality, Time, and Cost Performance Measurements To Chart Your Company's Future.* New York: Amacom/American Management Association, 1993.

Langley, Gerald J., Kevin M. Nolan, Thomas W. Nolan, Clifford L. Norman, and Lloyd P. Provost. *The Improvement Guide: A Practical Approach to Enhancing Organizational Performance.* San Francisco: Jossey-Bass Publishers, 1996.

PART III

Key Issues with the Measures

CHAPTER 12

How to Isolate the Effects of Project Management Solutions

When a significant increase in project performance is noted after a project management solution has been implemented, the two events may appear to be linked. A key manager may ask, "How much of this improvement was caused by the project management solution?" When this potentially embarrassing question is posed, it is rarely answered with any degree of accuracy and credibility. While the change in performance may be linked to the project, other non-project factors usually contribute to the improvement as well. This chapter explores useful techniques for isolating the effects of project management solution. These techniques are used by some of the most successful organizations as they attempt to measure the return on investment for project management solutions.

WHY THE CONCERN WITH THIS ISSUE?

In almost every project management solution there are multiple influences that will drive the business measures that the project targets to influence. With multiple influences, an attempt to measure the actual effect of each of the different factors is imperative. The results will be inappropriate and overstated if it is suggested that all of the change in the business impact measures are attributed to the actual project management solution. When isolating the influence of the project management solution is ignored, the impact study is considered to be invalid and inconclusive. This places tremendous pressure on project managers to show the actual value of their projects in comparison to other factors.

PRELIMINARY ISSUES

The cause-and-effect relationship between the project solution and performance can be very confusing and difficult to prove, but can often be shown with an acceptable degree of accuracy. The challenge is to develop one or more specific techniques to isolate the effects of the project management solution early in the process, usually as part of an evaluation plan. Up-front attention ensures that appropriate techniques will be used with minimal costs and time commitments. The most important issues in isolating the effects of a project management solution are covered below.

Chain of Impact

Before presenting the techniques, it is helpful to examine the chain of impact implied in the different levels of evaluation. Project team members should be applying the project management processes and skills to the job. Continuing with this logic, successful application of the project skills on the job should stem from project team members learning new skills or acquiring new knowledge from the project solution, which is measured as a Level 2 evaluation. Therefore, for a business impact improvement (Level 4 evaluation), this chain of impact implies that measurable, on-the-job application and implementation are realized (Level 3 evaluation), and new knowledge and skills are learned (Level 2 evaluation). Without this preliminary evidence, it is difficult to isolate the effects of a project management solution. In other words, if there is no learning or application on the job, it is virtually impossible to conclude that any performance improvements at Level 4 were caused by the project solution.

From a practical standpoint, this issue requires data collection at four levels for an ROI calculation. If data are collected on business impact, they should also be collected for other levels of evaluation to ensure that the project solution helped produce the business results. While this requirement is a prerequisite to isolating the effects of a project solution, it does not prove that there was a direct connection, nor does it pinpoint how much of the improvement was caused by the project solution. It merely shows that without improvements at previous levels, it is difficult to make a connection between the ultimate outcome and the project solution.

Identifying Other Factors: A First Step

As a first step in isolating a project solution's impact on organizational results, all key factors that may have contributed to the organizational results should be identified. This step communicates to interested parties that other factors may have influenced the results, underscoring that the project is not the sole source of improvement. Consequently, the credit for improvement is shared with several possible variables and sources—an approach that is likely to gain the respect of the key stakeholders of the project.

There are several potential sources available to identify major influencing variables. If the solution is implemented on request, the stakeholders may be able to identify factors that will influence the output variable. The stakeholders of the project will usually be aware of other initiatives or factors that may influence the results.

Project team members involved in the solution implementation are usually aware of other influences that may have caused organizational performance improvement. After all, it is the impact of their collective efforts that is being monitored and measured. In many situations, they have witnessed previous movements in the performance measures and can pinpoint reasons for change.

The project leaders involved in the process are another source for identifying variables that impact results. Although the needs analysis will usually uncover these influencing variables, project leaders typically analyze these variables while addressing the issues in the project.

In some situations, immediate managers of project team members (work unit managers) may be able to identify variables that influence the organizational performance improvements. This is particularly useful when project team members are non-exempt employees (operatives) who may not be fully aware of the variables that can influence performance.

Finally, middle and top management may be able to identify other influences based on their experience and knowledge of the situation. Perhaps they have monitored, examined, and analyzed the variables previously. The authority of these individuals often increases the data's credibility.

Taking time to focus attention on variables that may influence performance brings additional accuracy and credibility to the process. It moves beyond presenting results with no mention of other influences— a situation that often destroys the credibility of a project impact study. It also provides a foundation for some of the techniques described in this book by identifying the variables that must be isolated to show the effects of the project management solution. A word of caution is appropriate here. Halting the process after this step would leave many unknowns about the solution impact and might leave a negative impression with management, since the process may have identified variables not previously considered. Therefore, it is recommended that project managers go beyond this initial step and utilize one or more of the available techniques to isolate the impact of the solution, which are discussed next.

USE OF CONTROL GROUPS

The most accurate approach for isolating the impact of a project management solution is the use of control groups such as in an experimental design process. This approach involves the use of an experimental group that experiences the project solution and a control group that does not. The composition of both groups should be as identical as possible (job type, experience, etc.); however, placement in the two groups should be random. When this is achieved, and both groups are subjected to the same environmental influences, the difference in the performance of the two groups can be attributed to the project solution.

As illustrated in Figure 12-1, the control group and experimental groups do not necessarily have pre-project measurements. Measurements can be taken after the project, and the difference in the performance of the two groups shows the amount of improvement that is directly related to the project.

One caution to keep in mind is that the use of control groups may create an image that the project managers are producing a laboratory setting, which can cause a problem for some executives. To avoid this stigma, some organizations conduct a pilot project using project team members as the experimental group. A similarly matched non-participating control group is selected but does not receive any communication about the project.

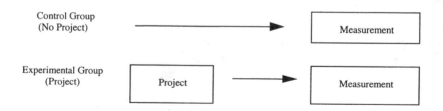

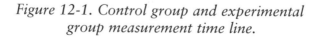

Figure 12-1. Control group and experimental group measurement time line.

The control group approach does have some inherent problems that may make it difficult to apply in practice. The first major problem is the selection of the groups. From a theoretical perspective, it is virtually impossible to have identical control and experimental groups. Dozens of factors can affect employee performance, some of them individual, others contextual. To address this issue on a practical basis, it is best to select four to six variables that will have the greatest influence on performance. For example, in a project designed to boost direct sales in a large retail store chain, three stores were selected, and their performances were compared to three similar stores that constituted the control group. The selection of these particular groups of stores was based on four variables that store executives thought would have the greatest influence on sales performance from one store to another: actual market area, store size, customer traffic, and previous store performance. Although there are other factors that could have influenced performance, these four variables were used to make the selection.

Another problem is contamination, which can develop when project team members in the project group (experimental group) actually communicate with others who are in the control group. Sometimes, the reverse situation occurs when members of the control group model the behavior of the experimental group. In either case, the experiment becomes contaminated as the influence of the project is passed on to the control group. This problem can be minimized if the control groups and project groups are at different locations, have different shifts, or are on different floors in the same building. When this is not possible, it may be helpful to explain to both groups that one group will be involved in the project now, and the other will be involved at a later date. Also, it may be helpful to appeal to the sense of responsibility of those involved in the project and ask them not to share the information with others.

Another problem occurs when the different groups function under different environmental influences. This is usually the case when groups are at different locations. Sometimes, the selection of the groups can help prevent this problem from occurring. Another tactic is to use more groups than necessary and discard those with some environmental differences.

Because the use of control groups is an effective approach for isolating the impact of project management solutions, it should be considered as a technique when a major ROI impact study is planned. In these situations, it is important that the project impact be isolated with a high level of accuracy, and the primary advantage of the control group process is accuracy.

TREND-LINE ANALYSIS

Another useful technique for approximating the impact of project solutions is trend-line analysis. With this approach, a trend line is drawn to predict the future, using previous performance as a base. When the project solution is implemented, actual performance is compared to the trend-line prediction. Any improvement of performance over what the trend line predicted can then be reasonably attributed to the project. While this is not an exact process, it provides a reasonable estimation of the project's impact.

Figure 12-2 shows an example of a trend-line analysis taken from a shipping department of a large book distribution company. The percentage reflects the level of actual shipments compared to scheduled shipments. Data are presented before and after a project solution was conducted in July. As shown in the figure, there was an upward trend on the data prior to conducting the project solution. Although the project solution apparently had a dramatic effect on shipment productivity, the trend line shows that some improvement would have continued anyway, based on the trend that had previously been established. It is tempting to measure the improvement by comparing the average six months' shipments prior to the project (87.3 percent) to the average six months after the project (94.4 percent), yielding a 7.1 percent difference. However, a more accurate comparison is the six-month average after the project compared to the trend line (92.3 percent). In this example, the difference is 2.1 percent. Using this more conservative measure increases the accuracy and credibility of the process to isolate the impact of the project solution.

A primary disadvantage of the trend-line approach is that it is not always accurate. This approach assumes that the events that influenced the performance variable prior to the project solution are still in place after the project solution, except for the implementation of the project solution (i.e., the trends that were established prior to the project solution will continue in the same relative direction). Also, it assumes that no new influences entered the situation at the time the project was conducted. This may not always be the case.

The primary advantage of this approach is that it is simple and inexpensive. If historical data are available, a trend line can quickly be drawn and differences estimated. While not exact, it does provide a quick assessment of the project impact.

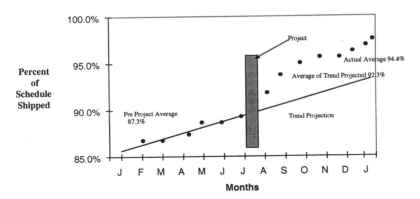

Figure 12-2. Example trend-line analysis.

Forecasting Methods

A more analytical approach to trend-line analysis is the use of forecasting methods that predict a change in performance variables. This approach represents a mathematical interpretation of the trend-line analysis when other variables enter a situation at the time of the project. With this approach, the output measure targeted by the project assignment is forecasted based on the influence of other variables that have changed during the implementation or evaluation period of the project assignment. The actual value of the measure is compared to the forecasted value. The difference reflects the contribution of the project solution. Because of the unlikely opportunity for this technique to be used, the presentation of specific techniques is beyond the scope of this book (Makridakis, 1989).

Project Team Members' Estimate of Impact

An easily implemented method for isolating the impact of project management solutions is to obtain information directly from project team members during the process. The effectiveness of this approach rests on the assumption that project team members are capable of determining or estimating how much of a performance improvement is related to the project solution. Because their actions have produced the improvement, project team members may have highly accurate input on the issue. They should know how much of the change was caused by implementing the project solution. Although an estimate, this value will usually have considerable credibility with management because they know project team members are at the center of the change or improvement. After describing the improvement, project team member estimation is obtained by asking project team members the series of questions in Table 12-1. For an example with one project team member's estimations, see Table 12-2.

Project team members who do not provide information on these questions are excluded from the analysis. Also, erroneous, incomplete, and extreme information should be discarded before analysis. To be conservative, the confidence percentage can be factored into the values. The confidence percentage is actually a reflection of the error in the estimate. Thus, an 80 percent confidence level equates to a potential error range of ±20 percent. With this approach, the level of confidence is multiplied by the estimate using the lower side of the range. In the example, the project team member allocates 60 percent of the improvement to the project and is 80 percent confident in the estimate. The confidence percentage is multiplied by the estimate to develop a usable project factor value of 48 percent. This adjusted percentage is then multiplied by the actual amount of the improvement (post-project minus pre-project value) to isolate the portion attributed to the project. The adjusted improvement is now ready for conversion to monetary values and, ultimately, use in the return on investment calculation.

Although an estimate, this approach does have considerable accuracy and credibility. Five adjustments are effectively applied to the project team member estimation to reflect a conservative approach:

Table 12-1. Questions for Project Team Member Estimation

What percentage of this improvement can be attributed to the implementation of the project?

What is the basis for this estimation?

What other factors contributed to this improvement in performance?

What confidence do you have in this estimate, expressed as a percentage? (0% = No confidence; 100% = Complete confidence)

What other individuals or groups could estimate this percentage to determine the amount of credit various factors should receive?

Table 12-2. Example of a Project Team Member's Estimation

Factor That Influenced Improvement	% of Improvement	Confidence Expressed as %	Adjusted % of Improvement
Project	60%	80%	48%
System changes	15%	70%	10.5%
Environmental changes	5%	60%	3%
Compensation changes	20%	80%	16%
Other	__%	__%	__%
Total	100%		

1. Project team members who do not provide usable data are assumed to have experienced no improvements.
2. Extreme data and incomplete, unrealistic, and unsupported claims are omitted from the analysis, although they may be included in the intangible benefits.
3. For short-term projects, it is assumed that no benefits from the project solutions are realized after the first year of implementation. For long-term projects it may be several years after the project solution before a benefit is realized.
4. The improvement amount is adjusted by the amount directly related to the project solution, expressed as a percentage.
5. The confidence level, expressed as a percentage, is multiplied by the improvement value to reduce the amount of the improvement by the potential error.

When presented to senior management, the result of an impact study is perceived to be an understatement of the solution's success. The data and the process are considered to be credible and accurate. As an added enhancement to this method, the next level of management above the project team members may be asked to review and approve the estimates from project team members.

An example will illustrate the process for project team member estimates. A restaurant chain initiated a project on performance improvement. The project was designed to improve the operating performance of the restaurant chain using a variety of tools to establish measurable goals for employees, provide performance feedback, measure progress toward goals, and take action to ensure that goals are met. As part of the project solution, each store manager developed an action plan for improvement. Managers also learned how to convert measurable improvements to an economic value for the restaurant. Their action plans could focus on any improvement area as long as they considered the content in the project and converted the improvements to either cost savings or restaurant profits. Some of the improvement areas were inventory, food spoilage, cash shortages, employee turnover, absenteeism, and productivity.

As part of the follow-up evaluation, each action plan was thoroughly documented showing results in quantitative terms, which were converted to monetary values. The annual monetary value of each improvement for each project team member was calculated from action plans. Realizing that other factors could have influenced the improvement, managers were asked to estimate the percentage of the improvement that resulted directly from the project solution (the contribution estimate). Restaurant managers are aware of factors that influence costs and profits and usually know how much of an improvement is traceable to a particular project solution. Each manager was asked to be conservative and provide a confidence estimate for the above contribution estimate (100 percent = certainty, and 0 percent = no confidence). The results are shown in Table 12-3.

Estimation of the project solution impact can be calculated using the conservative approach of adjusting for the contribution of the solution and adjusting for the error of the contribution estimate. For example, the $5,500 annual value for labor savings is adjusted to consider the project contribution ($5,500 × 60% = $3,300). Next, the value is adjusted for the confidence in this value ($3,300 × 80% = $2,640). The conservative approach yields an overall improvement of $68,386. Project Team Member 5 did not submit a completed action plan and was discarded from the analysis, although the costs are still included in the ROI calculation.

Another interesting observation emerges from this type of analysis. When the average of the three largest improvements is compared with the average of the three smallest values, important information is revealed about the potential for return on investment. If all the store managers involved in the solution had focused on high-impact improvements, a substantially higher ROI could have been achieved. This information can be helpful to the management group, whose support is often critical to the success of projects. While an impressive ROI is refreshing, a potentially greater ROI is outstanding.

Table 12-3. Estimates of Project Impact from Project Team Members

Participant	Total Annual Improvement (Dollar Value)	Basis	Contribution Estimate from Manager (Participants)	Confidence Estimate from Store Managers (Participants)	Conservative Value Reported
1	$5,500	Labor savings	60%	80%	$2,640
2	15,000	Turnover	50%	80%	6,000
3	9,300	Absenteeism	65%	80%	4,836
4	2,100	Shortages	90%	90%	1,701
5	0	—	—	—	—
6	29,000	Turnover	40%	75%	8,700
7	2,241	Inventory	70%	95%	1,490
8	3,621	Procedures	100%	80%	2,897
9	21,000	Turnover	75%	80%	12,600
10	1,500	Food spoilage	100%	100%	1,500
11	15,000	Labor savings	80%	85%	10,200
12	6,310	Accidents	70%	100%	4,417
13	14,500	Absenteeism	80%	70%	8,120
14	3,650	Productivity	100%	90%	3,285
Total	$128,722				$68,386

This process has some disadvantages. It is an estimate and, consequently, it does not have the accuracy desired by some project stakeholders. Also, the input data may be unreliable since some project team members are incapable of providing these types of estimates. They may not be aware of exactly which factors contributed to the results.

Several advantages make this technique attractive. It is a simple process, easily understood by most project team members and by others who review evaluation data. It is inexpensive, takes very little time and analysis and, thus, results in an efficient addition to the evaluation process. Also, these estimates originate from a credible source—the individuals who produced the improvement, the project team members.

The advantages of this approach seem to offset the disadvantages. Isolating the effects of a project management solution will never be precise, and this estimate may be accurate enough for most stakeholders and management groups. The process is appropriate when the project team members are managers, supervisors, team leaders, sales associates, engineers, and other professional or technical employees.

Managers' Estimate of Impact

In lieu of, or in addition to, project team member estimates, the project team members' manager may be asked to provide input as to the extent of the project solution's role in producing improved performance. In some settings, the project team members' manager may be more familiar with the other factors influencing performance. Consequently, they may be better equipped to provide estimates of impact. The recommended questions to ask managers, after describing the improvement caused by the project management solution, are provided in Table 12-4.

These questions are essentially the same ones described in the project team member's questionnaire. Manager estimates should be analyzed in the same manner as project team member estimates. To be more conservative, actual estimates may be adjusted by the confidence percentage. When project team members' estimates have also been collected, the decision of which estimate to use becomes an issue. If there is some compelling reason to think that one estimate is more credible than the other, then it should be used. The most conservative approach is to use the lowest value and include an appropriate explanation. Another potential option is to recognize that each source has its own unique perspective and that an average of the two is appropriate, placing an equal

Table 12-4. Questions for Managers' Estimates

What percentage of the improvement in performance measures of the participant resulted from the project?

What is the basis for this estimate?

What other factors could have contributed to this success?

What is your confidence in this estimate, expressed as a percentage? (0% = No confidence; 100% = Complete confidence)

What other individuals or groups would know about this improvement and could estimate this percentage?

weight on each input. If feasible, it is recommended that input be obtained from both project team members and their managers.

In some cases, upper management may estimate the percent of improvement that should be attributed to a project. After considering additional factors that could contribute to an improvement, such as technology, procedures, and process changes, management applies a subjective factor to represent the portion of the results that should be attributed to the project. While this is quite subjective, the input is typically accepted and can lead to funding for the project. Sometimes their comfort level with the process is the most important consideration.

This approach of using management estimates has the same disadvantages as project team member estimates. It is subjective and, consequently, may be viewed with skepticism by senior management. Also, managers may be reluctant to participate or may be incapable of providing accurate impact estimates. In some cases, they may not know about other factors that contributed to the improvement.

The advantages of this approach are similar to the advantages of project team member estimation. It is simple, inexpensive, and enjoys an acceptable degree of credibility because it comes directly from the managers of individuals who are involved in the project. When combined with project team member estimation, the credibility is enhanced considerably. Also, when factored by the level of confidence, its value further increases.

Customer Input on Project Management Solution Impact

Another helpful approach in some narrowly focused situations is to solicit input on the impact of the project management solution directly from customers. In these situations, customers are asked why they chose a particular product or service. In addition, they are asked to explain how their reaction to the product or service has been influenced by individuals or systems involved in the project management solution. This technique often focuses directly on what the solution is designed to improve. For example, after a customer service project was conducted with an electric utility, market research data showed that the percentage of customers who were dissatisfied with response time was reduced by 5 percent when compared to market survey data before the project. Since response time was reduced by the project and no other factor contributed to the reduction, the 5 percent reduction in dissatisfied customers was directly attributable to the project management solution.

Routine customer surveys provide an excellent opportunity to collect input directly from customers concerning their reaction to an assessment of a new or improved product, service, process, or procedure. Pre- and post-data can pinpoint the changes related to an improvement driven by a solution.

When collecting customer input, it is important to link it with the current data collection methods and avoid creating surveys or feedback mechanisms if at all possible. This measurement process should not add to the data collection systems.

Customer input could, perhaps, be the most powerful and convincing data if they are complete, accurate, and valid.

Expert Estimation of Project Solution Impact

External or internal experts can sometimes estimate the portion of results that can be attributed to a project solution. When using this technique, experts must be carefully selected based on their knowledge of the process, program, and situation. For example, an expert in quality might be able to provide estimates of how much change in a quality measure can be attributed to a project solution and how much can be attributed to other factors.

This approach does have disadvantages. It can be inaccurate unless the project solution and setting in which the estimate is made are quite similar to the project in question. Also, this approach may lose credibility because the estimates come from external sources and may not necessarily involve those who are close to the process.

This process has an advantage in that its credibility often reflects the reputation of the expert. It is a quick source of input from a reputable expert. Sometimes top management will place more confidence in external experts than its own internal staff.

Calculating the Impact of Other Factors

Although not appropriate in all cases, sometimes it is possible to calculate the impact of factors (other than the project management solution) that influence a portion of the improvement and credit the solution with the remaining portion. In this approach, the project management solution takes credit for the unknown, or improvement that cannot be attributed to other factors.

An example will help explain the approach. In a consumer-lending improvement project for a large bank, a significant increase in consumer loan volume was generated after the project was completed. Part of the increase in volume was attributed to the project management solution, and the remaining was due to the influence of other factors in place during the same time period. Two other factors were identified: an increase in marketing and sales promotion and falling interest rates, which caused an increase in consumer volume.

With regard to the first factor, as marketing and sales promotion increased, so did consumer loan volume. The amount of this factor was estimated using input from several internal experts in the marketing department. For the second factor, industry sources were used to estimate the relationship between increased consumer loan volume and falling interest rates. These two estimates together accounted for a modest percentage of increased consumer loan volume. The remaining improvement was attributed to the project.

This method is appropriate when the other factors are easily identified and the appropriate mechanisms are in place to calculate their impact on the improvement. In some cases, it is just as difficult to estimate the impact of other factors as it is the impact of the project solution, leaving this approach less advantageous. This process can be very credible if the method used to isolate the impact of other factors is credible.

USING THE TECHNIQUES

With all these techniques available to isolate the impact of projects management solutions, selecting the most appropriate technique can be difficult. Some techniques are simple and inexpensive, while others are more time-consuming and costly. When attempting to make the selection decision, the following factors should be considered:

- ☐ Feasibility of the technique
- ☐ Accuracy provided with the technique
- ☐ Credibility of the technique with the target audience
- ☐ Specific cost to implement the technique
- ☐ Amount of disruption in normal work activities as the technique is implemented
- ☐ Project team member, staff, and management time needed for the particular technique

Multiple techniques or multiple sources for data input should be considered since two sources are usually better than one. When multiple sources are utilized, a conservative method is recommended for combining the inputs. The reason is that a conservative approach builds acceptance. The target audience should always be provided with explanations of the process and the various subjective factors involved. Multiple sources allow an organization to experiment with different strategies and build confidence with a particular technique. For example, if management is concerned about the accuracy of project team members' estimates, a combination of a control group arrangement and project team members' estimates could be attempted to check the accuracy of the estimation process.

It is not unusual for the ROI of a project to be extremely large. Even when a portion of the improvement is allocated to other factors, the numbers are still impressive in many situations. The audience should understand that, although every effort is made to isolate the impact, it is still a figure that is not precise and may contain error. It represents the best estimate of the impact given the constraints, conditions, and resources available. Chances are it is more accurate than other types of analysis regularly used in other functions within the organization.

SHORTCUT WAYS TO ISOLATE THE EFFECTS OF THE PROJECT MANAGEMENT SOLUTION

Because of the importance of this issue, it cannot be ignored, omitted, or disregarded. At least one technique must be used to isolate the effects of the project management solution. However, for smaller, low-cost projects, estimates will have to be used and will normally be acceptable under these circumstances. The challenge is to be able to collect the estimates in the most credible and accurate way, using many of the techniques described in this chapter. If the client desires a more sophisticated method, then one of the other techniques may be applicable. Obviously, this would take more time and effort and perhaps cost the project stakeholders additional funds.

FINAL THOUGHTS

This chapter presents a variety of techniques for isolating the effects of project management solutions. The techniques represent the most effective approaches to address this issue and are used by some of the most progressive organizations. Too often, results are reported and linked with the project without any attempt to isolate the exact portion that can be attributed to project solutions. If professionals in the project management field are committed to improving their image, as well as meeting their responsibility for obtaining results, this issue must be addressed early in the process for all major project implementation solutions.

REFERENCES

Makridakis, S. *Forecasting Methods for Management*, 5th ed. New York: Wiley, 1989.

Tesoro, Ferdinand. "Implementing an ROI Measurement Process." In *Action: Implementing Evaluation Systems and Processes*, Jack J. Phillips, ed. Alexandria, Va.: American Society for Training and Development, 1998, 179-192.

FURTHER READING

Fetterman, David M., Shakeh J. Kaftarian, and Abraham Wandersman (Eds.). *Empowerment Evaluation: Knowledge and Tools for Self-Assessment & Accountability*. Thousand Oaks, CA: Sage Publications, 1996.

Gummesson, Evert. *Qualitative Methods in Management Research*. Newbury Park, CA.: Sage Publications, Inc., 1991.

Hronec, Steven M. and Arthur Anderson & Co. *Vital Signs: Using Quality, Time, and Cost Performance Measurements to Chart Your Company's Future*. New York: Amacom/American Management Association, 1993.

Langdon, Danny G., Kathleen S. Whiteside, and Monica M. McKenna (Eds.). *Intervention Resource Guide: 50 Performance Improvement Tools*. San Francisco: Jossey-Bass/Pfeiffer, 1999.

Phillips, Jack J. *Handbook of Training Evaluation and Measurement Methods*, 3rd ed. Boston: Butterworth-Heinemann, previously published by Gulf Publishing, 1997.

Rea, Louis M. and Richard A. Parker. *Designing and Conducting Survey Research: A Comprehensive Guide*, 2nd ed. San Francisco: Jossey-Bass Publishers, 1997.

CHAPTER 13

How to Convert Business Measures to Monetary Values

Transforming or converting data into monetary values is an essential step in calculating the return on investment for a project management solution. Many project evaluations stop with a tabulation of business results. While these results are important, it is even more valuable to convert the positive outcomes into monetary values and weigh them against the cost of the project management solution. This step is necessary to develop the ultimate level in the five-level evaluation framework. This chapter explains how progressive project managers are moving beyond simply tabulation of business results to developing monetary values used in calculating ROI.

WHY CONVERT DATA TO MONETARY VALUES?

The answer to this question is not always clearly understood by some project managers. A project management solution could be labeled a success without converting business results to monetary values, just by using business impact data to show the amount of change directly attributed to the project solution. For example, a change in quality, cycle time, market share, or customer satisfaction could represent significant improvements linked directly to a management solution. For some project solutions this may be sufficient. However, if the stakeholders desire a return on investment calculation with the actual monetary benefits compared to the costs, then this extra step of converting data to monetary values will be necessary. Also, the stakeholders may need additional information about the value of the business impact data. Sometimes, the monetary value has more impact on the stakeholders of a solution than just the change in the number itself. For example, project success in terms of a reduction of ten customer complaints per month may not seem to be significant. However, if the value of a customer complaint had been determined to be $3,000, this converts to a monthly improvement of at least $30,000—a more impressive improvement.

The Five Key Steps to Converting Data to Monetary Values

Before describing specific techniques to convert both hard and soft data to monetary values, there are five general steps that should be completed every time data needs to be converted to a monetary value.

1. **Focus on a unit of measure.** First, define a unit of measure. For output data, the unit of measure is the item produced, service provided, or sale consummated. Time measures might include the time to complete a project, cycle time, or customer-response time, and the unit is usually expressed in minutes, hours, or days. Quality is a common measure, with a unit being defined as one error, reject, defect, or reworked item. Soft data measures vary, with a unit of improvement representing such things as an absence, a turnover statistic, or a one-point change in the customer satisfaction index.

2. **Determine the value of each unit.** Place a value (V) on the unit identified in the first step. For measures of production, quality, cost, and time, the process is relatively easy. Most organizations maintain records or reports that can pinpoint the cost of one unit of production, or one defect. Soft data are more difficult to convert to dollars. For example, the value of one customer complaint or a one-point change in an employee attitude value is often difficult to determine. The techniques described in this chapter provide an array of approaches for making this conversion. When more than one value is available, usually the most credible or the lowest value is used in the calculation.

3. **Calculate the change in performance data.** Calculate the change in output data after the effects of the project management solution have been determined through the isolation step. The change (Δ) is the performance improvement, measured as hard or soft

data, which is directly attributed to the project management solution. The value may represent the performance improvement for an individual, a team, a group of project team members, or several groups of project team members.

4. **Determine an annual amount for the change.** Annualize the Δ value to develop a total change in the performance data for at least one year (ΔP). Using annual values has become a standard approach for organizations seeking to capture the benefits of a project, although the benefits may not remain constant through the entire year. First-year benefits are used even when the solution produces benefits beyond one year. This approach is considered conservative.

5. **Calculate the annual value of the improvement.** Arrive at the total value of improvement by multiplying the annual performance change (ΔP) by the unit value (V) for the complete group in question. For example, if one group of project team members is involved in a solution being evaluated, the total value will include total improvement for all project team members in the group. This value for annual project benefits is then compared to the cost of the project solution, usually with the ROI formula.

HOW DOES IT WORK?

An example taken from a grievance reduction project at a manufacturing plant describes the five-step process of converting data to monetary values. This project was developed and implemented after the initial needs assessment and analysis revealed that a lack of understanding, teamwork, and cooperation was causing an excessive number of labor grievances. Thus, the actual number of grievances resolved at Step 2 in the four-step grievance process was selected as an output measure. Table 13-1 shows the steps taken in assigning a monetary value to the data, arriving at a total project impact of $546,000.

TECHNIQUES FOR CONVERTING DATA TO MONETARY VALUES

Several strategies for converting data to monetary values are available. Some are appropriate for a specific type of data or data category, while others may be used with virtually any type of data. The project manager's challenge is to select the strategy that best suits the situation. These strategies are presented next, beginning with the most credible approach.

Table 13-1. An Example Illustrating the Steps for Converting Data to Monetary Values

Setting: Team-Building Project in a Manufacturing Plant

Step 1   **Focus on a Unit of Measure.**
One grievance reaching Step 2 in the four-step grievance resolution process

Step 2   **Determine the Value of Each Unit.**
Using internal experts (i.e., the labor relations staff), the cost of an average grievance was estimated to be $6,500, when time and direct costs are considered. (V = $6,500)

Step 3   **Calculate the Change in Performance Data.**
Six months after the project was completed, total grievances per month reaching Step 2 declined by 10. Seven of the 10 reductions were related to the project, as determined by supervisors (Isolating the Effects of the Project).

Step 4   **Determine an Annual Amount for the Change.**
Using the six-month value of seven grievances per month yields an annual improvement of 84 ($\Delta P = 84$).

Step 5   **Calculate the Annual Value of the Improvement.**
Annual Value = $\Delta P \times V$
= 84 × $6,500
= $546,000

CONVERTING OUTPUT DATA

When a project management solution produces a change in output, the value of the increased output can usually be determined from the organization's accounting or operating records. For organizations operating on a profit basis, this value is typically the marginal profit contribution of an additional unit of production or service provided. For example, a team within a major appliance manufacturer is able to boost the production of small refrigerators after a comprehensive project. The unit of improvement is the profit margin of one refrigerator. For organizations that are performance-driven rather than profit-driven, this value is usually reflected in the savings accumulated when an additional unit of output is realized for the same input. For example, in the visa section of a government office, an additional visa application is processed at no additional cost. Thus, an increase in output translates into a cost savings equal to the unit cost of processing a visa application.

The formulas and calculations used to measure this contribution depend on the type of organization and the status of their record-keeping. Most organizations have standard values readily available for performance monitoring and setting goals. Managers often use marginal cost statements and sensitivity analyses to pinpoint values associated with changes in output. If the data are unavailable, the project team must initiate or coordinate the development of appropriate values.

In one case involving a commercial bank, a project in the consumer-lending department produced increased consumer loan volume. To measure the ROI for the project, it was necessary to calculate the value (profit contribution) of one additional consumer loan. This was relatively easy to calculate from the bank's records. As shown in Table 13-2, the calculation involved several components.

The first step was to determine the yield, which was available from bank records. Next, the average spread between the cost of funds and the yield realized on the loan was calculated. For example, the bank could obtain funds from depositors at 5.5 percent on average, including the cost of operating the branches. The direct costs of making the loan—such as advertising expenditures and salaries of employees directly involved in consumer lending—were subtracted from this difference. Historically, these direct costs amounted to 0.82 percent of the loan value. To cover overhead costs for other corporate functions, an additional 1.61 percent was subtracted from the value. The remaining 1.82 percent of the average loan value represented the bank's profit

Table 13-2. Loan Profitability Analysis

Profit Component	Unit Value
Average loan size	$15,500
Average loan yield	9.75%
Average cost of funds (including branch costs)	5.50%
Direct costs for consumer lending	0.82%
Corporate overhead	1.61%
Net Profit Per Loan	**1.82%**

margin on a loan. The good news in this situation, and with this approach, is that these calculations are already completed for the most important data items and are reported as standard values.

CALCULATING THE STANDARD COST OF QUALITY

Quality and the cost of quality are important issues in most manufacturing and service firms. Since many project solutions are designed to increase quality, the project team must place a value on the improvement in certain quality measures. For some quality measures, the task is easy. For example, if quality is measured with the defect rate, the value of the improvement is the cost to repair or replace the product. The most obvious cost of poor quality is the scrap or waste generated by mistakes. Defective products, spoiled raw materials, and discarded paperwork are all the result of poor quality. Scrap and waste translate directly into a monetary value. In a production environment, for example, the cost of a defective product is the total cost incurred to the point the mistake is identified, minus the salvage value.

Employee mistakes and errors can cause expensive rework. The most costly rework occurs when a product is delivered to a customer and must be returned for correction. The cost of rework includes both labor and direct costs. In some organizations, rework costs can be as much as 35 percent of operating expenses.

In one example, a project focused on customer service provided by dispatchers in an oil company. The dispatchers processed orders and scheduled deliveries of fuel to service stations. A measure of quality that was considered excessive was the number of pullouts experienced. A pullout occurs when a delivery truck cannot fill an order for fuel at a service station. The truck must then return to the terminal for an adjustment to the order. This is essentially a rework item. The average cost of a pullout is developed by tabulating the cost from a sampling of actual pullouts. The elements in the tabulation included driver time, the cost of using the truck for adjusting the load, the cost of terminal use, and estimated administrative expenses. This value became the accepted standard following completion of the project.

Organizations have made great progress in developing standard values for the cost of quality. Quality costs can be grouped into four major categories: internal failure, external failure, appraisal, and prevention (Campanella, 1999).

1. **Internal failure.** Internal failure represents costs associated with problems detected prior to product shipment or service delivery. Typical costs are reworking and re-testing.
2. **External failure.** External failure refers to problems detected after product shipment or service delivery. Typical items are technical support, complaint investigation, remedial upgrades, and fixes.
3. **Appraisal costs.** Appraisal costs are the expenses involved in determining the condition of a particular product or service. Typical costs are testing and related activities, such as product-quality audits.
4. **Prevention costs.** Prevention costs include efforts undertaken to avoid unacceptable product or service quality. These efforts include service quality administration, inspections, process studies, and improvements.

Perhaps the costliest element of inadequate quality is customer and client dissatisfaction. In some cases, serious mistakes result in lost business. Customer dissatisfaction is difficult to quantify, and arriving at a monetary value may be impossible using direct methods. The judgment and expertise of sales, marketing, or quality managers are usually the best resources to draw upon when measuring the impact of dissatisfaction. More and more quality experts are measuring customer and client dissatisfaction with market surveys (Rust *et al.*, 1994). However, other strategies discussed in this chapter may be more appropriate for the task.

Another useful technique is finding a correlation between a customer satisfaction measure and another measure that can easily be converted to a monetary value. Figure 13-1 shows a relationship between customer satisfaction and customer loyalty that ultimately relates to profits (Bhote, 1996). As the figure illustrates, there is a strong correlation between customer satisfaction and customer loyalty. Many organizations are able to show a strong connection between these two measures. Furthermore, there is often a strong correlation between customer loyalty—which may be defined in terms of customer retention or defection—and the actual profit per customer. By connecting these two variables, it becomes possible to estimate the actual value of customer satisfaction by linking it to other measures. This technique is explored in greater detail later in this chapter.

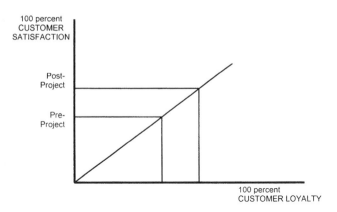

Figure 13-1. Correlation between customer satisfaction and customer loyalty.

CONVERTING EMPLOYEE TIME USING COMPENSATION

Decreasing the workforce or employee time is a common objective for projects. In a team environment, a project may enable the team to complete tasks in less time or with fewer people. A major project could effect a reduction of several hundred employees. On an individual basis, projects may be designed to help professional, sales, supervisory, and managerial employees save time in performing daily tasks. The value of the time saved is an important measure, and determining the monetary value is a relatively easy process.

The most obvious time savings are from reduced labor costs for performing the same amount of work. The monetary savings are found by multiplying the hours saved by the labor cost per hour. For example, after participating in a personal time-management project, project team members estimated that they saved an average of 74 minutes per day, worth $31.25 per day or $7,500 per year. The time savings were based on the average salary plus benefits for the typical project team members.

The average wage, with a percent added for employee benefits, will suffice for most calculations. However, employee time may be worth more. For example, additional costs in maintaining an employee (office space, furniture, telephones, utilities, computers, secretarial support, and other overhead expenses) could be included in calculating the average labor cost. Thus, the average wage rate may escalate quickly. In a large-scale employee reduction effort, calculating additional employee costs may be more appropriate for showing the value. However, for most projects the conservative approach of using salary plus employee benefits is recommended.

Beyond reducing the labor cost per hour, time savings can produce benefits such as improved service, avoidance of penalties for late projects, and additional profit opportunities. These values can be estimated using other methods discussed in this chapter.

A word of caution is in order when developing time savings. Savings are only realized when the amount of time saved translates into a cost reduction or profit contribution. Even if a project produces savings in a manager's time, a monetary value is not realized unless the manager puts the additional time to productive use. If a team-based project sparks a new process that eliminates several hours of work each day, the actual savings will be based on a reduction in staff or overtime pay. Therefore, an important preliminary step in developing time savings is determining whether the expected savings will be genuine.

USING HISTORICAL COSTS FROM RECORDS

Sometimes, historical records contain the value of a measure and reflect the cost (or value) of a unit of improvement. This strategy relies on identifying the appropriate records and tabulating the actual cost components for the item in question. For example, a large construction firm initiated a project to improve safety. The implementation of the project improved several safety-related performance measures, ranging from government fines to total worker's compensation costs. By examining the company's records using one year of data, the average cost for each safety measure was developed.

Historical cost data are usually available for most hard data. Unfortunately, this is generally not true for soft data, so other techniques explained in this chapter must be employed to convert the data to monetary values.

USING INPUT FROM INTERNAL AND EXTERNAL EXPERTS

When faced with converting soft data items, for which historical cost data are not available, it might be feasible to consider input from experts on the processes. Internal experts provide the cost (or value) of one unit of improvement. Individuals with knowledge of the situation and the respect of management are often the best prospects for expert input. They must understand the processes and be willing to provide estimates—as well as the assumptions made in arriving at the estimates. Most experts have their own methodology for developing these values. So when requesting their input, it is important to explain the full scope of what is needed, providing as many specifics as possible.

In the grievance-reduction project, the company had no records reflecting the total cost of grievances other than actual settlement costs and direct external expenses (e.g., there were no data for the time required to resolve a grievance). Therefore, an expert estimate was needed. The manager of labor relations, who had credibility with senior management and thorough knowledge of the grievance process, provided a cost estimate. He based it on the average settlement when a grievance was lost; the direct costs related to the grievances (arbitration, legal fees, printing, research); the estimated amount of supervisor and employee time expended; and a factor for reduced morale. This internal estimate, although not a precise figure, was appropriate for the analysis and had credibility with management.

When internal experts are unavailable, external experts are sought. External experts must be selected based on their experience with the unit of measure. Fortunately, there are many available experts working directly with important measures such as employee attitudes, customer satisfaction, turnover, absenteeism, and grievances. They are often willing to provide estimates of the cost (or value) of these intangibles. Because the accuracy and credibility of the estimates are directly related to the expert's reputation, his or her reputation is critical.

Using Values from External Databases

For some soft data, it may be appropriate to use cost (or value) estimates based on the research of others. This technique taps external databases that contain studies and research projects focusing on the cost of data items. Fortunately, there are many databases that include cost studies of many data items related to projects, and most are accessible through the Internet. Data are available on the cost of turnover, absenteeism, grievances, accidents, and even customer satisfaction. The difficulty is in finding a database with studies or research appropriate for the current project. Ideally, the data should come from a similar setting in the same industry, but that is not always possible. Sometimes, data on all industries or organizations are sufficient, perhaps with some adjustments to suit the project at hand.

An example illustrates the use of this process. A project was designed to reduce turnover of branch managers in a financial services company. To complete the evaluation and calculate the ROI, the cost of turnover was needed. To develop the turnover value internally, several costs were identified, including the expense of recruiting, employment processing, orientation, training new managers, lost productivity while training new managers, quality problems, scheduling difficulties, and customer satisfaction problems. Additional costs included the time regional managers spent working with turnover issues and, in some cases, the costs of litigation, severance, and unemployment. Obviously, these expenses are significant. Most project team members do not have time to calculate the cost of turnover, particularly if it is needed for a one-time event, such as evaluating a project. In this example, turnover cost studies in the same industry placed the value at about one and a half times the average annual salary of employees. Most turnover cost studies report the cost of turnover as a multiple of annual base salaries. In this example, management decided to be conservative and adjust the value downward to equal the average base salary of branch managers.

LINKING WITH OTHER MEASURES

When standard values, records, experts, and external studies are unavailable, a feasible approach might be developing a relationship between the measure in question and some other measure that may be easily converted to a monetary value. This involves identifying existing relationships, if possible, that show a strong correlation between one measure and another with a standard value.

For example, a classical relationship is a correlation between increasing job satisfaction and employee turnover. In a project designed to improve job satisfaction, a value is needed for changes in the job satisfaction index. A predetermined relationship showing the correlation between improvements in job satisfaction and reductions in turnover can link the changes directly to turnover. Using standard data or external studies, the cost of turnover can easily be developed as described earlier. Thus, a change in job satisfaction is converted to a monetary value or, at least, an approximate value. It is not always exact because of the potential for error and other factors, but the estimate is sufficient for converting the data to monetary values.

In some situations, a chain of relationships may be established to show the connection between two or more variables. With this approach, a measure that may be difficult to convert to a monetary

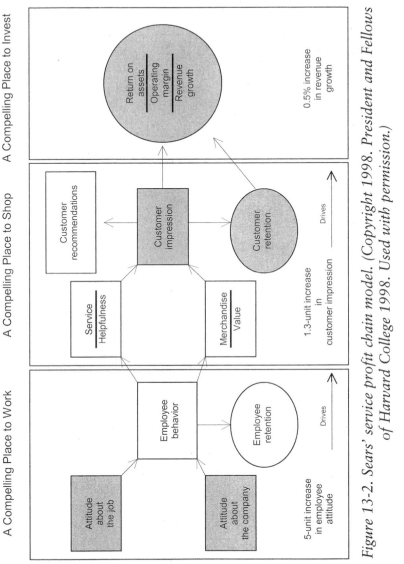

Figure 13-2. Sears' service profit chain model. (Copyright 1998. President and Fellows of Harvard College 1998. Used with permission.)

value is linked to other measures that, in turn, are linked to measures that a value can be placed on. Ultimately, these measures are traced to a monetary value often based on profits. Figure 13-2 shows the model used by Sears, one of the world's largest retail chains (Ulrich, 1998). The model connects job attitudes (collected directly from the employees) to customer service, which is directly related to revenue growth. The rectangles in the chart represent survey information, while the ovals represent hard data. The shaded measurements are collected and distributed in the form of Sears' total-performance indicators.

As the model shows, a five-point improvement in employee attitudes will drive a 1.3-point improvement in customer satisfaction. This, in turn, drives a 0.5 percent increase in revenue growth. Thus, if employee attitudes at a local store improved by 5 points, and previous revenue growth was 5 percent, the new revenue growth would be 5.5 percent.

These links between measures create a promising way to place monetary values on hard-to-quantify measures. This research practice is significant, and the opportunity for customized work is tremendous.

USING ESTIMATES FROM PROJECT TEAM MEMBERS

In some cases, project team members should estimate the value of soft data improvement. This technique is appropriate when project team members are capable of providing estimates of the cost (or value) of the unit of measure improved through the project. When using this approach, project team members should be provided clear instructions, along with examples of the type of information needed. The advantage of this approach is that the individuals closest to the improvement are often capable of providing the most reliable estimates of its value.

An example illustrates this process. A group of supervisors was involved in a major absenteeism reduction project. Successful application of the project should produce a reduction in absenteeism. To calculate the ROI for the project, it was necessary to determine the average value of one absence in the company. As is the case with most organizations, historical records for the cost of absenteeism were not available. Experts were not available, and external studies were sparse for this particular industry. Consequently, supervisors (project team members) were asked to estimate the cost of an absence. In a focus group format, each project team member was asked to recall the last time an employee in his or her work group was unexpectedly absent and describe what was necessary to adjust to the absence. Because the impact of an absence varies considerably from one employee to another within the same work unit, the group listened to all explanations. After reflecting on what actions to take when an employee is absent, each supervisor was asked to provide an estimate of the average cost of an absence in the company.

Although some supervisors are reluctant to provide estimates, with prodding and encouragement they usually will. The group's values are averaged, and the result is the cost of an absence that may be used in evaluating the project. Although this is an estimate, it is probably more accurate than data from external studies, calculations using internal records, or estimates from experts. And, because it comes from supervisors who wrestle with the issue daily, it will carry weight with senior management.

Using Estimates from the Management Team

In some situations, project team members may be incapable of placing a value on the improvement. Their work may be so far removed from the output of the process that they cannot reliably provide estimates. In these cases, the team leaders, supervisors, or managers of project team members may be capable of providing estimates. Consequently, they may be asked to provide a value for a unit of improvement linked to the project.

For example, a project involving customer service representatives was designed to reduce customer complaints. While the project resulted in a reduction of complaints, the value of a single customer complaint was still needed to determine the value of improvement. Although customer service representatives had knowledge of some issues surrounding customer complaints, they could not gauge the full impact, so their managers were asked to provide a value. In other situations, managers are asked to review and approve participants' estimates and confirm, adjust, or discard the values.

In some cases, senior management provides estimates of the value of data. With this approach, senior managers interested in the project solution are asked to place a value on the improvement based on their perception of its worth. This approach is used when it is difficult to calculate the value or when other sources of estimation are unavailable or unreliable.

An example illustrating this strategy is a hospital chain that was attempting to improve patient satisfaction with a particular project. Patient satisfaction was measured by an external customer satisfaction index. To determine the value of the project, the value of a unit of improvement (one point on the index) was needed. Because senior managers were interested in improving the index, they were asked to provide input on the value of a unit before the project was completed. In a regular executive meeting, each senior manager and hospital administrator was asked to describe what it means for a hospital when the index increases. After some discussion, each individual was asked to provide an estimate of the monetary value gained when the index moves one point. Although the senior managers were initially reluctant to provide the information, with some encouragement they finally did so. The values were then averaged. The result was a monetary estimate of one unit of improvement, and it was used in calculating the benefit of the project. Although this process is subjective, it does have the benefit of ownership from senior executives—the same executives who approved the project budget.

SELECTING THE TECHNIQUES AND FINALIZING THE VALUES

With so many techniques available, the challenge is selecting one or more strategies appropriate for the situation and available resources. It may be helpful to develop a table, or a list of values or techniques, appropriate for the situation. Table 13-3 shows the common conversion process for a group of output measures in a manufacturing firm. This process could be expanded to other categories and tailored specifically to the organization. The following guidelines may help determine the proper selection and finalize the values.

Use the Technique Appropriate for the Type of Data

Some strategies are designed specifically for hard data, while others are more appropriate for soft data. Consequently, the type of data often dictates the strategy. Hard data, while always preferred, are not always available. Soft data are often required and, thus, must be addressed using appropriate strategies.

Move from Most Accurate to Least Accurate

The strategies are presented in order of accuracy, beginning with the most accurate. Working down the list, each strategy should be considered for its feasibility for the situation. The strategy with the most accuracy is always recommended if it is feasible for the situation.

Table 13-3. Common Measures and the Methods to Convert to Monetary Values

Output Measures	Example	Strategy	Comments
Production unit	One unit assembled	Standard value	Available in almost every manufacturing unit
Service unit	Parts delivered on time	Standard value	Developed for most service providers when it is a typical service delivery unit
Sales	Monetary increase in revenue	Margin (profit)	The profit from one additional dollar of sales is a standard item.
Market share	10% increase in market share in one year	Margin of increased sales	Standard for most units
Productivity measure	10% change in productivity index	Standard value	This measure is very specific to the type of production or productivity measured. It may include per unit of time.

Consider Availability and Convenience

Sometimes, the availability of a particular source of data will drive the selection. In other situations, the convenience of a technique may be an important selection factor.

Use the Source with the Broadest Perspective

When using estimate, the individual providing the estimate must be knowledgeable of the processes and the issues surrounding the value of the data.

Use Multiple Techniques When Feasible

Sometimes, it is helpful to have more than one technique for obtaining values for the data. When multiple sources are feasible, they should be used to serve as comparisons or to provide additional perspectives. The data must be integrated using a convenient decision rule, such as the lowest value. A conservative approach must be taken.

Minimize the Amount of Time to Use a Technique

As with other processes, it is important to keep the time invested in this phase to a minimum, so that the total effort for the ROI study does not become excessive. Some techniques can be implemented in less time than others. Too much time on this step may dampen otherwise enthusiastic attitudes about the process.

Apply the Credibility Test

The techniques presented in this chapter assume that each data item collected and linked with project management solutions can be converted to a monetary value. Although estimates can be developed using one or more strategies, the process of converting data to monetary values may lose credibility with the target audience, which may question its use in analysis. Highly subjective data, such as changes in employee attitudes or a reduction in the number of employee conflicts, are difficult to convert. The key question in making this determination is: "Could these results be presented to senior management with confidence?" If the process does not meet this credibility test, the data should not be converted to monetary values but, rather, listed as intangibles. Other data, particularly hard data items, may be used in the ROI calculation, leaving the highly subjective data expressed in intangible terms.

Review the Stakeholders' Needs

The accuracy of data and the credibility of the conversion process are important concerns. Project managers sometimes avoid converting data because of these issues. They are more comfortable reporting that a solution reduced absenteeism from 6 percent to 4 percent, without attempting to place a value on the improvement. They may assume that the client will place a value on the absenteeism reduction. Unfortunately, the target audience may know little about the cost of absenteeism and will usually underestimate the actual value of the improvement. Consequently, there should be some attempt to include this conversion in the ROI analysis.

Consider a Potential Management Adjustment

In organizations where soft data are used and values are derived with imprecise methods, senior management is sometimes offered the opportunity to review and approve the data. Because of the subjective nature of this process, management may factor (reduce) the data so that the final results are more credible. In one example, senior managers at Litton Industries adjusted the value for the benefits derived from implementing self-directed teams (Graham, 1994).

Consider an Adjustment for the Time Value of Money

Since a project investment is made in one time period, and the return is realized at a later time, some organizations adjust project benefits to reflect the time value of money using discounted cash-flow techniques. The actual monetary benefits of the projects are adjusted for this time period. The amount of adjustment, however, is usually small when compared with the typical benefits of projects.

Shortcut Ways to Convert Data to Monetary Values

Converting data to monetary values is essential only if the ROI is being calculated or if the stakeholder needs to know the actual value of the data. Otherwise, it may be optional. If it is required and the project is small, or if resources are scarce, some of the techniques outlined in this chapter may be appropriate. Some of the options are (1) locating a standard value internally, (2) finding someone internally to estimate the value, or (3) identifying an external expert to provide a value. The individual providing the estimate must have credibility and be considered an expert on the issue. This is usually a reasonable task in most organizations, as there are individuals or departments with expertise on the particular issue in question.

Final Thoughts

In implementing project management solutions, money is an important value. Project managers are striving to be more aggressive in defining the monetary benefits of a project. Progressive project managers are no longer satisfied with simply reporting the business performance results from project solutions. Instead, they are taking additional steps to convert impact data to monetary values and weigh them against the project solution cost. In doing so, they achieve the ultimate level of evaluation: the return on investment. This chapter presented several strategies used to convert business results to monetary values, offering an array of techniques to fit any situation and project solution.

REFERENCES

Bhote, Keki R. *Beyond Customer Satisfaction to Customer Loyalty: The Key to General Profitability*. New York: Amacom/American Management Association, 1996.

Campanella, Jack (Ed.). *Principles of Quality Costs*, 3rd ed. Milwaukee: American Society for Quality, 1999.

Graham, Morris, Ken Bishop, and Ron Birdsong. "Self-Directed Work Teams." In *Action: Measuring Return on Investment*, vol. 1., Jack J. Phillips (Ed.). Alexandria, VA: American Society for Training and Development, 1994, 105–122.

Rust, Roland T., Anthony J. Zahorik, and Timothy L. Keiningham. *Return on Quality: Measuring the Financial Impact of Your Company's Quest for Quality*. Chicago: Probus Publishers, 1994.

Ulrich, Dave, ed. *Delivering Results*. Boston: Harvard Business School Press, 1998.

FURTHER READING

Anton, Jon. *CallCenter Management: By the Numbers*. West Lafayette, Ind.: Purdue University Press, 1997.

Heskett, James L., Earl Sasser, Jr., and Leonard A. Schlesinger. *The Service Profit Chain*. New York: The Free Press, 1997.

Hronec, Steven M. and Arthur Anderson & Co. *Vital Signs: Using Quality, Time, and Cost Performance Measurements to Chart Your Company's Future*. New York: Amacom/American Management Association, 1993.

Jones, Steve, ed. *Doing Internet Research*. Thousand Oaks, CA: Sage Publications, 1999.

Kaplan, Robert S. and Robin Cooper. *Cost and Effect: Using Integrated Cost Systems to Drive Profitability and Performance*. Boston: Harvard Business School Press, 1997.

Phillips, Jack J. *Return on Investment in Training and Performance Improvement Programs*. Boston: Butterworth-Heinemann, previously published by Gulf Publishing, 1997.

Stalk, George, Jr. and Thomas M. Hout. *Competing Against Time: How Time-Based Competition Is Reshaping Global Markets*. New York: The Free Press, 1990.

PART IV

Challenges

CHAPTER 14

Forecasting ROI: How to Build a Business Case for the Project Management Solution

Determining the appropriate time to develop the ROI for a project management solution is often confusing. The traditional and recommended approach, described in previous chapters, is to base ROI calculations strictly on business results obtained from the solution. Business performance measures (Level 4 data) are easily converted to monetary values, which are necessary for an ROI calculation. Sometimes these measures are not available, and it is usually assumed that an ROI calculation is out of the question. This chapter will illustrate that ROI calculations are possible at several different stages—even before the solution is initiated.

WHY FORECAST ROI?

Although calculation based on post-project data is the most accurate way to assess and develop an ROI calculation for a project manager, it is sometimes valuable to know the forecast before the final results are tabulated. Forecasting the impact of a project management solution, even before the solution is initiated, is important when critical issues drive the need for a forecasted ROI. There are five key reasons for doing so, as follows.

Reduce Uncertainty

Reducing uncertainty with new project management solutions is always beneficial to the client. In a perfect world, the client would like to know the expected payoff before any action is taken. Realistically, knowing the exact payoff may not be possible and, from a practical standpoint, it may not be feasible. However, there is still the desire to take the uncertainty out of the equation and act on the best data available. This sometimes pushes the project to a forecasted ROI before any resources are expended. Some project managers will simply not budge without a pre-project forecast for a project management solution; they need some measure of expected success before allocating any resources to the solution.

Support the Pursuit of Expensive Solutions

In some cases, even a pilot project management solution is not practical until some analysis has been conducted to examine the potential ROI. For example, if the project involves a significant amount of work or costs, a project manager may not want to expend the resources, even for a pilot, unless there is some assurance of a positive ROI. Although there may be some trade-offs with a lower-profile and lower-cost pilot, the pre-project ROI nevertheless becomes an important issue in these situations, prompting some clients to stand firm until an ROI forecast is produced.

Compare with Post-Project Data

Whenever there is a plan to collect data on the success of the application and implementation, impact, and ROI of the project management solution, it is helpful to compare actual results to pre-project expectations. In an ideal world, a forecasted ROI should have a defined relationship with the actual ROI, or they should be very similar—or at least one should predict the other with some adjustments. One important reason for forecasting ROI is to see how well the forecast holds up under the scrutiny of post-project analysis.

Save Costs

Several cost-saving issues may prompt the ROI forecast. First, the forecast itself is often a very inexpensive process because it involves estimations and several assumptions. Second, if the forecast itself becomes a reliable predictor of the post-project results, then the forecasted ROI might substitute for the actual ROI, at least with some adjustments. This could save the costs of the post-project analysis. Finally, the forecasted ROI data might be used for comparisons in other areas, at least as a beginning point for other types of projects. Thus, the forecasted ROI might be transferable to other project applications.

Comply with Policy

Many organizations are developing policy statements and, in the case of government agencies, sometimes even passing regulations to require a forecasted ROI before major project management solutions are undertaken. For example, in one organization, any project management solution exceeding $300,000 must have a forecasted ROI before it can be approved. As another example, in one foreign government, project managers can receive partial refunds on a project management solution if the ROI forecast is positive and likely to enhance the organization. These formal policies and legal structures are a growing reason for developing the ROI forecast.

Collectively, these five reasons are causing more organizations to examine ROI forecasts (or at least during a project) so that the client and the project manager will have some estimate of the expected payoff.

THE TRADE-OFFS OF FORECASTING

The ROI can be developed at different times and at different levels. Unfortunately, the ease, convenience, and low cost involved in capturing a forecasted ROI create trade-offs in accuracy and credibility. As shown in Figure 14-1, there are five distinct time intervals during the implementation of a project management solution when the ROI can actually be developed. The figure also shows the relationship with credibility, accuracy, cost, and difficulty.

The time intervals are:

1. *A pre-project forecast* can be developed using estimates of the impact of the project management solution. This approach lacks credibility and accuracy, but it is also the least expensive and least difficult ROI to calculate. There is value in developing the ROI on a pre-project basis. This will be discussed in the next section.
2. *Reaction and satisfaction data* can be extended to develop an anticipated impact, including the ROI. These data are collected after team members have been exposed to the solution through a briefing, explanation, or training session. In this case, team

ROI with:	Data Collection Timing (Relative to Project)	Credibility	Accuracy	Cost to Develop	Difficulty
1. Pre-Project Forecast	Before project is started	Not Very Credible	Not Very Accurate	Inexpensive	Not Difficult
2. Reaction and Satisfaction Data	At the beginning of the project, after team members have been exposed to the solution				
3. Learning Data	At the beginning of the project, after team members learn how to implement the solution				
4. Application and Implementation Data	During project implementation, after team members have applied the solution				
5. Business Impact Data	After project is complete	Very Credible	Very Accurate	Expensive	Very Difficult

Figure 14-1. Suggested time intervals for developing an ROI.

members actually anticipate the chain of impact as a project management solution is applied, implemented, and influences specific business measures. While the accuracy and credibility increase from that of the pre-project basis, this approach still lacks the credibility and accuracy desired in most situations.

3. *Learning data* in some project solutions can be used to forecast the actual ROI. These data are collected after team members learn how to use the solution, usually following a training program. This approach is applicable only when learning data show a relationship between acquiring certain skills or knowledge and subsequent business performance. When this correlation is available (it is usually developed to validate a test), test data can be used to forecast subsequent performance. The performance can then be converted to monetary impact and the ROI can be developed. This has less potential as an evaluation tool due to the lack of situations in which a predictive validation can be developed. Because of the limited use of this forecasting situation, additional detail is not provided in this chapter.

4. In some limited situations, when frequency of skills and actual use of skills and knowledge are critical, the *application and implementation* of those skills or knowledge can be converted to a monetary value using estimations. This is particularly helpful in situations where competencies are being developed as a major part of the solution and values are placed on improving competencies. Because of the limited use of this application and the preference to use business data, this approach is not explored further.

5. Finally, the ROI can be developed from *business impact data* converted directly to monetary values and compared to the cost of the solution. This post-project evaluation is the basis for the other ROI calculations in this book and has been the principal approach used in previous chapters. It is the preferred approach, but because of the pressures outlined above, it is critical to examine ROI calculations at other times and at levels other than Level 4.

This chapter will discuss, in detail, pre-project evaluation and the ROI calculations based on reactions. To a lesser degree, the chapter will also discuss the ROI calculations developed from learning and application data.

PRE-PROJECT ROI FORECASTING

Forecasting the ROI for the project management solution is one of the most useful steps in convincing a client that the expense for the project management solution is beneficial. The process is very similar to the post-project analysis, except that the extent of the impact must be estimated along with the forecasted cost of the solution.

Basic Model

Figure 14-2 shows the basic model for capturing the necessary data for a pre-project forecast. This model is a modification of the post-project project management scorecard model, except that data and influence factors are projected instead of being collected during different time frames. In place of the data collection is an estimation of the change in impact data that is expected to be influenced by the solution. Isolating the effects of the project management solution becomes a non-issue, as the estimate of output takes the isolation factor into consideration. For example, when a person is asked to indicate how much of the particular improvement can be driven by a solution, the influence of other factors is already taken into consideration. Only the solution factor is an issue, as the other factors have been isolated in the estimation process.

The method to convert data to monetary values is the same because the data items examined in a pre- and post-analysis should be the same. Estimating the project management solution's cost should be an easy step, as costs can easily be anticipated based on previous solutions using reasonable assumptions about the current solution. The anticipated intangibles are merely speculation in forecasting but can be reliable indicators of which measures may be influenced in addition to those included in the ROI calculation. The formula used to calculate the ROI is the same as in the post-analysis. The amount of monetary value from the data conversion is included as the numerator, while the estimated cost of the solution is inserted as the denominator. The projected benefit-cost ratio can be developed along with the ROI value (percent). The steps to develop the process are detailed next.

Steps to Develop the Pre-Project ROI

The detailed steps to develop the pre-project ROI forecast are presented in simplified form below:

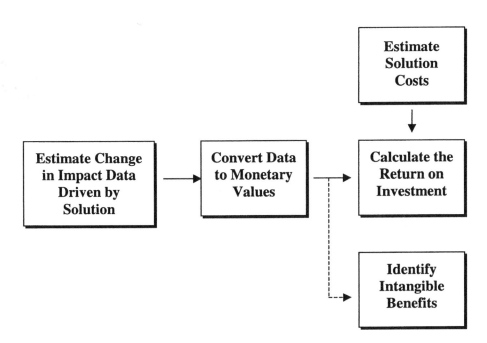

Figure 14-2. Basic model for capturing data for pre-project forecasting.

1. Develop the implementation (Level 3) and impact (Level 4) objectives with as many specifics as possible. Developed from the initial needs assessment and analysis, these objectives detail what would actually change as the project is implemented and identifies which business measures would actually be influenced. If these are unknown, the entire forecasting process is in jeopardy. There must be some assessment of which measures will change as a result of the solution, and someone must indicate the extent to which this change will materialize.
2. Estimate or forecast the total/monthly improvement in the business impact data. This is considered to be the amount of change directly related to the solution and is denoted by ΔP.
3. Convert the business impact data to monetary values using one or more of the methods described in Chapter 13. These are the same techniques, using the same processes as a post-project analysis; the value is denoted by V.
4. Develop the estimated annual impact for each business measure. In essence, this is the first-year improvement from the project

management solution, showing the value for the change in the business impact measures directly related to the solution. In formula form, this is $\Delta I = \Delta P \times V \times 12$.

5. For longer-term project management solutions, improvements may be forecasted for a period greater than one year. In this case, factor additional years into the analysis if a project will have a significant useful life beyond the first year. These values may be discounted to reflect a diminished benefit in subsequent years. The client or owner of the project should provide some indication as to the amount of improvement expected in years two, three, and so forth. However, it is helpful to obtain input from as many team members as possible.

6. Estimate the fully loaded costs of the project management solution, using the cost categories discussed in Chapter 11. The fully loaded cost would be estimated and projected for the solution. This is denoted as C. Again, all direct and indirect costs should be included in the calculation.

7. Calculate the forecasted ROI using the total projected benefits and the estimated cost in the standard ROI formula:

$$\text{ROI} (\%) = \frac{\Delta I - C}{C3} \times 100$$

8. Use sensitivity analysis to develop several potential ROI values with different levels of improvement (ΔP). When more than one measure is changing, that analysis should be developed using a spreadsheet showing different possible scenarios for output and subsequent ROI values.

9. Identify potential intangible benefits by securing input from the individuals most knowledgeable of the project and solutions. These are only anticipated and based on assumptions from previous experience with this type of solution.

10. Communicate the ROI projection and anticipated intangibles with much care and caution. The target audience must clearly understand that the forecast is based on several assumptions (clearly defined), and that the values are the best possible estimates. However, there is still a lot of room for error.

These ten steps make the ROI forecast possible. The most difficult part of the process is the initial estimate of performance improvement. Several sources of data are available for this purpose, described next.

Forecasting/Estimating Performance Improvement

Several sources of input are available when attempting to estimate the actual business performance improvement that will be influenced by a project management solution. As shown in Figure 14-3, the business improvement from the solution is in two categories; project impact measures (related directly to project improvement) and business impact measures (improvement in the business unit directly influenced by the solution project). The following six important considerations should be explored when estimating performance improvement:

1. Previous experience in the organization with a similar project management solution or solutions may help form the basis of the estimate. Utilizing the breadth of experience can be an important factor as comparisons are rarely, if ever, exact.

2. The project team may have experience with similar solutions in other organizations or in other situations. Here, the experience of the designers, developers, and implementers involved in the solution will be helpful as they reflect on their experiences.

3. The input of external experts (usually project management consultants) who have worked in the field or tackled similar project solutions in other organizations can be extremely valuable. These may be consultants, suppliers, designers, or others who have earned a reputation as being knowledgeable about this type of solution in this type of situation.

4. Estimates can be obtained directly from a subject matter expert (SME) in the organization. This is an individual who is familiar with the internal processes being altered, modified, or improved by the solution. Internal SMEs are very knowledgeable and sometimes the most favored source for obtaining conservative estimates.

5. Estimates can be obtained directly from the client or the sponsor of the project. This is the individual who is ultimately making the purchasing decision and is providing data or input on the anticipated change in a measure linked to the actual project management solution. This influential position makes him or her a very credible source.

6. Individuals who are directly involved in the project management solution, often the project team, are sometimes in a position to know how much of a measure can be changed or improved with a particular type of solution. These individuals understand the

processes, procedures, and performance measurements being influenced. Their close proximity to the situation makes them highly credible and often the most accurate sources for estimating the amount of change.

Collectively, these sources provide an appropriate array of possibilities to help estimate the value of an improvement. This is the weakest link in the ROI forecasting process and deserves the most attention. The target audience, needing a proposal that includes a forecasted ROI, should understand where the estimates came from—as well as who made them. More importantly, the target audience must view the source as credible. Otherwise, the forecasted ROI has no credibility.

Case Example

It may be helpful to illustrate how a forecasted ROI can be developed using the processes explained here. A global financial services company was interested in purchasing project management software to enable its project managers to keep track of projects in the sales and marketing division. According to the needs assessment and initial analysis, there was a need for the software. The analysis involved detailing the exact needs, selecting an appropriate software package, and implementing the software along with appropriate job aids, job training, and classroom

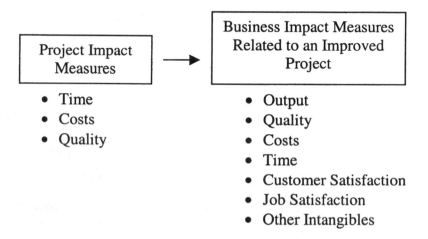

Figure 14-3. Business improvement linked to a solution.

training, if necessary. However, before purchasing the software, a forecasted ROI was needed. A project involving the improvement of customer contact management was selected to forecast the impact of the project management software. Following the steps outlined earlier in this chapter, it was determined that one project impact measure would be influenced by the software (time to complete the project), and three business impact measures would be influenced by the implementation of this project:

1. Increase in sales to existing customers
2. Reduction in customer complaints due to missed deadlines, late responses, and failure to complete transactions
3. Increase in customer satisfaction composite survey index

In examining the potential project, several individuals provided input. With improved customer contact management in place, relationship managers should benefit from quick and effective customer communication and have easy access to customer databases. To determine the extent to which the four measures would change, input was collected from four sources:

1. Internal project management software developers with expertise in various software applications provided input on expected changes in each of the measures.
2. Relationship managers provided input on expected changes in the variables if the project was successful.
3. The individual interested in pursuing the project, namely the client, provided some input on what could be expected from the project management software.
4. Finally, a survey of project management software developers provided some input.

When input is based on estimates, the actual results may differ greatly. However, this client was interested in a forecast based on very limited analysis but strengthened with the best expert opinions available. After some discussion of the availability of data and examining the techniques to convert data to monetary values, the following conclusions were reached:

☐ The reduction in project time in days could easily be converted into monetary values using two parts: time of the team using the

fully loaded compensation costs *and* opportunity costs as the
project is completed early (using an estimation).

☐ The increase in sales could easily be converted to a monetary
value using the profit margin for revenue linked to the particular
project if applied directly.

☐ The cost of a customer complaint had not been fully developed
internally and, therefore, was not used as a generally accepted
cost of a complaint; it was listed as a potential intangible benefit.

☐ There is no generally accepted value for increasing customer satisfaction, so customer satisfaction impact data were listed as a
potential intangible benefit.

The forecasted ROI calculation was developed for this single project
in the organization. After reviewing the possible scenarios, it was
decided that there could be a range of possibilities for reducing time
and increasing sales. Time reduction was expected to be in the range of
five to ten days, so three scenarios were developed for the reduction,
using five, seven and a half, and ten in the ROI calculation. The sales
increase should be in the range of 3–9 percent. Thus, three scenarios
were developed using 3 percent, 6 percent, and 9 percent as the
increase in sales.

The increase in sales was easily converted to monetary values using
the margin rates, and the reduction in time was easily converted using
the compensation cost for the team and omitting the opportunity cost
or value. The cost for the project software solution was easily estimated,
based upon input from those who briefly examined the situation. The
total cost was developed to include software, acquisition costs, facilities for meetings, lost time for learning activities, and coordination and
evaluation. This fully loaded projected cost, when compared to the
benefits, yielded a range of expected ROI values. Table 14-1 shows a
matrix of the nine possible scenarios using payoffs on the two measures. The ROI values range from a low of 60 percent to a high of 180
percent. With these values in hand, the decision to move forward was
a relatively easy one, as even the worst-case scenarios were very positive, and the best case was approximately three times that ROI
amount. Thus, the decision was made to move forward with the project. As this example illustrates, the process needs to be kept simple,
using the most credible resources available to quickly arrive at estimates for the process. Recognizing this is an estimate, its advantage is
simplicity and low cost, and these factors should be considered when
developing the processes.

Table 14-1. Expected ROI Values for Different Outputs

Potential Time Reduction (Number of Days)	Potential Sales Increase (Existing Customers, %)	Expected ROI (%)
5.0	3	60
7.5	3	90
10.0	3	120
5.0	6	90
7.5	6	120
10.0	6	150
5.0	9	120
7.5	9	150
10.0	9	180

FORECASTING WITH A PILOT PROGRAM

Although the steps listed above provide a process for estimating the ROI when a pilot or trial implementation is not conducted, a more favorable approach is to develop a small-scale version of the project management solution and develop the ROI based on post-project data. This scenario involves the following five steps:

1. As in the previous process, develop implementation (Level 3) and impact (Level 4) objectives.
2. Initiate the project management solution on a very small-scale sample as a pilot project, without all the bells and whistles. This keeps the cost extremely low without sacrificing the fundamentals of the project solution.
3. Conduct the pilot solution, fully implementing it with one or more of the typical projects that can benefit from the project management solution.
4. Develop the ROI using the project management scorecard for post-project analysis. This is the scorecard used in the previous chapters.
5. Finally, decide whether to implement the project management solution throughout the organization based on the results of the pilot implementation.

This approach provides a much more accurate analysis based on a pilot project, withholding full implementation until results can be developed from the pilot study. In this scenario, data can be developed using all six types of measures outlined in this book.

FORECASTING ROI WITH REACTION DATA

After project team members are exposed to the project management solution, usually through training or briefings, a reaction questionnaire is administered. When a reaction evaluation includes planned applications from a project management solution, this important data can ultimately be used in ROI forecast calculations. With questions concerning how project team members will use what they learned, higher-level evaluation information can be developed. The questions presented in Table 14-2 illustrate how these types of data are collected with a reaction questionnaire. Project team members are asked to state specifically how they plan to use the project management solution and the results they expect to achieve with it. They are asked to convert their planned accomplishments into annual monetary values and show the basis for developing the values. Team members can adjust their responses with a confidence factor to make the data more credible and allow them to reflect their uneasiness with the process. With some advance notice and discussion of the questions—including explanation of the use of the data, encouragement to provide data, a simple and typical example, and sample time to complete the form—a high participation rate (normally 80 to 90 percent) can be achieved.

When tabulating data, the confidence levels are multiplied by the annual monetary values, which produces a more conservative estimate for use in the data analysis. For example, if a team member estimated that the monetary impact of the project management solution would be $50,000 but the confidence level in this member's estimation was only 50 percent, a $25,000 value would be used in the ROI calculations.

To develop a summary of the expected benefits, several steps are taken. First, any data that are incomplete, unusable, extreme, or unrealistic is discarded. Next, an adjustment is made to the estimate for confidence level as previously described. Individual data items are then totaled. Finally, as an optional exercise, the total value is adjusted again by a factor that reflects the subjectivity of the process and the possibility that team members will not achieve the results anticipated. The

Table 14-2. Important Questions to Ask on Feedback Questionnaires

Planned Improvements

As a result of this project management solution, what specific actions will you attempt as you apply what you have learned?

1. _____

_____

2. _____

_____

3. _____

_____

Please indicate what specific business unit outcomes or project measures will change as a result of your actions.

1. _____

_____

2. _____

_____

3. _____

_____

As a result of anticipated changes above, please estimate (in monetary terms) the benefits to your organization over a period of one year. $_____

What is the basis of this estimate? Please be as specific as possible.

_____

_____

_____

_____

What confidence, expressed as a percentage, can you put in your estimate? (0% = No Confidence; 100% = Certainty) _____ %

project team can estimate this adjustment factor. One organization divided the benefits by two to develop a number to use in the equation. Finally, the ROI forecast is calculated using the anticipated net benefits from the project management solution divided by the solution costs. This value, in essence, becomes the expected return on investment once the confidence adjustment for accuracy and the adjustment for subjectivity have been made.

This process can best be described using an actual case. Large Scale Systems Company (LSSC) designs and builds large commercial systems for communications. To improve the current level of project management, they initiated a training program for project managers and team members. The program focused on leadership, planning, work breakdown, scheduling, tracking, communication, task relationships, resources, and budgets. After completing the project management training, project managers and team members were expected to improve project performance. Several project and business unit performance measures used in the company were discussed and analyzed during the training program. At the end of the project management training, team members completed a comprehensive reaction feedback questionnaire, which probed specific action items planned as a result of the training and provided estimated monetary values of the planned actions. In addition, project team members explained the basis for estimates and placed a confidence level on their estimates. Table 14-3 presents data provided by the first group of program participants. Only eighteen of the twenty-two team members supplied data, representing approximately 80 percent of participants. The total cost of the training, including participants' salaries, was $35,000. Prorated development costs were included in this figure.

The monetary value of the planned improvements was extremely high, reflecting the project team members' optimism and enthusiasm at the end of a very effective training session from which specific actions were planned. As a first step in the analysis, extreme data items were omitted. Data such as "millions," "unlimited," and "significant" are discarded, and each remaining value is multiplied by the confidence value and totaled. This adjustment is one way of reducing highly subjective estimates. The resulting tabulations yielded a total improvement of $836,050. Because of the subjective nature of the process, the values were adjusted by a factor of two, an arbitrary number suggested by the principal project management consultant and supported by the project manager. This "adjusted" value was $418,025, rounded to $418,000. The projected ROI, which was based

Table 14-3. Level 1 Data for ROI Calculations

Participant No.	Estimated Value	Basis	Confidence Level	Adjusted Value
	$ 80,000	Reduction in Time	90%	$72,000
	100,000	Project Quality	80%	80,000
	50,000	Time Reduction	85%	42,500
	10,000	Increased Opportunity	60%	6,000
	50,000	Reduction in Time	95%	47,500
	150,000	Total Project Cost	75%	112,500
	75,000	Team Compensation	80%	60,000
	7,500	Cost Savings	75%	56,250
	50,000	Reduction in Time	50%	25,000
	30,000	Project Team Compensation	80%	24,000
	150,000	Reduction in Total Project Costs	90%	135,000
	20,000	Business Unit Output	70%	14,000
	40,000	Project Time Reduction	70%	28,000
	75,000	Total Cost of Project	90%	67,500
	65,000	Total Team Compensation	50%	32,500
	Unlimited	Output of Business Unit	90%	—
	2,000	Quality in Unit	90%	1,800
	45,000	Revenues in Unit	70%	31,500
			TOTAL	$ 836,050

on the feedback questionnaire at the end of the project but before job application, is as follows:

$$ROI = \frac{\$418,000 - \$35,000}{\$35,000} \times 100 = 1094\%$$

The project management consultant communicated these projected values to the CEO but cautioned that the data was very subjective, although they had twice been adjusted downward. The consultant also emphasized that the project team members in the training program, who should presumably be aware of what they could accomplish, generated the forecasted results. In addition, the consultant mentioned that a follow up was planned to determine the results actually delivered by the group.

A word of caution is in order when using Level 1 ROI forecasting: the calculations are highly subjective and may not reflect the extent to which project team members will apply what they have learned to achieve results. A variety of influences in the work environment can enhance or inhibit the attainment of project performance goals. Having high expectations at the end of training is no guarantee that those expectations will be met. Disappointments are documented regularly in training programs throughout the world and reported in research findings.

While the process is subjective and possibly unreliable, it does have some usefulness. First, if evaluation must stop at Level 1, this approach provides more insight into the value of the solution than data from typical reaction questionnaires. Managers usually find these data more useful than a report stating, "40 percent of participants rated the training above average." Unfortunately, there is evidence that a high percentage of evaluations stop at this first level. Reporting Level 1 ROI data provides a more useful indication of the potential impact of a project management solution than the alternative, which is to report attitudes and feelings about the solution.

Second, these data can form a basis for comparing different projects of the same type. If one solution forecasts an ROI of 300 percent and another projects 30 percent, it would appear that one solution may be more effective than the other. The project team members in the first solution have more confidence in the planned application of the solution.

Third, collecting these data focuses increased attention on solution outcomes. Project team members involved in the solution will have an understanding that specific behavior change is expected, which produces results for the organization. This issue becomes very clear to team members as they anticipate results and convert them to monetary values. Even if this projected improvement is ignored, the exercise is productive because of the important message sent to the project team.

Fourth, if a follow up is planned to pinpoint post-project results, the data collected in the Level 1 evaluation can be very helpful for comparison. The data collection helps project team members plan the implementation of the solution. Incidentally, when a follow up is planned, team members are more conservative with their projected estimates.

The calculation of the ROI at Level 1 is being used more frequently. Some organizations base many of their ROI calculations on Level 1 data. Although they may be very subjective, the calculations do add value, particularly if they are included as part of a comprehensive evaluation system.

FINAL THOUGHTS

This chapter presented the techniques for forecasting ROI at four different time frames using different levels of evaluation data. Two of these techniques, pre-project forecasting and forecasting with learning data, are useful for very simple and inexpensive projects. They may be helpful even in short-term, low-profile projects. Forecasting using learning data at Level 2 and application data at Level 3 is rare and should be reserved only for large-scale projects involving significant learning events.

Pre-project forecasting may be necessary, and actually desired, even if it is not required. Because business data are the drivers of the project management solution, business impact measures should be identified up front. Estimating the actual change in these measures is a recommended and highly useful exercise, as it shows the client the perceived value of the project solution. This simple exercise should take no more than one or two days. The result can be extremely valuable when communicating to the client and in providing some clear direction and focus for the project manager.

In almost every project management solution, reaction data is collected from the project team members involved in the solution. A worthwhile extension of reaction data is to include several questions that allow those individuals to project the actual success of the project. Chapter 5, How to Measure Reaction and Satisfaction, discussed this as an option. This chapter recommended it as another simple tool for forecasting the actual ROI. This planned action provides some additional insight into the potential worth of the solution and alerts the project manager to potential problems or issues that may need attention as the remaining issues are addressed in the solution. The additional questions are very simple and the project team can answer them easily in fifteen to twenty minutes. For the process to be successful and usable, members must be committed to it. This can usually be achieved by exploring ways to increase the response rate for the various instruments described in this book.

As would be expected, pre-project forecast calculations are the lowest in terms of credibility and accuracy but have the advantage of being inexpensive and relatively easy to develop. ROI calculations using business impact data (Level 4) are rich in credibility and accuracy but are very expensive and difficult to develop. Although ROI calculations at Level 4 are preferred, ROI development at earlier stages with other levels of data is an important part of a comprehensive and systematic project evaluation process.

FURTHER READING

Dean, Peter J., Ph.D. and David E. Ripley (Eds.). *Performance Improvement Interventions: Performance Technologies in the Workplace: Volume Three of the Performance Improvement Series: Methods for Organizational Learning.* Washington, D.C.: The International Society for Performance Improvement, 1998.

Esque, Timm J. and Patricia A. Patterson. *Getting Results: Case Studies in Performance Improvement,* vol. 1. Washington, DC: HRD Press, Inc./International Society for Performance Improvement, 1998.

Friedlob, George T. and Franklin J. Plewa, Jr. *Understanding Return on Investment.* New York: John Wiley & Sons, 1991.

Hale, Judith. *The Performance Consultant's Fieldbook: Tools and Techniques for Improving Organizations and People.* San Francisco: Jossey-Bass/Pfeiffer, 1998.

Kaufman, Roger, Sivasailam Thiagarajan, and Paula MacGillis. *The Guidebook for Performance Improvement: Working with Individuals and Organizations.* San Francisco: Jossey-Bass/Pfeiffer, 1997.

Phillips, Jack J. *Return on Investment in Training and Performance Improvement Programs.* Boston: Butterworth-Heinemann, previously published by Gulf Publishing, 1997.

Price Waterhouse Financial & Cost Management Team. *CFO: Architect of the Corporation's Future.* New York: John Wiley & Sons, 1997.

Swanson, Richard A. *Analysis for Improving Performance: Tools for Diagnosing Organizations & Documenting Workplace Expertise.* San Francisco: Berrett-Koehler Publishers, 1994.

CHAPTER 15

How to Provide Project Feedback and Communicate Results to the Client

With data in hand, what's next? Should the data be used to modify the project management solution, change the process, show the contribution, justify new projects, gain additional support, or build goodwill? How should the data be presented? The worst course of action is to do nothing. Communicating results is as important as achieving results. This chapter provides useful information to help present evaluation data to the various audiences using both oral and written reporting methods.

WHY BE CONCERNED ABOUT COMMUNICATING RESULTS?

Communicating results is a critical issue for the project management scorecard. While it is important to communicate achieved results to interested stakeholders once the project is complete, it is also important to communicate throughout the project. Communication throughout the project ensures that information is flowing so adjustments can be made and so that all stakeholders are aware of the success and issues surrounding the project solution implementation. There are at least five key reasons for being concerned about communication in a project management solution.

Measurement and Evaluation Mean Nothing Without Communication

As Mark Twain once said, "Collecting data is like collecting garbage—pretty soon we will have to do something with it." If success is measured and evaluation data are collected, they mean nothing unless the findings are communicated promptly to the appropriate audiences so they will be aware of what is occurring and can take action if necessary. Communication allows a full loop to be made from the project solution results to the necessary actions based on those results.

Communication Is Necessary to Make Improvements

Because information is collected at different points during the process, the communication or feedback to the various groups who will take action is the only way adjustments can be made. Thus, the quality and timeliness of communication become critical issues for making necessary adjustments or improvements. Even after the project is completed, communication is necessary to make sure the target audience fully understands the results achieved and how the results could either be enhanced in future projects or in the current project, if it is still operational. Communication is the key to making these important adjustments at all phases of the project.

Communication Is Necessary to Explain Contributions

The contribution of the project management solution surrounding the six major types of measures is a confusing issue at best. The different target audiences will need a thorough explanation of the results. A communication strategy, including techniques, media, and the overall process, will determine the extent to which they understand the contribution. Communicating results, particularly with business impact and ROI, can quickly become confusing for even the most sophisticated target audiences. Communication must be planned and implemented with the goal of making sure the audiences understand the full contribution.

Communication Is a Sensitive Issue

Communication is one of those important issues that can cause major problems. Because the results of a solution can be closely linked to the political issues in an organization, communication can upset some individuals while pleasing others. If certain individuals do not receive the information or it is delivered inconsistently from one group to another, problems can quickly surface. Not only is it an understanding issue, it is also a fairness, quality, and political correctness issue to make sure communication is properly constructed and effectively delivered to all key individuals who need the information.

A Variety of Target Audiences Need Different Information

Because there are so many potential target audiences for receiving communication on the success of a project management solution, it is important for the communication to be tailored directly to their needs. A varied audience will command varied needs. Planning and effort are necessary to make sure the audience receives all of the information it needs, in the proper format, and at the proper time. A single report for all audiences may not be appropriate. The scope, size, media, and even the actual information of different types and different levels will vary significantly from one group to another, making the target audience the key to determining the appropriate communication process.

Collectively, these reasons make communication a critical issue, although it is often overlooked or underestimated in the evaluation of project management solutions. This chapter builds on this important issue and shows a variety of techniques for accomplishing all types of communication for various target audiences.

PRINCIPLES OF COMMUNICATING RESULTS

The skills required to communicate results effectively are almost as delicate and sophisticated as those needed to obtain results. The style is as important as the substance. Regardless of the message, audience, or medium, a few general principles apply and are explored next.

Communication Must Be Timely

Usually, solution results should be communicated as soon as they are known. From a practical standpoint, it may be best to delay the communication until a convenient time, such as the publication of the next stakeholder newsletter or the next general management meeting. Questions about timing must be answered: Is the audience ready for the results in light of other things that may have happened? Are they expecting results? When is the best time for having the maximum effect on the audience? Are there circumstances that dictate a change in the timing of the communication?

Communication Should Be Targeted to Specific Audiences

Communication will be more effective if it is designed for a particular group. The message should be specifically tailored to the interests, needs, and expectations of the target audience.

The results of a particular project are used in this chapter and reflect outcomes at all levels, including the six types of data developed in this book. Some of the data are developed earlier in the project and communicated during the project. Other data are collected after the project's implementation and communicated in a follow-up study. Thus, the results, in their broadest sense, may involve early feedback in qualitative terms to ROI values in varying quantitative terms.

Media Should Be Carefully Selected

For particular groups, some media may be more effective than others. Face-to-face meetings may be better than special bulletins. A memo distributed exclusively to top management may be more effective than the company newsletter. The proper method of communication can help improve the effectiveness of the process.

Communication Should Be Unbiased and Modest

It is important to separate fact from fiction and accurate statements from opinions. Various audiences may accept communication from project managers with skepticism, anticipating biased opinions. Boastful statements sometimes turn off recipients, and most of the content is lost. Observable, believable facts carry far more weight than extreme or sensational claims. Although such claims may get audience attention, they often detract from the importance of the results.

Communication Must Be Consistent

The timing and content of the communication should be consistent with past practices. A special communication at an unusual time during the project may provoke suspicion. Also, if a particular group, such as top management, regularly receives communication on project outcomes, it should continue receiving communication—even if the results are not positive. If some results are omitted, it might leave the impression that only positive results are reported.

Testimonials Are More Effective Coming from Individuals the Audience Respects

Opinions are strongly influenced by others, particularly those who are respected and trusted. Testimonials about project results, when solicited from individuals respected by others in the organization, can influence the effectiveness of the message. This respect may be related to leadership ability, position, special skills, or knowledge. A testimonial from an individual who commands little respect and is regarded as a sub-standard performer can have a negative impact on the message.

The Audience's Opinion of the Project Manager Will Influence the Communication Strategy

Opinions are difficult to change, and a negative opinion of the project manager may not change with the mere presentation of facts. However, the presentation of facts alone may strengthen the opinions held by those who already agree with the project results. It helps reinforce their position and provides a defense in discussions with others. A project manager with a high level of credibility and respect may have a relatively easy time communicating results. Low credibility can create problems when trying to be persuasive.

These general principles are important to the overall success of the communication effort. They should serve as a checklist for the project team when disseminating program results.

A MODEL FOR COMMUNICATING RESULTS

The process of communicating project management solutions results must be systematic, timely, and well planned, as illustrated in the model in Figure 15-1. The model represents seven components of the communication process that should normally occur in the sequence shown.

The first step is one of the most important and consists of an analysis of the need to communicate results from a project. Possibly, a lack of support for the project solution was identified, and perhaps the need for making changes to or continuing to fund the project was uncovered. There may be a need to restore confidence or build credibility for the project solution. Regardless of the triggering events, an important first

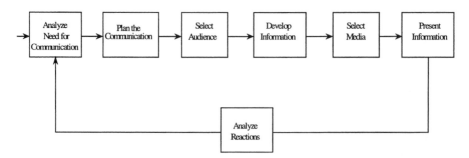

Figure 15-1. Process for planning communication of project results.

step is to outline the specific reasons for communicating the results of the project.

The second step focuses on a plan for communication. Planning is very important and usually involves three types of plans rather than an overall plan for communicating results in all types of projects:

1. The first plan includes numerous issues to be addressed in communication about all project management solutions.
2. The second plan covers the communication around the specific project management solution, detailing exactly what will be communicated, when, and to which groups.
3. The third plan covers communicating specific types of data, such as the results, conclusions, and recommendations produced through the evaluation process.

The third step involves selecting the target audiences for communication. Audiences range from top management to past project team members, all of which have their own special communication needs. All groups should be considered in the communication strategy. An artfully crafted, targeted communication may be necessary to win the approval of a specific group.

The fourth step involves developing written material to explain solution results. This can include a wide variety of possibilities, from a brief summary of the results to a detailed research report on the evaluation effort. Usually, a complete report is developed, and then selected parts or summaries from the report are used for different audiences.

Selecting the medium is the fifth step. Some groups respond more favorably to certain methods of communication. A variety of approaches, both oral and written, are available to the project management professional.

Information is presented in the sixth step. The product is delivered with the utmost care, confidence, and professionalism.

The last step, but not the least significant, is analyzing reactions to the communications. Positive reactions, negative reactions, and a lack of comments are all indicators of how well the information was received and understood. An informational but unscientific analysis may be appropriate for many situations. Tuning in to the reaction of a specific group may often suffice. For an extensive and more involved communication effort, a formal and structured feedback process may be necessary. Reactions could trigger an adjustment to the communication of the same project results or provide input to make adjustments for future project communications.

This communications model is not intended to make the process complicated. Rather, it is a process to ensure clear, accurate information is provided to the appropriate audiences. More than one audience usually receives the results of a project management solution evaluation, and each audience has its own unique needs. Each of the components in the model should be given consideration, if only informally, before the communications strategy is developed. Otherwise, the full impact of the effort may be diminished. The various steps in the model are amplified in the remainder of this chapter.

Analyzing the Need for Communication

Because there may be other reasons for communicating results, a list should be tailored to the organization and adjusted as necessary. The reasons for communicating project management results depend on the specific project, the setting, and the unique needs. The most common reasons are:

- ☐ **To secure approval for the project management solution and allocate resources of time and money.** The initial communication presents a proposal, projected ROI, or other data intended to secure the project approval. This communication may not have very much data but rather anticipates what is to come.
- ☐ **To gain support for the project management solution and its objectives.** It is important to have support from a variety of groups. This communication is intended to build the necessary support to make the project solution successful.
- ☐ **To secure agreement on the issues, solutions, and resources.** As the project solution begins, it is important for all those directly

involved to have some agreement and understanding of the important elements and requirements surrounding the project.

☐ **To build credibility for the project management organization, its techniques, and the finished products.** It is important early in the process to make sure that those involved understand the approach and reputation of the project management organization, and, based on the approach taken, the commitments made by all parties.

☐ **To reinforce the processes used in the project management solution.** It is important for key managers to support the project and reinforce the various processes used in the project solution. This communication is designed to enhance those processes.

☐ **To drive action for improvement in the project management solution.** This early communication is designed as a process improvement tool to effect changes and improvements as the needs are uncovered and as suggestions are made by various individuals.

☐ **To prepare project team members for the project management solution.** It is necessary for those most directly involved in the project, the project team members, to be prepared for assignments, roles, and responsibilities that will be required of them as they bring success to the project.

☐ **To enhance results throughout the project management solution and the quality of future feedback.** This communication is designed to show the status of the project and to influence decisions, seek support, or communicate events and expectations to the key stakeholders. In addition, it will enhance both the quality and quantity of information as stakeholders see the feedback cycle in action.

☐ **To show the complete results of the project management solution.** This is perhaps the most important communication, where all of the results involving all six types of measures are communicated to the appropriate individuals so they have a full understanding of the success or shortcomings of the project.

☐ **To underscore the importance of measuring results.** Some individuals need to understand the importance of measurement and evaluation and see the need for having important data on different measures.

☐ **To explain techniques used to measure results.** Several individuals on the project and support staff need to understand the techniques used in measuring results. In some cases, these techniques may be transferred internally to use with other projects. In short, these individuals need to understand the soundness and theoretical framework of the process used.

☐ **To stimulate desire in project team members to be involved in the project management solution.** Ideally, project team members want to be involved in the project. This communication is designed to pique their interest in the project, the assignment, and their importance to the project.

☐ **To stimulate interest in the project management organization's products.** From a project management organization's perspective, some communications are designed to create interest in all of the products and services based on the results obtained by the current product or process.

☐ **To demonstrate accountability for stakeholder expenditures.** It is important for a broad group to understand the need for accountability and the approach of the project manager or the project management organization. This ensures accountability for expenditures on the project.

☐ **To market future project management solutions.** From a project management organization's perspective, it is important to build a database of successful projects to use in convincing others that the project management process can add value.

Because there may be other reasons for communicating results, the list should be tailored to the individual organization.

Planning the Communication

Any type of successful activity must be carefully planned for it to produce the maximum results. This is a critical part of communicating the results of project assignments. The actual planning of the communications is important to ensure that each audience receives the proper information at the right time and that appropriate actions are taken. Three separate issues are important in planning the communication of results, as presented next.

Communication Policy Issues

In examining the complete project process, policy issues need to be developed around the communication of results. These range from providing feedback during a project to communicating the ROI from an impact study. Policy issues rest with both the stakeholder and the project manager. Internally, the stakeholder group may want to develop the policy around communication results as part of an overall policy on project assignments. From the project management organization's standpoint, the policy may be developed as part of the overall results-based approach to projects. Seven different areas will need some attention as the policies are developed:

1. **What will actually be communicated?** It is important to detail the types of information communicated throughout the project—not only the six types of data generated from the project management scorecard process, but the overall progress with the project may be a topic of communications as well.

2. **When will the data be communicated?** With communications, timing is critical. If adjustments in the project need to be made, the information should be communicated quickly so that swift actions can be taken.

3. **How will the information be communicated?** This shows the preferences toward particular types of communication media. For example, some organizations prefer to have written documents sent out as reports, while others prefer face-to face-meetings, and still others want electronic communications utilized as much as possible.

4. **Where will the communication take place?** Some prefer that the communication take place close to the project, others prefer stakeholder offices, and still others prefer the external facilities. The location can be an important issue in terms of convenience and perception.

5. **Who will communicate the information?** Will the project team, an independent person, or an individual involved on the stakeholder team communicate the information? The person communicating must have credibility so that the information is believable.

6. **Who will be the target audience?** Identify specific target audiences that should always receive information and others that will receive information when appropriate.

7. **What specific actions are required or desired?** When information is presented, in some cases no action is needed; in others, changes are desired and sometimes even required.

Collectively these seven issues frame the policy around communication as a whole.

Planning the Communication Around the Specific Project Management Solution

When a project is approved, the communication plan is usually developed. This details how specific information is developed and communicated to various groups and the expected actions. In addition, this plan details how the overall results will be communicated, the time frames for communication, and the appropriate groups to receive information. The stakeholder and project manager need to agree on the extent of detail in the plan. Additional information on this type of planning is provided later.

Communicating an Impact Study

The third type of plan is aimed at presenting the results of the project management solution evaluation—the impact study. This occurs when a major project is completed and the overall, detailed results are known. One of the major issues is who should receive the results and in what form. This is more specialized than the plan for the entire project because it involves the final study from the project. Table 15-1 shows the communication plan for a major team-based project that had a stress-reduction solution. Teams were experiencing high levels of stress and, through a variety of activities and job changes, stress began to diminish among the teams. The same process was made available to other teams who were experiencing similar symptoms.

Five different communication pieces were developed for different audiences. The complete report was an ROI impact study, a seventy-five-page report that served as the historical document for the project. It went to the stakeholders, the project staff, and the particular manager of each of the teams involved in the studies. An executive summary, a much smaller document, went to some of the higher-level executives. A general interest overview and summary without the ROI calculation went to the project team members. A general-interest article was developed for company publications, and a brochure was developed to show the success of the project. That brochure was used in marketing the same process internally to other teams and served as additional marketing material for the project management organization. This detailed plan may be part of the overall plan for the project assignment but may be fine-tuned during the actual project process.

Collectively, these three types of plans underscore the importance of organizing the communication strategy for a particular project or the overall project management process in an organization.

Table 15-1. Project Management Results Communication Plan

Communication Document	Communication Target(s)	Distribution Method
Complete Report with Appendices (75 pages)	☐ Stakeholder Team ☐ Project Team Members ☐ Project Manager	Distribute and discuss in a special meeting
Executive Summary (8 pages)	☐ Senior Management ☐ in the Business Units ☐ Senior Corporate Management	Distribute and discuss in routine meeting
General Interest Overview and Summary without the Actual ROI Calculation (10 pages)	☐ Project Team Members ☐ Other Interested parties	Mail with letter
General Interest Article (1 page)	☐ All Employees	Publish in company publication
Brochure highlighting project, objectives, and specific results	☐ Team Leaders with an Interest in the Project Solution ☐ Other Clients	Include with other marketing materials

SELECTING THE AUDIENCE FOR COMMUNICATIONS

When approaching a particular audience, the following questions should be asked about each potential group:

☐ Are they interested in the project management solution?
☐ Do they really want to receive the information?
☐ Has someone already made a commitment to them regarding communication?
☐ Is the timing right for this audience?
☐ Are they familiar with the project management solution?

☐ How do they prefer to have results communicated?
☐ Do they know the project team members? The project management organization?
☐ Are they likely to find the results threatening?
☐ Which medium will be most convincing to this group?

For each target audience, three actions are needed:

1. To the greatest extent possible, the project managers should know and understand the target audience.
2. The project managers should find out what information is needed and why. Each group will have its own needs relative to the information desired. Some want detailed information while others want brief information. Rely on the input from others to determine audience needs.
3. The project managers should try to understand audience bias. Each will have a particular bias or opinion. Some will quickly support the results, whereas others may be against them or be neutral. The staff should be empathetic and try to understand differing views. With this understanding, communications can be tailored to each group. This is especially critical when the potential exists for the audience to react negatively to the results.

Selecting the audience is a critical step in planning the communication of results. Addressing the above issues will help ensure that the appropriate audience receives the appropriate information.

Basis for Selecting the Audience

The potential target audiences to receive information on project results are varied in terms of job levels and responsibilities. Determining which groups will receive a particular communication piece deserves careful thought, as problems can arise when a particular group receives inappropriate information or when another is omitted altogether. A sound basis for proper audience selection is to analyze the reason for communication, as discussed in an earlier section. Table 15-2 shows common target audiences and the basis for selecting the audience.

Perhaps the most important audience is the stakeholders. This group (or individual) initiates the project, reviews data, selects the project manager, and weighs the final assessment of the effectiveness of the project. Another important target audience is the top management

Table 15-2. Common Target Audiences

Reason for Communication	Primary Target Audience
To Secure Approval for the Project Solution	Stakeholders, Top Executives
To Gain Support for the Project Solution	Immediate Managers, Team Leaders
To Secure Agreement with the Issues	Participants, Team Leaders
To Build Credibility for the Project Management	Top Executives
To Enhance Reinforcement of the Processes	Immediate Managers
To Drive Action for Improvement	Project Managers
To Prepare Project Team Members for the Project Solution	Team Leaders
To Enhance Results and Quality of Future Feedback	Participants
To Show the Complete Results of the Project Solution	Stakeholder Team
To Underscore the Importance of Measuring Results	Stakeholders, Project Managers
To Explain Techniques Used to Measure Results	Stakeholders, Project Support Staff
To Create Desire for Project Team Members to Be Involved	Team Leaders
To Stimulate Interest in the Consulting Firm's Products	Top Executives
To Demonstrate Accountability for Stakeholder Expenditures	All Employees
To Market Future Project Solutions	Prospective Clients

group. This group is responsible for allocating resources to the project and needs information to help justify expenditures and gauge the effectiveness of the efforts.

Selected groups of managers (or all managers) are also important target audiences. Management's support and involvement in the project management process and the department's credibility are important to success. Effectively communicating program results to management can increase both support and credibility.

Communicating with the project members' team leaders or immediate managers is essential. In many cases, they must encourage project team members to implement the project solution. Also, they often support and reinforce the objectives of the project. An appropriate return on investment improves the commitment to projects and provides credibility for the project team members.

Occasionally, results are communicated to encourage participation in the project solution. This is especially true for those projects offered on a volunteer basis. The potential project team members are important targets for communicating results.

Project team members need feedback on the overall success of the effort. Some individuals may not have been as successful as others in achieving the desired results. Communicating the results adds additional pressure to effectively implement the project and improve results for the future. For those achieving excellent results, the communication will serve as a reinforcement of the project. Communicating results to project team members is often overlooked, with the assumption that since the project is over, they do not need to be informed of its success.

The project staff must receive information about project results. Whether for small projects where project managers receive a project update, or for larger projects where a complete team is involved, those who design, develop, facilitate, and implement the project must be given information on the project's effectiveness. Evaluation information is necessary so adjustments can be made if the program is not as effective as it could be.

The support staff should receive detailed information about the process to measure results. This group provides support services to the project team, usually in the department where the project is conducted.

Company employees and stockholders may be less likely targets. General-interest news stories may increase employee respect. Goodwill and positive attitudes toward the organization may also be byproducts of communicating project results. Stockholders, on the other hand, are more interested in the return on their investment.

While Table 15-2 shows the most common target audiences, there can be others in a particular organization. For instance, management or employees could be subdivided into different departments, divisions, or even subsidiaries of the organization. The number of audiences can be large in a complex organization. At a minimum, four target audiences are always recommended: a senior management group, the project team members' immediate manager, the project team members, and the project staff.

DEVELOPING THE INFORMATION: THE IMPACT STUDY

The type of formal evaluation report depends on the extent of detailed information presented to the various target audiences. Brief summaries of project results with appropriate charts may be sufficient for some communication efforts. In other situations, particularly with significant projects requiring extensive funding, the amount of detail in the evaluation report is more crucial. A complete and comprehensive impact study report may be necessary. This report can then be used as the basis of information for specific audiences and various media. The report may contain the following sections.

Management/Executive Summary

The management summary is a brief overview of the entire report, explaining the basis for the evaluation and the significant conclusions and recommendations. It is designed for individuals who are too busy to read a detailed report. It is usually written last but appears first in the report for easy access.

Background Information

The background information provides a general description of the project management solution. If applicable, the needs assessment that led to the implementation of the project is summarized. The project is fully described, including the events that led to the implementation of the project management solution. Other specific items necessary to provide a full description of the project are included. The extent of detailed information depends on the amount of information the audience needs.

Objectives

The objectives for both the project and project solutions are outlined. Sometimes, they are the same but may be separate. This distinction is presented in Chapter 3, on planning the evaluation process. The report details the particular objectives of the study itself so that the reader clearly understands desired accomplishments for the assignment or project. In addition, if there were specific project management solutions implemented during this process, they are detailed here, as these are the issues or objectives from which the different types or levels of data will be collected.

Evaluation Strategy/Methodology

The evaluation strategy outlines all of the components that make up the total evaluation process. Several components of the results-based model and the project management scorecard process presented in this book are discussed in this section of the report. The specific purposes of evaluation are outlined, and the evaluation design and methodology are explained. The instruments used in data collection are also described and presented as exhibits. Any unusual issues in the evaluation design are discussed. Finally, other useful information related to the design, timing, and execution of the evaluation is included.

Data Collection and Analysis

This section explains the methods used to collect data as outlined in earlier chapters. The data collected are usually presented in the report in summary form. Next, the methods used to analyze data are presented with interpretations.

Project Solution Costs

Project costs are presented in this section. A summary of the costs by category is included. For example, analysis, development, implementation, and evaluation costs are recommended categories for cost presentation. The assumptions made in developing and classifying costs are discussed in this section of the report.

Reaction and Satisfaction

This section details the data collected from key stakeholders, particularly the project team members involved in the process, to measure the reaction to the project and a level of satisfaction with various issues and parts of the process. Other input from the stakeholder groups is also included to show the level of satisfaction.

Learning

This section shows a brief summary of the formal and informal methods for measuring learning. It explains how project team members have learned new processes, skills, tasks, procedures, and practices from the project.

Application and Implementation

This section shows how the project was actually implemented and illustrates the success with the application of new skills and knowledge. Implementation issues are addressed, including any major success and/ or lack of success.

Business Impact

This section shows the actual business impact measures representing the business needs that initially drove the project solution. This shows the extent to which performance has changed during the implementation of the project.

Return on Investment

This section shows the actual ROI calculation along with the benefit/cost ratio. It compares the value to what was expected and provides an interpretation of the actual calculation.

Intangible Measures

This section shows the various intangible measures directly linked to the project. Intangibles are those measures not converted to monetary values or included in the actual ROI calculation.

Barriers and Enablers

The various problems and obstacles affecting the success of the project are detailed and presented as barriers to implementation. Also, those factors or influences that had a positive effect on the project are included as enablers. Together, they provide tremendous insight into what can hinder or enhance projects in the future.

Conclusions and Recommendations

This section presents conclusions based on all of the results. If appropriate, brief explanations are presented on how each conclusion was reached. A list of recommendations or changes in the project, if appropriate, is provided with brief explanations for each recommendation. It is important that the conclusions and recommendations are consistent with one another and with the findings described in the previous section.

These components make up the major parts of a complete evaluation report.

Developing the Report

Table 15-3 shows the table of contents from a typical evaluation report for an ROI evaluation. This specific study was conducted for a large financial institution and involved an ROI analysis on a project for commercial banking. The typical report provides background information, explains the processes used and, most importantly, presents the results.

While this report is an effective, professional way to present ROI data, several cautions need to be followed. Since this document reports the success of a solution involving a group of employees, complete credit for the success must go to the project team members and their immediate leaders. Their performance generated the success. Another important caution is to avoid boasting about results. Although the project management scorecard may be accurate and credible, it still may have some subjective issues. Huge claims of success can quickly turn off an audience and interfere with the delivery of the desired message.

A final caution concerns the structure of the report. The methodology should be clearly explained, along with assumptions made in the analysis. The reader should readily see how the values were developed and how the specific steps were followed to make the process more conservative, credible, and accurate. Detailed statistical analyses should be placed in the appendix.

SELECTING THE COMMUNICATION MEDIA

There are many options available to communicate program results. In addition to the impact study report, the most frequently used media are meetings, interim and progress reports, the organization's publications, and case studies.

Table 15-3. Format of an Impact Study Report

- ☐ General Information
  - — Background
  - — Objectives of Study

- ☐ Methodology for Impact Study
  - — Levels of Evaluation
  - — ROI Process
  - — Collecting Data
  - — Isolating the Effects of Project Solutions
  - — Converting Data to Monetary Values

- ☐ Data Analysis Issues

- ☐ Costs

- ☐ Results: General Information
  - — Response Profile
  - — Success with Objectives

- ☐ Results: Reaction and Satisfaction
  - — Data Sources
  - — Data Summary
  - — Key Issues

- ☐ Results: Learning
  - — Data Sources
  - — Data Summary
  - — Key Issues

- ☐ Results: Application and Implementation
  - — Data Sources
  - — Data Summary
  - — Key Issues

- ☐ Results: Business Impact
  - — General Comments
  - — Linkage with Business Measures
  - — Key Issues

- ☐ Results: ROI and Its Meaning

- ☐ Results: Intangible Measures

- ☐ Barriers and Enablers
  - — Barriers
  - — Enablers

- ☐ Conclusions and Recommendations

Meetings

Meetings are fertile opportunities for communicating program results, if used properly. All organizations have a variety of meetings, and, in each, the proper context and project results are an important part. A few examples illustrate the variety of meetings.

MANAGER MEETINGS

Regular meetings with the first-level management group are quite common. Typically, items are discussed that will possibly help their work units. A discussion of a project and the subsequent results can be integrated into the regular meeting format.

PANEL DISCUSSIONS

Although not common in all organizations, panel discussions can be very helpful in showing how a problem was solved. A typical panel might include two or more managers or team leaders discussing their approach to a solution of a problem common to other areas. A successful discussion based on the results of a recent project can provide convincing data to other managers.

BEST-PRACTICES MEETINGS

Some organizations have best-practices meetings or video conferences to discuss recent successes and best practices. This is an excellent opportunity to learn and share methodologies and results.

BUSINESS UPDATE MEETINGS

A few organizations have initiated a periodic meeting for all members of management, in which the CEO reviews progress and discusses plans for the coming year. A few highlights of project results can be integrated into the CEO's speech, showing interest, commitment, and support by a top executive. Project results are mentioned along with operating profit, new facilities and equipment, new company acquisitions, and next year's sales forecast.

Whenever a management group convenes in significant numbers, evaluate the appropriateness of communicating project results.

Interim and Progress Reports

Although usually limited to large project management solutions, a highly visible way to communicate results is through interim and routine memos and reports. Published or disseminated via computer intranet on a periodic basis, they usually have several purposes:

- ☐ To inform management about the status of the project management solution
- ☐ To communicate the interim results achieved in the project management solution
- ☐ To activate needed changes and improvements

A more subtle reason for the report is to gain additional support and commitment from the management group and to keep the project intact. This report is produced by the project management staff and distributed to a select group of managers in the organization. Format and scope vary considerably.

The Organization's Publications and Standard Communication Tools

To reach a wide audience, project managers can use in-house publications. Whether a newsletter, magazine, newspaper, or electronic file, these types of media usually reach all employees. The information can be quite effective if communicated appropriately. The scope should be limited to general interest articles, announcements, and interviews.

E-mail and Electronic Media

Internal and external Web pages on the Internet, company-wide intranets, and e-mail are excellent vehicles for releasing results, promoting ideas, and informing employees and other target groups of project results. E-mail, in particular, provides a virtually instantaneous means with which to communicate and solicit response from large numbers of people.

Project Brochures and Pamphlets

A brochure might be appropriate for projects conducted on a continuing basis, where project team members have produced excellent results. It should be attractive and present a complete description of the project, with a major section devoted to results obtained from previous project team members, if available. Measurable results and reactions from project team members, or even direct quotes from individuals, could add spice to an otherwise dull brochure.

Case Studies

Case studies represent an effective way to communicate the results of a project. Consequently, it is recommended that a few projects be developed in a case study format. A typical case study describes the situation, provides appropriate background information (including the events that led to the intervention), presents the techniques and strategies used to develop the study, and highlights the key issues in the project. Case studies tell an interesting story of how the evaluation was developed and the problems and concerns identified along the way.

Case studies have many useful applications in an organization. First, they can be used in group discussions, where interested individuals can react to the material, offer different perspectives, and draw conclusions about approaches or techniques. Second, the case study can serve as a self-teaching guide for individuals trying to understand how evaluations are developed and utilized in the organization. Finally, case studies provide appropriate recognition for those involved in the actual case. More importantly, they recognize the project team members who achieved the results, as well as the managers who allowed the project team members to be involved in the project. The case study format has become one of the most effective ways to learn about project evaluation.

COMMUNICATING THE INFORMATION

Perhaps the biggest challenge of communication is the actual delivery of the message. This can be accomplished in a variety of ways and settings based on the actual target audience and the media selected for the message. Three particular approaches deserve additional coverage. The first approach is providing insight into how to provide feedback throughout the project to make sure information flows so changes can be made. The second is presenting an impact study to a senior management team. This may be one of the most challenging tasks for the project manager. The third is communicating regularly and routinely with the executive management group. Each of these three approaches is explored in more detail.

Providing Feedback

One of the most important reasons for collecting reaction, satisfaction, and learning data is to provide feedback so adjustments or changes can be made throughout the project. In most projects, data is routinely collected and quickly communicated to a variety of groups. Table 15-4 shows a feedback action plan designed to provide information to several feedback audiences using a variety of media.

As the plan shows, data are collected during the project at four specific time intervals and communicated back to at least four audiences—and sometimes six. Some of these feedback sessions result in identifying specific actions that need to be taken. This process becomes comprehensive and needs to be managed in a very proactive way. The following steps are recommended for providing feedback and managing the feedback process. Many of the steps and issues follow the recommendations of Peter Block in his successful consulting book, *Flawless Consulting* (1981).

1. **Communicate quickly.** Whether it is good news or bad news, it is important to let individuals involved in the project have the information as soon as possible. The recommended time for providing feedback is usually a matter of days and certainly no longer than a week or two after the results are known.
2. **Simplify the data.** Condense data into a very understandable, concise presentation. This is not the format for detailed explanations and analysis.
3. **Examine the role of the project managers and the stakeholders in the feedback situation.** Sometimes the project manager is the judge, and sometimes the project manager is the jury, prosecutor, defendant, or witness. On the other hand, sometimes the stakeholder is the judge, jury, prosecutor, defendant, or witness. It is important to examine the respective roles in terms of reactions to the data and the actions that need to be taken.
4. **Use negative data in a constructive way.** Some of the data will show that things are not going so well, and the fault may rest with the project management firm or the stakeholder. In either case, the story basically changes from "Let's look at the success we've made" to "Now we know which areas to change."
5. **Use positive data in a cautious way.** Positive data can be misleading and, if they are communicated too enthusiastically, they may create expectations beyond what may materialize later.

Table 15-4. Feedback Action Plan

Data Collection Item	Timing	Feedback Audience	Media	Timing of Feedback	Action Required
1. Pre-Project Survey ☐ Climate/Environment ☐ Issue Identification	Beginning of the Project	Stakeholder Team Project Team Members Team Leaders Project Managers	Meeting Survey Summary Survey Summary Meeting	One Week Two Weeks Two Weeks One Week	None None Communicate Feedback Adjust Approach
2. Implementation Survey ☐ Reaction to Plans ☐ Issue Identification	Beginning of Actual Implementation	Stakeholder Team Project Team Members Team Leaders Project Managers	Meeting Survey Summary Survey Summary Meeting	One Week Two Weeks Two Weeks One Week	None None Communicate Feedback Adjust Approach
3. Implementation Reaction Survey/Interviews ☐ Reaction to Solution ☐ Suggested Changes	One Month into Implementation	Stakeholder Team Project Team Members Support Staff Team Leaders Immediate Managers Project Managers	Meeting Study Summary Study Summary Study Summary Study Summary Meeting	One Week Two Weeks Two Weeks Two Weeks Three Weeks Three Days	Comments None None Support Changes Support Changes Adjust Approach
4. Implementation Feedback Questionnaire ☐ Reaction (Satisfaction) ☐ Barriers ☐ Projected Success	End of Implementation	Stakeholder Team Project Team Members Support Staff Team Leaders Immediate Managers Consultants	Meeting Study Summary Study Summary Study Summary Study Summary Meeting	One Week Two Weeks Two Weeks Two Weeks Three Weeks Three Days	Comments None None Support Changes Support Changes Adjust Approach

Positive data should be presented in a cautious way—almost in a discounting mode.

6. **Choose the language of the meeting and communication very carefully.** Use language that is descriptive, focused, specific, short, and simple. Avoid language that is too judgmental, macro, stereotypical, lengthy, or complex.

7. **Ask the stakeholders for reactions to the data.** After all, the stakeholders are the number one customers, and their reaction is critical since it is most important that they are pleased with the project.

8. **Ask the stakeholders for recommendations.** The stakeholders may have some very good recommendations of what needs to be changed to keep a project on track or put it back on track if it derails.

9. **Use support and confrontation carefully.** These two issues are not mutually exclusive. There may be times when support and confrontation are needed for the same group. The stakeholders may need support and yet be confronted for lack of improvement or sponsorship. The project management group may be confronted on the problem areas that are developed but may need support as well.

10. **React and act on the data.** Weigh the different alternatives and possibilities to arrive at the adjustments and changes that will be necessary.

11. **Secure agreement from all key stakeholders.** This is essential to make sure everyone is willing to make adjustments and changes that seem necessary.

12. **Keep the feedback process short.** Don't let it become bogged down in long, drawn-out meetings or lengthy documents. If this occurs, stakeholders will avoid the process instead of being willing to participate in the future.

Following these twelve steps will help move the project forward and provide important feedback, often ensuring that adjustments are supported and made.

Presenting Impact Study Data to Management

Perhaps one of the most challenging and stressful communications is presenting an impact study to the management team, which also serves as the stakeholder in a project solution. The challenge is convincing this highly skeptical and critical group that outstanding results have been achieved (assuming they have), in a very reasonable time frame, addressing the salient points, and making sure the managers understand the process. Two particular issues can create challenges. First, if the results are very impressive, it may be difficult to make the managers believe the data. On the other extreme, if the data is negative, it will be a challenge to make sure managers don't overreact to the negative results and look for someone to blame. Following are guidelines that can help make sure this process is planned and executed properly:

- ☐ Plan a face-to-face meeting with senior team members for the first one or two major impact studies. If they are unfamiliar with the complete project management scorecard, a face-to-face meeting is necessary to make sure they understand the process. The good news is that they will probably attend the meeting because they have not seen ROI data developed for this type of project. The bad news is that it takes a lot of time, usually one to two hours for this presentation.

- ☐ After a group has had a face-to-face meeting with a couple of presentations, an executive summary may suffice. At this point they understand the process, so a shortened version may be appropriate.

- ☐ After the target audience is familiar with the process, a brief version may be necessary, which will involve a one- to two-page summary with charts and graphs showing all six types of measures.

- ☐ In making the initial presentation, the results should not be distributed beforehand or even during the session but saved until the end of the session. This will allow enough time to present the process and react to it before the target audience sees the actual ROI number.

- ☐ Present the process step by step, showing how the data were collected, when they were collected, who provided the data, how the data were isolated from other influences, and how they were converted to monetary values. The various assumptions, adjustments, and conservative approaches are presented along with the total cost of the project. The costs are fully loaded so that the target audience will begin to buy into the process of developing the actual ROI.

- ☐ When the data are actually presented, the results are presented step by step, starting with Level 1, moving through Level 5, and ending with the intangibles. This allows the audience to see the reaction and satisfaction, learning, application and implementation, business impact, and return on investment. After some discussion on the meaning of the ROI, the intangible measures are presented. Allocate time to each level as appropriate for the audience. This helps overcome the potentially negative reactions to a very positive or negative ROI.

☐ Show the consequences of additional accuracy if it is an issue. The trade-off for more accuracy and validity often means more expense. Address this issue whenever necessary, agreeing to add more data if required.

☐ Collect concerns, reactions, and issues for the process and make adjustments accordingly for the next presentation.

Collectively, these steps will help prepare for and present one of the most critical meetings in the process.

Communicating with Executive Management and Clients

No group is more important than top executives when it comes to communicating project solution results. In many situations, this group is also the stakeholder. Improving communications with this group requires developing an overall strategy, which may include all or part of the actions outlined next.

STRENGTHEN THE RELATIONSHIP WITH EXECUTIVES

An informal and productive relationship should be established between the project manager responsible for the project solution and the top executive at the location where the project is taking place. Each should feel comfortable discussing needs and project results. One approach is to establish frequent, informal meetings with the executive to review problems with current projects and discuss other performance problems/opportunities in the organization. Frank and open discussions can provide the executive with insight not possible from any other source. Also, it can be very helpful to the project management organization in determining the direction of the project.

SHOW HOW PROJECTS HAVE HELPED SOLVE MAJOR PROBLEMS

While hard results from recent projects are comforting to an executive, solutions to immediate problems may be more convincing. This is an excellent opportunity to discuss a possible future intervention.

Distribute Memos on Project Management Solution Results

When a project management solution has achieved significant results, make appropriate top executives aware of them. This can easily be done with a brief memo or summary outlining what the solution was supposed to accomplish, when it was implemented, who was involved, and the results achieved. This should be presented in a for-your-information format that consists of facts rather than opinions. A full report may be presented later.

All significant communications on projects, plans, activities, and results should include the executive group. Frequent information from the projects, as long as it is not boastful, can reinforce credibility and accomplishments.

Ask the Executive to Be Involved in the Review

An effective way to enhance commitment from top executives is to ask them to serve on a project review committee. A review committee provides input and advice to the project staff on a variety of issues, including needs, problems with the present project, and project evaluation issues. This committee can be helpful in letting executives know what the projects are achieving.

Analyzing Reactions to Communication

The best indicator of how effectively the results of a solution have been communicated is the level of commitment and support from the management group. The allocation of requested resources and strong commitment from top management are tangible evidence of management's perception of the results. In addition to this macro-level reaction, there are a few techniques project managers can use to measure the effectiveness of their communication efforts.

Whenever results are communicated, the reaction of the target audiences can be monitored. These reactions may include non-verbal gestures, oral remarks, written comments, or indirect actions that reveal how the communication was received. Usually, when results are presented in a meeting, the presenter will have some indication of how the results were received by the group. The interest and attitudes of the audience can usually be quickly evaluated.

During the presentation, questions may be asked or, in some cases, the information is challenged. In addition, a tabulation of these challenges and questions can be useful in evaluating the type of information to include in future communications. Positive comments about the results are certainly desired and, when they are made—formally or informally—they should also be noted and tabulated.

Project staff meetings are an excellent arena for discussing the reaction to communicating results. Comments can come from many sources depending on the particular target audiences. Input from different members of the staff can be summarized to help judge the overall effectiveness.

When major program results are communicated, a feedback questionnaire may be used for an entire audience or a sample of the audience. The purpose of this questionnaire is to determine the extent to which the audience understood and/or believed the information presented. This is practical only when the effectiveness of the communication has a significant impact on the future actions of the project management organization.

Another approach is to survey the management group to determine its perceptions of the results. Specific questions should be asked about results: What does the management group know about the results? How believable are the results? What additional information is desired about the project? This type of survey can help provide guidance in communicating results.

The purpose of analyzing reactions is to make adjustments in the communication process—if adjustments are necessary. Although the reactions may involve intuitive assessments, a more sophisticated analysis will provide more accurate information to make these adjustments. The net result should be a more effective communication process.

SHORTCUT WAYS TO PROVIDE FEEDBACK AND COMMUNICATE WITH STAKEHOLDERS

While this chapter has presented a full array of possibilities for all types of projects, a simplified and shortcut approach may be appropriate for small-scale projects and inexpensive project assignments. The following five issues can be addressed with minimal time.

1. Planning can be very simple and occupy only one block in the evaluation planning document. It is helpful to reach an agreement as to who will see the data and when they will receive it.
2. Feedback during a project should be simplified using a questionnaire, followed by a brief meeting to communicate the results.

This is almost informal but should address as many of the issues outlined in this chapter as possible. Most importantly, it should be kept simple and should lead to action if it is needed.

3. An impact study should be developed showing the actual success of the project, preferably with all six types of data. If certain types of data have been omitted, the impact study should be developed with the data that are available, following the appropriate areas or topics contained in an impact study, as outlined in this chapter.

4. The impact study results should be presented in a face-to-face meeting with the stakeholders and perhaps with the executive group, if they are not the same group. This is usually a meeting that will be easy to schedule and necessary from the perspectives of both the stakeholders and the project manager. A one-hour meeting can show the results of the project and respond to various issues. Using suggestions for conducting this meeting, as outlined in this chapter, would be helpful in this situation.

5. Keep impact study data for marketing purposes. From the perspective of the project manager, this is excellent marketing data that can be used in a generic way to convince others that the project is successful. From the stakeholders' perspective, this is a historical document that leaves a permanent record of success and can be used as a reference in the future. When communicating results from past studies, client confidentiality and protection of sensitive information should be honored.

FINAL THOUGHTS

This chapter presented the final step in the results-based approach to project accountability. Communicating results is a crucial step in the overall evaluation process. If this step is not taken seriously, the full impact of the results will not be realized. The chapter began with general principles for communicating program results. A communications model was presented, which can serve as a guide for any significant communication effort. The various target audiences were discussed and, because of its importance, emphasis was placed on the executive group. A suggested format for a detailed evaluation report was also provided. Much of the remainder of the chapter included a detailed presentation of the most commonly used media for communicating project results, including meetings, client publications, and electronic media. Numerous examples illustrated these concepts.

FURTHER READING

Bleech, J.M. and D.G. Mutchler. *Let's Get Results, Not Excuses!* Hollywood, FL: Lifetime Books Inc., 1995.

Block, Peter. *Flawless Consulting.* San Diego: Pfeiffer and Co., 1981.

Connors, R., T. Smith, and C. Hickman. *The OZ Principle.* Englewood Cliffs, NJ: Prentice Hall, 1994.

Fradette, Michael and Steve Michaud. *The Power of Corporate Kinetics: Create the Self-Adapting, Self-Renewing, Instant-Action Enterprise.* New York: Simon & Schuster, 1998.

Fuller, Jim. *Managing Performance Improvement Projects: Preparing, Planning, and Implementing.* San Francisco: Pfeiffer and Co., 1997.

Hale, Judith. *The Performance Consultant's Fieldbook: Tools and Techniques for Improving Organizations and People.* San Francisco: Jossey-Bass/Pfeiffer, 1998.

Kaufman, Roger, Sivasailam Thiagarajan, and Paula MacGillis. *The Guidebook for Performance Improvement: Working with Individuals and Organizations.* San Francisco: Pfeiffer and Co., 1997.

Kaufman, Roger. *Strategic Thinking: A Guide to Identifying and Solving Problems.* Washington, DC: American Society for Training and Development/International Society for Performance Improvement, 1996.

Kraut, A.I. *Organizational Surveys.* San Francisco: Jossey-Bass Publishers, 1996.

Labovitz, George and Victor Rasansky. *The Power of Alignment: How Great Companies Stay Centered and Accomplish Extraordinary Things.* New York: John Wiley & Sons, 1997.

Langdon, Danny G. *The New Language of Work.* Amherst, MA: HRD Press, Inc., 1995.

Phillips, Jack J. *The Consultant's Scorecard.* New York: McGraw-Hill, 2000.

Sujansky, J.C. *The Power of Partnering.* San Diego: Pfeiffer & Co., 1991.

CHAPTER 16

Overcoming Resistance and Barriers to the Project Management Scorecard

Even the best-designed process, model, or technique is worthless unless it is effectively and efficiently integrated into the organization. Often, there is resistance to the project management scorecard, equally from the stakeholder, the project manager, and the project management team. Some of this resistance is based on fear and misunderstanding. Some is real, based on actual barriers and obstacles. Although the project management scorecard process is presented in this book as a step-by-step, methodical, and simplistic procedure, it can fail if it is not integrated properly and fully accepted and supported by those who must make it work in the organization. This chapter focuses on the key issues needed to overcome resistance to implementing the project management scorecard in the organization and the project management firm.

WHY BE CONCERNED ABOUT OVERCOMING RESISTANCE?

With any new process or change, there is resistance. Resistance may be especially great when implementing a process as complex as calculating the project management scorecard. There are four key reasons why there should be a detailed plan to overcome resistance.

Resistance Is Always Present

There is always resistance to change. Sometimes, there are good reasons for resistance, but often it exists for the wrong reasons. The important point is to sort out both types and try to dispel the myths. When legitimate barriers are the basis for resistance, trying to minimize or remove them altogether is the challenge.

Implementation Is Key

As with any process, effective implementation is the key to its success. This occurs when the new technique or tool is integrated into the routine framework. Without effective implementation, even the best process will fail. A process that is never removed from the shelf will never be understood, supported, or improved. There must be clear-cut steps for designing a comprehensive implementation process that will overcome resistance.

Consistency Is Needed

As this process is implemented from one study to another, consistency is an important consideration. With consistency come accuracy and reliability. The only way to make sure consistency is achieved is to follow clearly defined processes and procedures each time the project management scorecard is used. Proper implementation will ensure that this occurs.

Efficiency

Cost control and efficiency will always be an issue in any major undertaking, and the project management scorecard process is no exception. Implementation must ensure that tasks are done efficiently as well as effectively. It will help ensure that the process cost is kept to a minimum and that time is utilized appropriately.

THE APPROACH TO OVERCOMING RESISTANCE

Resistance shows up in many ways—as comments, remarks, actions, or behaviors. Table 16-1 shows some comments that reflect open resistance to the project management scorecard. Each of these represents issues that need to be resolved or addressed in some way. A few of the comments are based on realistic barriers, while others are based on myths that must be dispelled. Sometimes, resistance to the process reflects underlying concerns. The individuals involved may have fear of losing control of their processes, and others may feel that they are vulnerable to actions that may be taken if the process is not successful. Still others may be concerned about any process that brings change or requires additional learning efforts.

Resistance can appear with both major audiences addressed in this book. It can occur with project management firms, as many project managers may resist the project management scorecard and openly make comments similar to those listed in Table 16-1. Heavy persuasion and evidence of tangible benefits may be needed to convince those in a project management firm that this is a process that must be done, should be done, and is in their best interest to undertake. The other major audience, stakeholders in the organization where the project occurs, will also experience resistance. Although most stakeholders would like to see the results of the project, they may have concerns about the information they are asked to provide and if their performance is being judged along with the evaluation of the entire project. In reality, they may express the same fears listed in Table 16-1.

Table 16-1. Typical Objections to the Project Management Scorecard

Open Resistance

1. It costs too much.
2. It takes too much time.
3. Who is asking for this?
4. It is not in my job duties.
5. I did not have input on this.
6. I do not understand this.
7. What happens when the results are negative?
8. How can we be consistent with this?
9. The project management scorecard is too subjective.
10. Our managers will not support this.
11. ROI is too narrowly focused.
12. This is not practical.

The challenge is to implement the process methodically and consistently for both project management firms and stakeholders so that it becomes normal business behavior and a routine, standard process that is built into projects. The implementation necessary to overcome resistance covers a variety of areas. Figure 16-1 shows nine actions outlined in this chapter that are presented as building blocks to overcoming resistance. They are all necessary to build the proper base or framework to dispel myths and remove or minimize actual barriers. The remainder of this chapter presents specific strategies and techniques around each of the nine building blocks identified in Figure 16-1. They apply equally to the project management firm and the stakeholder

*Figure 16-1. Strategies for building support for
the project management scorecard.*

organization, and no attempt is made to separate the two in this presentation. In some situations, a particular strategy would work best in a project management firm, while others may work best in stakeholder organizations. In reality, all nine may be appropriate for both groups in certain cases.

DEVELOPING ROLES AND RESPONSIBILITIES

Defining and detailing specific roles and responsibilities for different groups and individuals addresses many of the resistance factors and helps pave a smooth path for implementation. In this section, four key issues are addressed.

Identifying a Champion

As an early step in the process, one or more individual(s) should be designated as the internal leader or champion for the project management scorecard process. As with most change efforts, someone must take responsibility for ensuring that the process is implemented successfully. This leader serves as a champion for the project management scorecard and is usually the one who understands the process best and sees vast potential for its contribution. More importantly, this leader is willing to teach others and will work to sustain sponsorship.

The scorecard leader is a member of the project team who usually has this full-time responsibility in larger project management firms or part-time in smaller organizations. Organizations may also have a leader who pursues the project management scorecard from the stakeholders' perspective. The typical job title for a full-time project management scorecard leader is "manager of measurement and evaluation." Some organizations assign this responsibility to a team and empower it to lead the scorecard effort.

Developing the Scorecard Leader

In preparation for this assignment, individuals usually obtain special training that builds specific skills and knowledge for the project management scorecard process. The role of the scorecard leader is quite broad and serves a variety of specialized duties. In some organizations, the scorecard leader can take on as many as fourteen roles, as shown in Table 16-2.

Table 16-2. Roles of the Scorecard Leader

Technical Expert	Cheerleader
Consultant	Communicator
Problem Solver	Process Monitor
Initiator	Planner
Designer	Analyst
Developer	Interpreter
Coordinator	Teacher

Leading the project management scorecard effort is a difficult and challenging assignment that requires special skill-building. Fortunately, there are programs available that teach these skills. For example, one such program is designed to certify individuals who are assuming a leadership role in the implementation of the scorecard process. This certification is built around ten specific skill sets linked to successful project scorecard implementations. These are:

1. Planning for ROI calculations
2. Collecting evaluation data
3. Isolating the effects of the project management solutions
4. Converting data to monetary values
5. Monitoring project costs
6. Analyzing data, including calculating the ROI
7. Presenting evaluation data
8. Implementing the project management scorecard
9. Providing internal project management evaluation education and advice
10. Teaching others the project management scorecard

This process is quite comprehensive but may be necessary to build the appropriate skills for tackling this challenging assignment.

Establishing a Task Force

Making the process work well may require the use of a task force. A task force is usually a group of individuals from different parts of the project management process who are willing to develop the project management scorecard process and implement it in the organization. The selection of the task force may involve volunteers, or participation may be mandatory depending on specific job responsibilities. The task force should represent the necessary cross section for accomplishing stated goals. Task forces have the additional advantage of bringing more people into the process and developing more ownership and support for the project management scorecard process. The task force must be large enough to cover the key areas but not so large that it becomes cumbersome and difficult to function: six to twelve members is recommended. For the organization, the same approach may be necessary, utilizing a task force for evaluating project activities as well as other processes.

Assigning Responsibilities

Determining specific responsibilities is a critical issue because confusion can arise when individuals are unclear about their specific assignments for the project management scorecard. Responsibilities apply to two areas. The first is the measurement and evaluation responsibility of the entire project management team. It is important for everyone involved in projects to have some responsibility for measurement and evaluation. These responsibilities include providing input on the design of instruments, planning specific evaluations, analyzing data, and interpreting the results. Typical responsibilities include:

- ☐ Ensuring that the needs assessment includes specific business impact measures
- ☐ Developing specific application and implementation objectives (Level 3) and business impact objectives (Level 4) for each project
- ☐ Focusing the content of the project on the performance improvement, ensuring that exercises, case studies, and skill practices relate to the desired objectives
- ☐ Keeping project team members focused on application and impact objectives
- ☐ Communicating rationale and reasons for evaluation
- ☐ Assisting in follow-up activities to capture application and business impact data
- ☐ Providing technical assistance for data collection, data analysis, and reporting
- ☐ Designing instruments and plans for data collection and analysis

While it may be inappropriate to have each member of the staff involved in all of these activities, each individual should have at least one or more responsibilities as part of his or her routine job duties. This assignment of responsibility keeps the project management scorecard from being disjointed and separated from major project activities. More importantly, it brings accountability to those directly involved in projects.

Another issue involves the technical support function. Depending on the size of the project management firm or the organization where the project occurs, it may be helpful to establish a group of technical experts who provide assistance with the project management scorecard process. When this group is established, it must be clear that the experts are not there to relieve others of evaluation responsibilities but to supplement technical expertise. When this type of support is developed, responsibilities revolve around six key areas:

1. Designing data collection instruments
2. Providing assistance for developing an evaluation strategy
3. Analyzing data, including specialized statistical analyses
4. Interpreting results and making specific recommendations
5. Developing an evaluation report or case study to communicate overall results
6. Providing technical support in all phases of the project management scorecard process

The assignment of responsibilities for evaluation is also an issue that needs attention throughout the evaluation process. Although the project team must have specific responsibilities during an evaluation, it is not unusual to require others in support functions to have responsibility for data collection. These responsibilities are defined when a particular evaluation strategy plan is developed and approved.

ESTABLISHING GOALS AND PLANS

Establishing goals, targets, and objectives is critical to the implementation. This means having detailed planning documents for the overall process as well as for individual scorecard projects. Several key issues relating to goals and plans are covered here.

Setting Evaluation Targets

Establishing specific targets for evaluation levels is an important way to make progress with measurement and evaluation. Targets enable the staff to focus on improvements needed at specific evaluation levels. In this process, the percentage of projects planned for evaluation at each level is developed. The first step is to assess the present situation. The number of all projects, including repeated projects of a similar nature, is tabulated along with the corresponding level(s) of evaluation presently conducted for each project. Next, the percentage of projects using reaction questionnaires is calculated, which is probably 100 percent. The process is repeated for each level of evaluation.

After detailing the current situation, the next step is to determine a realistic target within a specific time frame. Many organizations set annual targets for changes. This process should involve the input of the entire project team to ensure that targets are realistic and that the staff is committed to the process. If the project team does not develop ownership for this process, targets will not be met. The improvement targets must be achievable, while at the same time challenging and motivating.

Target-setting is a critical implementation issue. It should be completed early in the process with the full support of the project team. Also, if practical and feasible, the targets should have the approval of key managers—particularly the senior management team.

Developing a Project Plan for Implementation

An important part of implementation is to establish timetables for the complete implementation process. This document becomes a master plan for the completion of the different elements presented in this chapter, beginning with assigning responsibilities and concluding with meeting the targets previously described. From a practical standpoint, this schedule is a project plan for transitioning from the present situation to the desired future situation. The items on the schedule include, but are not limited to, developing specific scorecard projects, building staff skills, developing policy, teaching managers the process, analyzing data, and communicating results. The more detailed the document, the more useful it becomes. The project plan is a living, long-range document that should be reviewed frequently and adjusted as necessary. More importantly, it should always be familiar to those who are working on the project management scorecard. As an example, Figure 16-2 shows a project management scorecard implementation project plan for a large petroleum company.

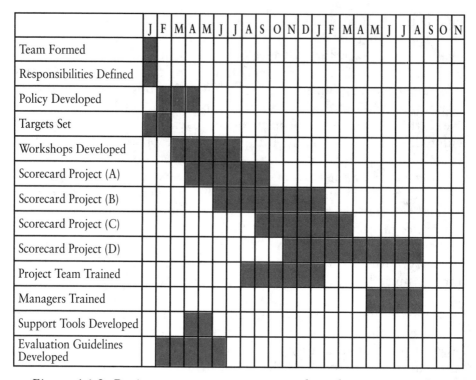

Figure 16-2. Project management scorecard implementation plan.

REVISING/DEVELOPING POLICIES AND GUIDELINES

Another key part of planning is revising (or developing) the organization's policy concerning measurement and evaluation for projects, which is often a project manager's function. The policy statement contains information developed specifically for the measurement and evaluation process. It is frequently developed with the input of the project team and key managers or stakeholders. Sometimes, policy issues are addressed during internal workshops designed to build skills for measurement and evaluation. The policy statement addresses critical issues that will influence the effectiveness of the measurement and evaluation process. Typical issues include adopting the five-level framework presented in this book, requiring Level 3 and 4 objectives for some or all projects, and defining responsibilities for the project's development.

Policy statements are very important because they provide guidance and direction for the staff and others who work closely with the project management scorecard. These individuals keep the process clearly focused and enable the group to establish goals for evaluation. Policy statements also provide an opportunity to communicate basic requirements and fundamental issues regarding performance and accountability. More than anything else, they serve as learning tools to teach others, especially when they are developed in a collaborative and collective way. If policy statements are developed in isolation and do not enjoy ownership from the staff and management, they will not be effective or useful.

Guidelines for measurement and evaluation are important for showing how to utilize the tools and techniques, guide the design process, provide consistency in the project management scorecard process, ensure that appropriate methods are used, and place the proper emphasis on each of the areas. The guidelines are more technical than policy statements and often contain detailed procedures showing how the process is actually undertaken and developed. They often include specific forms, instruments, and tools necessary to facilitate the process.

PREPARING THE PROJECT TEAM

Project managers often resist the project management scorecard. They often see evaluation as an unnecessary intrusion into their responsibilities, absorbing precious time and stifling their freedom to be creative. The cartoon character Pogo perhaps characterized it best when he said, "We have met the enemy, and he is us." This section outlines some important issues that must be addressed when preparing the project team for the implementation of the project management scorecard.

Involving the Staff

On each key issue or major decision, the staff should be involved in the process. As policy statements are prepared and evaluation guidelines developed, staff input is absolutely essential. It is difficult for the staff to resist something it helped design and develop. Using meetings, brainstorming sessions, and task forces, the staff should be involved in every phase of developing the framework and supporting documents for the project management scorecard.

Using the Scorecard as a Learning Tool

One reason the project team may resist the project management scorecard is that the effectiveness of its projects will be fully exposed, putting the project management organization's reputation on the line. The organization may have a fear of failure. To overcome this, the project management scorecard should be clearly positioned as a tool for learning and not a tool for evaluating project team performance—at least during its early years of implementation. Project managers will not be interested in developing a process that can be used against them.

Evaluators can learn as much from failures as successes. If the project is not working, it is best to find out quickly to understand the issues first-hand, not from others. If a project is ineffective and not producing the desired results, it will eventually be known to stakeholders and/or the management group, if they are not aware of it already. A lack of results will cause managers to become less supportive of projects. If the weaknesses of projects are identified and adjustments are made quickly, not only will more effective projects be developed, but the credibility and respect for project management will also be enhanced.

Teaching the Team

The project team usually has inadequate skills in measurement and evaluation and thus will need to develop some expertise in the process. Measurement and evaluation is not always a formal part of the preparation for becoming a project manager. Consequently, each project team member must be provided training on the project management scorecard to learn its systematic steps. In addition, project managers must know how to develop an evaluation strategy and specific plan, collect and analyze data from the evaluation, and interpret results from data analysis. Sometimes a one- to two-day workshop is needed to build adequate skills and knowledge to understand the process, appreciate what the process can do for the project managers and the organization, see the necessity for it, and participate in a successful implementation.

INITIATING THE SCORECARD PROJECT

The first tangible evidence of the project management scorecard may be the initiation of the first project in which an ROI calculation is planned. This section outlines some of the key issues involved in identifying the projects and keeping them on track.

Selecting Initial Projects

Selecting a project for scorecard implementation is an important and critical issue. Only specific types of projects should be selected for comprehensive, detailed analysis. Typical criteria for identifying projects for analysis are to select projects that:

- ☐ Involve large groups of employees
- ☐ Are linked to major operational problems/opportunities
- ☐ Are important to overall strategic objectives
- ☐ Are expensive
- ☐ Are time-consuming
- ☐ Have high visibility
- ☐ Have management's interest in evaluation

Using these or similar criteria, the project manager must select the appropriate projects to consider for the project management scorecard. Ideally, management should concur with or approve the criteria.

The next major step is determining how many projects to undertake initially and in which particular areas. A small number of initial projects are recommended, perhaps two or three projects. The selected projects may represent the functional areas of the business such as operations, sales, finance, engineering, and information systems. Another approach is to select projects representing functional areas of project management, such as productivity improvement, re-engineering, quality enhancement, technology implementation, and major change. It is important to select a manageable number so the process will be implemented.

Reporting Progress

As the projects are developed and the scorecard implementation is under way, status meetings should be conducted to report progress and discuss critical issues with appropriate team members. For example, if a project for operations is selected as one of the scorecard projects, the key staff involved meet regularly to discuss the status of the project. This keeps the project team focused on the critical issues, generates the best ideas for tackling particular problems and barriers, and builds a knowledge base for better implementation evaluations in future interventions. Sometimes, this group is facilitated by an external consultant, perhaps an expert in the project management scorecard. In other cases, the internal leader may facilitate the group.

In essence, these meetings serve three major purposes: reporting progress, learning, and planning. The meeting usually begins with a status report on each scorecard, describing what has been accomplished since the previous meeting. Next, the specific barriers and problems encountered are discussed. During the discussions, new issues are interjected in terms of possible tactics, techniques, or tools. Also, the entire group discusses how to remove barriers to success and focuses on suggestions and recommendations for next steps, including developing specific plans. Finally, the next steps are determined.

PREPARING THE MANAGEMENT TEAM

Perhaps no group is more important to the project management scorecard than the management team that must allocate resources for support of the project. In addition, the management team often provides input and assistance for the project management scorecard. Specific actions for training and developing the management team should be carefully planned and executed.

A critical issue that must be addressed before a project begins is the relationship between the project team and key managers. A productive partnership is needed, which requires each party to understand the concerns, problems, and opportunities of the other. Developing this type of relationship is a long-term process that must be deliberately planned and initiated by key project managers. Sometimes, the decision to commit resources and support for a project is based on the effectiveness of this relationship.

The Overall Importance of Project Management

Managers need to be convinced that project management is a mainstream function that is growing in importance and influence in modern organizations. They need to understand the results-based approach of today's progressive project management firms. Managers should perceive projects as a critical process in the organization and be able to describe how the process contributes to strategic and operational objectives. Data from the organization should be presented to show the full scope of projects in the organization. Tangible evidence of top management's commitment to the process should be presented in the form of memos, directives, or policies signed by the CEO or other appropriate top executives. Also, external data should be shared to illustrate the growth of project budgets and the increasing importance of project management.

The Impact of Project Management

Too often, managers are unsure about the success of project management. Managers need to be able to identify the steps to measuring the impact that project management has on important output variables. Reports and studies should be presented, showing the impact of the project using measures such as productivity, quality, cost, response time, and customer satisfaction. Internal evaluation reports, if available, should be presented to managers, revealing convincing evidence that project management is making a significant difference in the organization. If internal reports are not available, success stories or case studies from other organizations can be utilized. Managers need to be convinced that project management is a successful, results-based tool—not only to help with change, but to meet critical organizational goals and objectives as well.

Responsibility for Managing Projects

Defining who is responsible for what areas of the project is important to the success of the project. Managers should know their specific responsibilities, see how they can influence project management, and understand the degree of responsibility they must assume in the future. Multiple responsibilities for project management are advocated, including specific responsibilities for managers, project team members, project team member supervisors, and project managers. In some organizations, job descriptions are revised to reflect project management responsibilities. In other organizations, major job-related goals are established to highlight management's responsibility for the project.

Active Involvement

One of the most important ways to enhance managers' support for the project management scorecard is to actively involve them in the process, having them commit to one or more ways to become actively involved in the future. Figure 16-3 shows several forms of manager involvement identified in one company. The information in the figure was presented to managers with a request for them to commit to at least one area of involvement. After these areas are fully explained and discussed, each manager is asked to select one or more ways in which he or she will be involved in projects in the future. A commitment to sign up for at least one involvement role is required. If used properly, these

The following are areas for present and future involvement in the project. Please check your areas of planned involvement.

	In Your Area	Outside Your Area
☐ Provide Input on a Project Needs Analysis	☐	☐
☐ Serve on a Project Advisory Committee	☐	☐
☐ Provide Input on a Project Management Design	☐	☐
☐ Serve as a Subject-Matter Expert	☐	☐
☐ Serve on a Task Force to Develop a Project	☐	☐
☐ Provide Reinforcement to Your Employees as They Participate in Project Solutions	☐	☐
☐ Coordinate a Project Solution	☐	☐
☐ Assist in a Project Evaluation or Follow-Up	☐	☐

Figure 16-3. Possibilities for management involvement in projects.

commitments are a rich source of input and assistance from the management group. There will be many offers for involvement, and a quick follow-up on all offers is recommended.

REMOVING OBSTACLES

As the project management scorecard process is implemented, there will be obstacles to its progress. Many of the fears discussed in this chapter may be valid, while others may be based on unrealistic fears or misunderstandings. As part of the implementation, attempts should be made to dispel the myths and remove or minimize the barriers or obstacles. These myths should be discussed and debated in the organization so that they can be discounted, at least in the eyes of the project managers or other project support staff.

MONITORING PROGRESS

A final part of the implementation process is monitoring the overall progress made and communicating that progress. Although it is an often-overlooked part of the process, an effective communication plan can help keep the implementation on target and let others know what the project management scorecard process is accomplishing for the project management organization and the client organization.

The initial schedule for implementation of the project management scorecard provides a variety of key events or milestones. Routine progress reports should be developed to communicate the status and progress of these events or milestones. Reports are usually developed at six-month intervals, but may be more frequent for short-term projects. Two target audiences, the project team and senior managers, are critical for progress reporting. The entire project team should be kept informed of the progress, and senior managers need to know the extent to which the project management scorecard is being implemented and how it is working in the organization.

SHORTCUT WAYS TO MAKE THE SCORECARD PROCESS WORK

To address concerns about excessive time and resources for the project management scorecard, it is important to constantly pursue shortcut ways to make the process work. Throughout this book in nearly every chapter, shortcut ways were presented to save time and cost as a project management scorecard is applied and implemented. These serve as a helpful summary of the key issues involved in developing these shortcuts. It may be helpful to review these shortcuts now, as they are not reprinted here. In addition, at the end of each chapter is a section on shortcut ways to accomplish the objective of the chapter. Collectively, there are many shortcut ways with which time can be saved and cost can be reduced without seriously damaging the effectiveness of the project management scorecard.

FINAL THOUGHTS

In summary, the implementation of the project management scorecard is a very critical issue. If not approached in a systematic, logical, and planned way, the project management scorecard will not become an integral part of project management and, consequently, the accountability of projects will suffer. This final chapter presented the different elements that must be considered and issues that must be addressed to ensure that implementation is smooth and uneventful. The result provides a complete integration of the project management scorecard as a mainstream activity in the project management process.

FURTHER READING

Esque, Timm J. and Patricia A. Patterson. *Getting Results: Case Studies in Performance Improvement.* Vol. 1. Washington, DC: HRD Press, Inc./International Society for Performance Improvement, 1998.

Fuller, Jim. *Managing Performance Improvement Projects: Preparing, Planning, and Implementing.* San Francisco: Pfeiffer and Co., 1997.

Kaufman, Roger, Sivasailam Thiagarajan, and Paula MacGillis. *The Guidebook for Performance Improvement: Working with Individuals and Organizations.* San Francisco: Pfeiffer and Co., 1997.

Labovitz, George and Victor Rasansky. *The Power of Alignment: How Great Companies Stay Centered and Accomplish Extraordinary Things.* New York: John Wiley & Sons, 1997.

LaGrossa, Virginia and Suzanne Saxe. *The Consultative Approach: Partnering for Results!* San Francisco: Jossey-Bass/Pfeiffer, 1998.

Langley, Gerald J., Kevin M. Nolan, Thomas W. Nolan, Clifford L. Norman, and Lloyd P. Provost. *The Improvement Guide: A Practical Approach to Enhancing Organizational Performance.* San Francisco: Jossey-Bass Publishers, 1996.

Rackham, Neil, Lawrence Friedman, and Richard Ruff. *Getting Partnering Right: How Market Leaders Are Creating Long-Term Competitive Advantage.* New York: McGraw-Hill, 1996.

Segil, Larraine. *Intelligent Business Alliances: How to Profit Using Today's Most Important Strategic Tool.* New York: Times Business/Random House, 1996.

Redwood, Stephen, Charles Goldwasser, and Simon Street/PricewaterhouseCoopers. *Practical Strategies for Making Your Corporate Transformation a Success: Action Management.* New York: John Wiley & Sons, 1999.

Trout, Jack and Steve Rivkin. *The Power of Simplicity: A Management Guide to Cutting Through the Nonsense and Doing Things Right.* New York: McGraw-Hill, 1999.

Establishing an Effective PM Culture

Robert Happy, Director of Consulting and Technology, Project Management Practice, Franklin Covey Consulting

Carol Meyer, Abbott Laboratories

For people interested in setting up project/program management offices, practices, or centers for project excellence and toward establishing truly effective project management within an organization.

Just Do It . . . possibly the three most dangerous words for project management. How can three words, popularized by Nike Corporation's ad campaign throughout the 1990s, be so wrong for organizations implementing projects? Easy! Organizations are spending billions of dollars "just doing it" to the wrong things at the wrong time and in the wrong way. More often than not, organizations dive right into implementation, disregarding or misunderstanding the whole of project management as a practice, which requires undergoing critical steps prior to execution. Having had the privilege of working with hundreds of organizations and thousands of individuals with implementing effective project management, we sometimes see this erroneously disguised as being entrepreneurial. Think of the story of the project leader, who turns to his engineers and says, "You start development while I go find out what the customer really wants."

Understanding that implementing effective project management requires a framework with a process, tools, and skills to support it will go a long way to ensure success. Couple that with a clearly defined mission, vision, and strategy acting as the primary filter for project decision-making, and organizations can move past the "just do it" approach into doing the right projects at the right time and in the right way. All translate into optimizing the value of your organization.

Companies striving to maintain and improve their competitiveness, and expand their markets, will inevitably be faced with implementing project management as a practice. This comes in many different shapes and forms, depending on the nature of the business and maturity level of your organization.

Some organizations aspire to set up effective project management offices or simply choose to appoint project leaders/managers to manage cross-functional projects in addition to their existing responsibilities. Whatever the approach or the goal an organization may have, establishing an effective PM culture has proven to be an arduous task, to say the least. One thing is certain, in the next ten years successful organizations will be defined by those who have implemented project management effectively and have established a project management culture to the point where it becomes "muscle memory"—like riding a bicycle.

As global markets rapidly change and customers become more demanding, organizations that can respond more effectively are the ones that will achieve greatest financial success. Once you introduce the word "change" or "customer demands," you have opened the door for project management since it can respond to unique customer needs (internal or external) better than traditional management techniques. At its core, project management embraces principles, processes, and tools that are designed to account for unique and temporary endeavors to meet or exceed customer's expectations. In the end, project management practices are more responsive to meeting customer deliverables because they operate more effectively within the three constraints all organizations must manage—tradeoffs between time, cost, and performance.

CASE STUDY EXAMPLE

Working for a large, Fortune 500 healthcare company for over nineteen years, I've worked on a lot of projects run with the "just do it" approach. In our organization, groups or individuals were assigned to work on projects and they immediately start executing, trying to meet a deadline that is set without regard to the activities and resources required to get there successfully. After many years of trying to execute projects this way and experiencing a variety of results, I decided that there had to be a better solution.

I had recently been assigned the responsibility for improving the management of more than 40 small projects, involving the packaging of drug supplies for many different clinical studies being run in Europe. Managing multiple projects without a defined process was like trying to piece together a patchwork quilt without a design in mind. Each customer defined their needs and requirements for drug supplies differently, but these requirements all had to be met by the same organization. It was clear to me that I had to define a project management process, but at that time I didn't know where to begin. I thought the solution was using project management software, so I bought a software package and went to a training class.

The instructor of the class did a good job of training on the basics of using the software, but as I asked questions about fitting my many real-life projects into the software, she couldn't answer them for me. I went back to my job determined to make this software solve my problems, but quickly got stuck in the complexities of the application. In frustration, I went to the back of the software manual looking for the customer support "800" number. I called the customer service rep and asked a few questions, but after getting more confused, I pleaded, "Isn't there someone who can understand my projects and then teach me how to use this software to manage them? Please help me find a way to use this software in the 'real' world!"

That request changed the way I manage projects. I was referred by the software company to the Project Consulting Group and started working with Robert Happy and his partners. The first thing Rob did when we met was to put aside the software packages and begin teaching me the process of project management. I realized I had a lot to learn!

For more than ten years, we have been involved with implementing project management, partnering with hundreds of organizations and affecting thousands of employees. Large or small, private or public, each of these companies has their own unique needs. During this time, we have come to realize that PM evolves within an organization, and we have been able to identify three distinct stages that companies will go through on their quest for optimizing their resource utilization and achieving truly effective project management. It appears that these stages are part of a natural evolving process, which cannot be transcended but only accelerated. It can be compared to the "crawl, walk, run" analogy of human development. As with humans, we have to learn to crawl before we walk and walk before we run. Although there are exceptions, most organizations will go through a similar development process when trying to establish an effective PM culture. Organizations can benefit a great deal from "shared" experiences to accelerate this development, and become effective more rapidly.

A typical situation we encounter goes something like this: organizations start out with an ambitious entrepreneurial spirit and focus on getting things done—in other words, implementation. Little time is spent on initiating, planning, controlling, and closing of projects while all efforts focus on "just do it." For a while this may work due to the limited number of projects and people involved. Eventually, however, a critical mass of projects is reached; project challenges increase and begin to jeopardize the success of the organization. Challenges begin to appear in four different varieties that we will refer to as the "Big 4" as follows:

1. Cost overruns
2. Time overruns
3. Customer dissatisfaction
4. Staff turnover/low morale

CASE STUDY EXAMPLE

In working on new product development projects, the deadline was always the immovable constraint. Being first to market meant a market share that could "make or break" a product's success in the marketplace. As a result, project teams would stretch their people resources to the max, trying to fit all their activities into the timeline the deadline allowed. We lost a lot of good people that way and also ended up continuing to "tweak" or develop the product once it was on the market. One example of this was that process improvements to reduce manufacturing or support costs had to be made after the product was introduced, instead of being planned into the product development process.

Once an organization understands these problems exist, many of which are caused by poor or non-existent project management practices, they begin to take steps to deal with these problems. The development process that organizations move through as they try to solve these critical issues can be broken down into the following distinct stages:

☐ Stage 1—Recognition
☐ Stage 2—Acceptance
☐ Stage 3—Effectiveness

Each one of these stages represent, in general terms, the aggregate of our shared consulting experiences over the past ten years and describe the commonalties that were identified from one organization to another. Each organization is unique and therefore must be treated that way. We have found that we can map an organization's effort to implement effective project management to one of these stages. As a result, organizations can identify and accelerate an appropriate approach for implementing the right solutions to support their respective efforts in achieving their desired results.

STAGE 1—RECOGNITION

Recognition is the stage in which an organization realizes that project management is an issue and that they need to take action. This stage is typically initiated by a single person or small group in an organization and is typically not recognized as being a key strategic initiative by executive management. Project management is the "accidental profession," an assignment given to a department member who is viewed as a department expert. For these reasons, there is no real commitment nor are long-lasting solutions implemented. Usually, a "band aid" approach is taken by applying two days of PM training and perhaps purchasing Microsoft Project© for the desktop. Typically, no lasting results are obtained and key challenges still persist.

STAGE 1: SYMPTOMS (MOVING BEYOND "JUST DO IT")

The critical mass of projects is reached and the "Big 4" begin to occur in part or in all:

1. Cost Overruns Identified as Significant
2. Schedule Overruns Identified as Significant
3. Customer Complaints/Dissatisfaction Increase
4. Employee Conflict, Stress, Turnover Occurs

STAGE 1: TYPICAL SOLUTIONS

- ☐ Band-Aid Approach
- ☐ Purchase Scheduling Tool—MS Project Installed on Desktop
- ☐ Send Some People to PM Concepts and/or Tools (MSP) Training
- ☐ "Hit and Run" Solutions

STAGE 1: TYPICAL RESULTS

- ☐ Short-Term Feeling That Something Is Being Accomplished
- ☐ Islands of PM Approaches Created
- ☐ Non-Integrated—Disparate Data and Processes Created
- ☐ Some "Elitist" Project Managers Rise—Problems Still Persist
- ☐ No Committed Funding for Project Managers

CASE STUDY EXAMPLE

What I described earlier was definitely the Recognition phase of implementing a project management practice. The clinical drug supply group was unable to meet deadlines and had no way to prioritize projects. They also could not plan their resources for future projects. Because of these problems, their customers were complaining that they were not able to complete clinical studies on time. The vice president in charge of drug development recognized that something needed to be done to improve the delivery of drug supplies, and I was assigned to "fix it." With thirteen years of experience across many areas of product development, I thought I was well equipped to tackle the challenge.

I recognized that a consistent approach was needed to obtain visibility of all the projects, but did not recognize that this was more of a project management process issue. I had never thought of project management as a defined process or methodology, or, that this same process could be applied to all different types of projects. I thought that by collecting all the projects into one software application, I could solve the management problems. I was able to enter all the projects into the software, but when I discovered I needed twenty-seven Ule Johannsens (one of the drug supply center's employees) in the month of September to meet all the deadlines requested, I knew right away that the software wasn't going to be the answer to all our problems!

STAGE 2—ACCEPTANCE

Acceptance is the stage an organization goes through when it accepts the commitment of investing in expanded project management solutions beyond a "hit and run" approach. Experiences from Stage 1 gain some visibility and attention from higher levels of management. The organization begins to see that a process for managing projects is needed. Solutions include looking at process and tools together. However, there is still no funding dedicated to full-time internal resources to support project management practice. As a result, some benefits are obtained, but there are still major inconsistencies existing between departments.

STAGE 2: SYMPTOMS (MOVING PAST THE "BAND AID" TOWARD LASTING RESULTS)

- ☐ Problems Persist with Projects and Teams
- ☐ Disparate Approaches, Tools, and Processes Causing Inefficiencies
- ☐ Islands of Projects Defined
- ☐ Need for Standard Process and Tools Accepted
- ☐ Acceptance of PM as an Organizational Practice—Executive Sponsorship Obtained

STAGE 2: TYPICAL SOLUTIONS

- ☐ Identify Internal PM Champion(s) to Dedicate Part or All of Their Time to Implementing Standard PM Process and Tools (PM Solution)
- ☐ Customized Project Management Solution Defined to Meet Business Requirements
- ☐ Implemented with Focus—The "Crawl to Walk" Stage

STAGE 2: TYPICAL RESULTS

- ☐ Sense of Accomplishment Realized
- ☐ Some PM Benefit Attained—Initial Progress on Addressing "Big 4" Problems Realized
- ☐ Visibility Created for Projects, Risk, and Issues
- ☐ Not Complete Integration—Islands Still Exist, Some Push Back
- ☐ Some Slow to Adopt/Some Trendsetters—No Reward Structure and/or Feedback Mechanism to Support Project Efforts

CASE STUDY EXAMPLE

We implemented a project management process to improve delivery of clinical drug supplies, and we realized that improving one piece of the clinical study process (e.g., drug supplies) did not have a significant effect on the entire clinical study process. This was just one deliverable in a much larger project.

With the drug supply process, we had created visibility of all the projects and learned the entire process to manage them, most importantly starting with planning and prioritizing projects to meet customer deadlines before starting to execute, control, and close them. With initial success, I was motivated to tackle the larger, clinical study project. I jumped in with both feet and tried to bring a project management process to a group of twelve clinical project managers.

What I encountered was resistance. This group was largely satisfied with using an individual approach to managing their projects. Each project was distinct, supporting different products, and the outcome of each project did not impact the other projects. The experience level of the project managers was varied, and though they carried the title of project manager, many of them operated more as coordinators of tasks or activities. Also, in my enthusiasm to implement a project management process, I created a very detailed process. Combining this with the lack of interest and a lack of project management experience, it was a sure bet to fail.

The project managers also viewed the implementation as management's way to micro-manage what they were doing. As we struggled to implement the process, I also recognized that my upper management did not know how to best utilize the information that we were generating. There was a lack of appreciation for the benefits that implementing a project management process would generate and the upper management interest and support also waned. In the end, we were only partially successful in implementing a consistent process with only some of the project managers using the process effectively.

STAGE 3—EFFECTIVENESS

In the final stage of implementing project management, Stage 3— Effectiveness, organizations fund internal full-time resources to establish and maintain a common methodology (processes, tools, skills, and language) to support the overall mission, vision, and strategy of an (the) organization. Top management becomes a champion for the project management process and successful project managers are recognized as project management professionals within their organization.

STAGE 3: SYMPTOMS (MOVING TO AN EFFECTIVE PM ORGANIZATION)

- ☐ Problems Still Exist but Subsiding Enough to Realize ROI
- ☐ Discipline Not "Muscle Memory" Yet, but Starting to Be Accepted
- ☐ PM for Everyone—WIIFM Identified as the Way to Go for All Levels of the Organization

STAGE 3: TYPICAL SOLUTIONS

- ☐ Funding Approved for PM (PMO, PM Practice, Center for Excellence)
- ☐ Standards, Process, and Tools Established and Documented

☐ Accessible and Integrated to All
☐ Roles Defined—Accountability, Responsibility, and Authority Clear at All Levels (Executive, Functional Management; PMO; Project Sponsor PM; Team Members; Customers)
☐ Focus on Organization-Wide PM Culture—Move from "Walk" to "Run"

STAGE 3: TYPICAL RESULTS

☐ ROI Realized from Effective PM—Attacks All Aspects of the "Big 4"
☐ Organizational Acceptance—Inside Out and Outside In
☐ Benefits Obtained—Problems Minimized, Resources Optimized
☐ "Muscle Memory" Created—PM in Automatic Transmission

CASE STUDY EXAMPLE

Having had two years of experience implementing this process for clinical study projects supporting many different products for my company, I moved into a group focused on the development of one drug. I took on the responsibility for managing the entire drug development program for that drug. This was an opportunity to implement the process of project management to a much larger scope, a more complex project involving many more functional groups across the corporation.

I took the experiences I had had in the previous organization and tried to implement what I had learned from our successes and failures. First, I focused on getting the support and buy-in from my director for implementing a new process. Initially, this was a challenge as my director was very experienced in drug development and had a good understanding of all the critical activities for a successful drug development program. He didn't really see the need for a new process, but he respected my abilities and was willing to give me the chance to try a new approach. It was very helpful to have the experience of the Project Consulting Group with Rob to draw on to explain how this process could impact the drug development process. My director saw it as a good process to teach me all the aspects of drug development that I was unfamiliar with, as this was my first experience with managing a project with this large of a scope.

Next, I met with the team members to get their support. I explained that I wanted to try a team approach to planning the project to assure that each of their activities were identified and planned for. As I was new to leading the project, I also said that I could better support the needs of the individual functions if we had an integrated plan that we all understood and agreed to. The team was eager to try the approach, and Rob and his team coached me in planning a two-day planning workshop at an off-site location.

With Rob and another PCG partner as facilitators working with the team and myself, we planned the entire project. We used a hands-on approach that got everyone involved in the process. We started with the scope of the project and discussed strategy. Once we had agreement on the scope, we broke down the main deliverables and each of the team members planned out their activities. We used all the wall space in the room to develop a project schedule with colored "post-it notes," and along the way used flip charts to record any project risks and issues. This way we had a common note-taking process that was visible to all involved.

As we moved through the process, we inserted small segments of training to teach each of the project management concepts along the way. This was an effective way to teach concepts and then apply them in real life. Team members could see an immediate value to the application of the concept.

At the end of the two-day session, the team had a common understanding of the project. We knew the critical path to complete the project (i.e., file the application for the drug with the FDA) and also as a team agreed on what the top risks were to the project, and how we were going to manage those risks going forward. We had a communication plan on how we would manage the project going forward and, two years later, are still successfully managing this integrated plan.

EFFECTIVE PM APPROACH AND BEST PRACTICES

Our "Effective PM" approach was designed to accelerate the design and implementation of project management to get through the stages as efficiently and cost effectively as possible. An effective PM program directly impacts an organization's bottom line more rapidly than any other approach. It is based on the best practices in the following paragraphs.

1. Implement in Stages—"Crawl, Walk, Run"

CASE STUDY EXAMPLE

Starting with a very detailed work breakdown structure is difficult to manage with team members that are new to the process and who quickly lose motivation. I learned from my initial attempts with the clinical project managers that we needed to start out simple and get some success with managing a simple plan. With that success we could add additional detail and get benefits from managing down to that detail.

2. People and Process First, Tools Second

CASE STUDY EXAMPLE

I think this is the most important thing I learned in implementing an effective process. Obtaining buy-in from the team members and all other project stakeholders is the key to a successful project. If teams don't have a good understanding of the process, they can't define an effective project plan, and no software can take an ineffective plan and make it an effective one.

Getting everyone involved was also a strong motivating factor for the project. Our team developed a strong synergy and sense of a common purpose. It was also a team-building experience that enabled us to work more effectively together.

Initially, as a team we built a project plan and updated that plan using the colored "post-it note" on the wall approach, and I transferred those activities into a project management software tool that I continued to manage. At a certain point in the project, we experienced a significant change in scope that required a major revision to the project schedule. This offered the team members the opportunity to take ownership of their part of the project plan in the software tool. They were eager to do this, and with approximately eighteen months of experience in the project planning process, the transition to managing the plan via the software tool was a relatively easy one.

3. Be Inclusive at All Levels of the Organization—You Need Executive Level Support in Conjunction with Staff at All Levels

CASE STUDY EXAMPLE

At various points throughout all the projects I've worked on with this process, I have invited upper management to participate in the process. I have asked them to take part in planning meetings or come to meetings as observers, and have made management presentations on project deliverables and risks. It is especially important to include the team members' functional management as well as a project's executive management. I use top-level views of the project plan to report and focus on the key risks, issues, and milestones of the project.

4. Treat Implementing Effective PM as a Project

CASE STUDY EXAMPLE

The success of this drug development project has been the best advertisement for an effective project management process. It gained the interest and

support of the management team for a process improvement initiative looking for best practices within the organization. They have developed a project plan to implement this same process throughout the entire drug development organization. Again, we are using the "crawl, walk, run" approach
with the rollout of the plan starting with implementing the process in two
additional drug development projects and eventually covering thirty plus
projects over a period.

5. Make It Customizable/Flexible

We want to customize this process for individuals and departments,
bringing them on board as they are willing and able.

CASE STUDY EXAMPLE

I think the important thing to recognize here is that each project is
unique, and while certain activities may be consistent across projects, there
are always risks, constraints, or other factors that need to be considered
when developing and managing each project plan.

Agreeing on common top-level deliverables helps to communicate project
status consistently to upper management across projects, but allowing for
flexibility in further levels of detail gives project teams the means to manage
the unique aspects of the project and also the ability to address varying levels
of experience of the different team members.

6. Know Your Organization's Mission, Vision, and Strategy

CASE STUDY EXAMPLE

A common understanding of our mission, vision, and strategy helps to
assure that the projects with the highest value to the organization are the
ones being funded. For drug development, focusing our investment within
strategic business franchises helped to identify the projects that had the highest return on investment. A good project management process is only good
if it's being applied to the right projects. Knowing the mission, vision, and
strategy is central to funding the right projects at the right time.

7. Conduct Interviews—Gather Input from All Stakeholders

CASE STUDY EXAMPLE

I found with experience that gathering input throughout the project management process was essential to gain, and more importantly to maintain,
the buy-in from all stakeholders. Also, as projects move through various

stages of completion, stakeholder needs change and the process needs to accommodate those changes. Gathering input either from small group discussions or one-on-one meetings should be an ongoing activity for the project manager and the team members.

8. Present Feedback and Make It an Iterative Process

CASE STUDY EXAMPLE

This goes hand-in-hand with the previous best practice. Feedback from stakeholders and input of team members needs to be evaluated and, if needed, incorporated into the project plan to adjust to the changing needs of the project. One critical process, however, is assuring that the project scope is being managed and, as adjustments to the plan are made, the changes are still within the scope of the project. This helps to minimize "scope creep" and keeps the project on track.

9. Eliminate Burdensome Processes and Tools and Focus on Benefits

CASE STUDY EXAMPLE

As I discussed earlier, one important learning experience I had was to keep the process and tools simple, especially early on in implementation. If teams gain early success with the process and the use of the tools, they will focus on the benefits. With experience gained, they will be more eager to add complexity and take more ownership of the process.

10. Recognize Successful Project Managers Within an Organization

CASE STUDY EXAMPLE

As projects complete key deliverables or come to a close within the project scope and budget, the project manager responsible should be recognized by both the project team and the management organization. In my experience, the project managers that gain the most recognition and visibility are those always "saving the day" with firefighting tactics and heroics, while those that avoid the need for firefighting by planning and controlling their projects don't receive recognition. It is essential that top management gain an understanding of project management practices and key project metrics to better identify and reward project managers that are successful.

11. Develop a Career Development Ladder to Encourage Professionals to Stay in the Project Management Role

CASE STUDY EXAMPLE

First, recognize that project management is a profession that can transfer between functions and across organizations. Create a career ladder where project management talent can be recognized and promoted to positions of increasing responsibility as successful project managers gain experience. Provide opportunities for growth by challenging project managers experienced in one functional area to try projects in new areas where they need to rely on and leverage the experience of other team members.

12. Promote a Positive Perception—Promote Success and Communicate Benefits at All Levels

CASE STUDY EXAMPLE

Invite managers or members of other projects to participate in team meetings and planning sessions from teams that are operating successfully. When new teams are forming, invite members from more experienced teams to assist with a team kick-off meeting to help set the stage or share their enthusiasm for the process. Use management update presentations as an opportunity to communicate time or cost savings gained through the project management process. Recognize and reward team members when key deliverables are accomplished.

13. Understand It Is a Continuous Improvement Process

CASE STUDY EXAMPLE

Don't expect that everything will be right from the start of the process. Start with top-level plans that can be more easily managed and refine those plans to further detail over time. Learn from mistakes and make adjustments as you go along. With time and practice, the process will become easier to manage and the benefits will increase.

14. Make It Non-Elitist—Open to All as Career Enhancing

CASE STUDY EXAMPLE

Make sure that opportunities to learn the process are available to everyone and that people are aware of where to get support and training. Even if a person's career goal is not focused on the project management profession, project management practices and processes can enhance any professional career development plan. Team members should be encouraged to obtain further training in both processes and tools.

15. Strive to Create "Muscle Memory"—"Like Riding a Bike"

CASE STUDY EXAMPLE

Recently, I held a planning session focusing on the unique requirements for developing this same drug in Japan. As the cultural and language barriers are challenging with a team made up of Americans, Europeans, and Japanese, we found that using the colored "post-it notes" on the wall was an effective way to communicate across those barriers. As some of our more experienced team members were present, they automatically started collecting information using the process we had incorporated. It was very rewarding to see how these members took on their roles in the process, and the impact it had on getting these newer members (from a very different cultural background) involved in building an effective plan.

16. Strive for Cultural Consistency—Eliminate Islands of Project Management and Work Toward Integrated Solutions

CASE STUDY EXAMPLE

As we develop teams using the same process, it has become easier to communicate project status, to focus resources, and to support project managers using common tools. When I was initially trying to implement the process with my team, I had to teach the process, provide support for using the tools, and manage the project. With an integrated solution, the teaching and support can be shared across teams so that the project managers can focus on their individual projects. Functional areas whose members participate in product development teams gain from a common approach and are better able to respond to requirements. Even the terms and the language become consistent, which improves communication and acceptance.

SUMMARY

In conclusion, we realize that implementing project management requires the application of good project management skills. Over time, and with a vast array of project management engagements, we have been applying and cultivating the most current project management concepts, training techniques, and state-of-the-art technology. This has led to a very efficient and mature approach, using the best practices described above that can accelerate the evolution that an organization goes through when establishing a project management culture.

Index

Page numbers followed by "t" indicate tables; those followed by "f" indicate figures.

About the Authors

Jack J. Phillips, Ph.D.

As a world-renowned expert on measurement and evaluation, Dr. Jack J. Phillips provides consulting services for Fortune 500 companies and workshops for major conference providers throughout the world. Phillips is also the author or editor of more than 30 books—10 about measurement and evaluation—and more than 100 articles.

His expertise in measurement and evaluation is based on extensive research and more than 27 years of corporate experience in five industries (aerospace, textiles, metals, construction materials, and banking). Phillips has served as training and development manager at two Fortune 500 firms, senior HR officer at two firms, president of a regional federal savings bank, and management professor at a major state university.

In 1992, Phillips founded Performance Resources Organization (PRO), an international consulting firm providing comprehensive assessment, measurement, and evaluation services for organizations. In 1999, PRO was acquired by the Franklin Covey Company and is now known as The Jack Phillips Center for Research. Today, the center is an independent, leading provider of measurement and evaluation services to the global business community. Jack Phillips can be reached at roiresearch@mindspring.com.

Timothy W. Bothell, Ph.D.

As a consultant on Return on Investment for Franklin Covey's Jack Phillips Center for Research, Dr. Timothy W. Bothell provides consulting services for Fortune 500 companies and facilitates measurement workshops at conferences, public locations, and private locations. His expertise in measurement and evaluation is based on more than seven years of experience with educational institutions and three years of experience with corporate clients from many industries.

Bothell began working at the Franklin Covey Jack Phillips Center for Research in 1997. He facilitates approximately 14 impact studies a month that provide results across all five levels of evaluation, including ROI. Bothell leads Franklin Covey's one-day private and public workshops and is involved in research and publishing that supports the knowledge and development of assessment, measurement, and evaluation.

Bothell's most recent presentations include Measuring Return on Investment of Training, given at the most recent ASTD international conference, SHRM and ASTD local chapter meetings, the ASTD Tech Knowledge Conference, and at many custom seminars. His most recent publication was "Measuring the Impact of Learning and Performance" (In: Phillips J.J. (ed.), *Measuring Learning and Performance,* Alexandria, VA: ASTD, 1999).

Bothell has an undergraduate degree in psychology, a master's degree in technology education, and a Ph.D. in instructional psychology, all from Brigham Young University.

G. Lynne Snead

Lynne Snead is the program author and developer of Franklin Covey's "Planning for Results" project and workload management seminar. She is currently the Director of the Franklin Covey Center for Project and Workload Management. She has presented the program to thousands of individuals in major corporations throughout the United States, as well as Europe and Asia.

Prior to joining Franklin Covey, Snead served as Project Manager for a computer company specializing in the engineering, design, and manufacture of custom communications products. She noted dramatic positive changes in the productivity of individuals and the company after the managers had been trained in the Franklin Quest Time Management System.

Intrigued by the organizational capabilities of the Franklin Planner, Snead joined Franklin Quest, now Franklin Covey, as Director of Public Seminars in 1987. She worked closely with clients to help create tools and a process to make the Franklin Planner a practical and complete project and workload management system. She is the author of *To Do, Doing, Done: A Creative Approach to Managing Projects and Effectively Finishing What Matters Most* (Simon & Schuster, 1997). She helped design Franklin Covey's On Target 2.0, which incorporates the Planning for Results process into a simple-to-use software program. Her clients include Andersen Consulting, Boeing, Clorox, Disney, Dell Computer, IBM, and Starbucks.

Snead is on the Board of Directors for the Innovation Network, a network of consultants focusing on innovation and creativity in business. She has also taught learning skills at the University of Utah and has a background in both educational psychology and data processing. She says, "I enjoy helping individuals and organizations get focused on successfully accomplishing their most important strategic objectives and realize that they can actually enjoy the process with confidence."

About
Franklin Covey

Franklin Covey is a leading global provider of learning and performance solutions for individuals and organizations. Their mission is to inspire change by igniting the power of proven principles so people and organizations achieve what matters most.

Franklin Covey distinguishes itself with unique thought-leadership, and a holistic approach that creates breakthrough, measurable results. They create curriculum and thought leadership through the works of Stephen R. Covey, Hyrum W. Smith, and others. Covey is a leadership authority and author of *The 7 Habits of Highly Effective People.* Smith is the developer of the Franklin Planner system and author of *What Matters Most.*

The company provides expertise in leadership development; productivity, time, and project management; communication and collaboration; sales performance; managing organizational change and employee retention; measuring the return on investment for learning; and creating effective corporate universities.

With 19,000 facilitators worldwide teaching and training 750,000 people annually, their curriculum is carried out through customized consulting services, personal coaching, custom on-site training, client-facilitated training, online training, and open enrollment workshops. Franklin Covey also provides an array of products available in 33 languages to increase personal and organizational effectiveness.

Franklin Covey's proven strengths are:

☐ **Assessment and Measurement**—Leading the industry in measuring the impact of learning and performance improvement.

☐ **Consulting**—Bringing the best strategic thinking available and experienced application insight for the toughest and most critical business challenges.

☐ **Training and Education**—Providing award-winning content and learning experiences in a wide variety of formats including electronic and online.

☐ **Implementation Processes**—Assisting in the application of new knowledge and skills.

☐ **Application Tools**—Leveraging leading-edge technologies and tools to achieve desired learning and business results.

Franklin Covey's client portfolio includes 80 percent of the Fortune 100, 75 percent of the Fortune 500, thousands of smaller and mid-sized businesses, and government entities. Clients access Franklin Covey's products and services through professional consulting services, licensed client facilitators, public workshops, catalogs, 160 retail stores, and the Internet (www.franklincovey.com). With 45 offices in 38 countries, Franklin Covey employs over 3,000 associates.

For information on Franklin Covey, please call, write, or visit our website:

Franklin Covey Co.
2200 West Parkway Boulevard
Salt Lake City, Utah 84119-2331 • USA
Toll Free: 800-882-6839 (U.S. & Canada)
International callers: 001 801-817-7045
or fax 001 801-342-6664
http://www.franklincovey.com
http://www.franklinplanner.com

The Value of Belonging

ASTD membership keeps you up to date on the latest developments in your field, and provides top-quality, *practical* information to help you stay ahead of trends, polish your skills, measure your progress, demonstrate your effectiveness, and advance your career.

We give you what you need most from the entire scope of workplace learning and performance:

Information
We're your best resource for research, best practices, and background support materials – the data you need for your projects to excel.

Networking
We're the facilitator who puts you in touch with colleagues, experts, field specialists, and industry leaders – the people you need to know to succeed.

Technology
We're the clearinghouse for new technologies in training, learning, and knowledge management in the workplace – the background you need to stay ahead.

Analysis
We look at cutting-edge practices and programs and give you a balanced view of the latest tools and techniques – the understanding you need on what works and what doesn't.

Competitive Edge
ASTD is your leading resource on the issues and topics that are important to you. That's the value of belonging!

For more information, or to become a member, please call 1.800.628.2783 (U.S.) or +1.703.683.8100; visit our Website at **www.astd.org**; or send an email to customercare@astd.org.

ASTD
Linking People,
Learning & Performance

990-31410